EYE TO EYE

EYE TO EYE

Women Practising Development Across Cultures

Edited by Susan Perry
& Celeste Schenck

ZED BOOKS
London & New York

This book is dedicated to our sons:
Arnault Barichella, Lucas and Maxime Coleon

Eye to Eye: Women Practising Development Across Cultures
was first published in 2001 by
Zed Books Ltd, 7 Cynthia Street, London N1 9JF, UK,
and Room 400, 175 Fifth Avenue, New York, NY 10010, USA

Distributed in the USA exclusively by Palgrave, a division of St Martin's Press,
LLC, 175 Fifth Avenue, New York, NY 10010, USA

Designed and typeset in Monotype Joanna by Illuminati, Grosmont
Cover designed by Lee Robinson/Ad Lib Design, London N19
Cover photos: Masai woman © Betty Press/Panos Pictures;
Young Javanese woman © Anders Gunnartz/Panos Pictures
Printed and bound in the United Kingdom by Biddles Ltd,
Guildford and King's Lynn

A catalogue record for this book is available from the British Library

Library of Congress Cataloging-in-Publication Data available

ISBN 1 85649 846 8 (Hb)
ISBN 1 85649 847 6 (Pb)

Contents

Acronyms and Abbreviations   viii

Foreword
   Oidov Enhtuya   x

Introduction: Practising Theory Eye to Eye
   Susan Perry and Celeste Schenck   I

CHAPTER ONE
The Feminism of International Institutions

The World Bank and Women: 'Instrumental Feminism'
   Sophie Bessis   10

International Organizations: Women's Rights
and Gender Equality
   Aster Zaoudé and Joanne Sandler   25

Responses   41

CHAPTER TWO
The Politics of Women's NGOs in India,
Bangladesh and China

Gender and the Politics of Fatwas in Bangladesh
   Elora Shehabuddin   50

Gender Silences in the Narmada Valley
Jael Silliman   71

Between a Rock and a Hard Place: Women's Organizations
in China
Susan H. Perry   89

CHAPTER THREE
Women's Higher Education
in Ghana and South Africa

The Classroom or the Marketplace:
Survival Strategies of Ghanaian Women
Vijitha Mahadevan Eyango   106

'Blessed with the Necessity of Transformation':
Postgraduate Education in South Africa
Denise Newfield   119

CHAPTER FOUR
Making Peace as Development Practice

Dialogue in the War Zone:
Israeli and Palestinian Women For Peace
Sumaya Farhat-Naser and Gila Svirsky   134

Letters   149

CHAPTER FIVE
What's in a Name? (Re)contextualizing
Female Genital Mutilation

Abandoning Female Genital Cutting in Africa
Molly Melching   156

If Female Circumcision Did Not Exist,
Western Feminism Would Invent It
Obioma Nnaemeka   171

Female Genital Mutilation in France:
A Crime Punishable by Law
Linda Weil-Curiel   190

CHAPTER SIX
Reading the Local and the Global:
Literature as Development Practice

Testimonial and the Stories from the 'Stolen Generation'
in Australia
  Deirdre Gilfedder   200

'She Breastfed Reluctance into Me':
Hunger Artists in the Global Economy
  Françoise Lionnet   214

Developing Subjects
  Celeste Schenck   235

EPILOGUE
Resisting Development

Beyond Child Abuse
  Chinyere Grace Okafor   259

Notes on Contributors   277

Index   281

Acronyms and Abbreviations

ACWF	All-China Women's Federation
ADAB	Association of Development Agencies in Bangladesh
ANC	African National Congress
ATSIC	Aboriginal and Torres Strait Islander Commission
APRM	Anti-Price Rise Movement
BBC	British Broadcasting Corporation
BRAC	Bangladesh Rural Advancement Committee
CAMS	Comité pour l'Abolition des Mutilations Sexuelles
CEDAW	Convention on the Elimination of All Forms of Discrimination Against Women
CEDLA	Interuniversity Centre for Latin American Research and Documentation
CEDPA	Centre for Development and Population Activities
CNN	Cable News Network
FGC	Female Genital Cutting
FGM	Female Genital Mutilation
GAD	Gender and Development
GLSS	Ghana Living Standards Survey
GNP	Gross National Product
GOB	Government of Bangladesh
GOI	Government of India

HRC	Human Rights Commission
IACWGE	Interagency Committee on Women and Gender Equality
IDA	International Development Agency
IDS	Institute of Development Studies, University of Sussex
ILO	International Labour Organization
IMF	International Monetary Fund
INSTRAW	International Research and Training Institute for the Advancement of Women (United Nations)
JCW	Jewish Centre for Women
LEOS	Liberal Women's Brain Pool
NBA	Narmada Bachao Andolan
NGO	Non-Governmental Organization
OAU	Organization for African Unity
OFAD	Organisation de Formation et d'Appui au Développement
PAP	Project-affected persons
PLO	Palestine Liberation Organization
SADC	Southern African Development Community
SSMS	Shramik Sti Mukti Sanghatana
TOSTAN	Senegalese NGO
UAC	United Action Council
UN	United Nations
UNDAF	United Nations Development Assistance Framework
UNDG	United Nations Development Group
UNDP	United Nations Development Programme
UNICEF	United Nations Children's Fund
UNIFEM	United Nations Development Fund for Women
UNESCO	United Nations Education, Science and Culture Organization
UNRISD	United Nations Research Institute for Social Development
WAD	Women and Development
WID	Women in Development
WICSA	Women's Issues and Communication Services Agency

Foreword

As keynote speaker at the conference on 'Women, Culture and Development Practices' that prompted this book, I exhorted women from the nearly fifty countries represented to take the initiative to 'self-lead'. My experience as an elected official and NGO activist in Mongolia during the transition period from a Soviet-supported regime to a free-market democracy has convinced me that a creative and flexible response by women to this new opportunity has been an essential part of my country's development over the past decade.[1] The loose coalition of women politicians and activists with whom I have collaborated in Mongolia resembled the large, diverse community I encountered in Paris. The creative design of the conference pushed us all to think critically about the link between theory and practice, and served itself as a model for women's development. Theorists met with grassroots practitioners in the French Senate; lawyers argued with elected representatives; educators compared notes with researchers; literary critics presented novels as an explanation for economic realities. In short, the Paris conference served us all as a laboratory in which to experiment, try out new combinations of elements, see things in new ways.

In my experience, and in that of the contributors to this volume, women all over the world are redefining development as negotiable practice. The Liberal Women's Brain Pool (we use the acronym LEOS in Mongolia) was founded in 1992 to increase women's political participation in Mongolia. Our mission was to encourage people's participation in the decision-making process, to bolster the efficacy of NGOs in influencing public policy, and to promote leadership at all levels, especially in the rural areas. Concretely, we collected signatures to support revisions to the national electoral process; organized bipartisan campaigns to support women candidates and increase women's representation in the government, the courts and the Parliament; held leadership-training seminars; promoted health and education programmes; and – most important – created a pool of accurate statistical information on gender discrimination. For example, we determined and publicized the fact that rural women worked six more hours per day than rural men in their role as 'kitchen persons', the Mongolian term for wife!

Even in my own country, known for its relatively isolated nomadic culture with a demographically dispersed – and small – population, women's networking has changed the face of development. In just a few years, LEOS has grown from a handful of founders to 7,500 members in a society with no previous experience of independent associative behaviour. Our network has extended internationally through e-mail, fax, Internet and global conferencing. This description alone should challenge the view that some readers of this book may still have of 'the South' when they speak of development. The virtual community created by this volume is an excellent example of how women have seized the initiative offered by new technologies to share information and experience with an ever-wider audience, and to begin to think in terms of global dialogues rather than development as an imperative issued by well-intentioned Northerners. In Paris, I discovered a community of like-minded individuals, working in countless different disciplines, languages and terrains. There, we envisioned an alternative to traditional development models, one that explores the interstices between the public and the private, between the formal and the informal, between the demands and the compromises that make up women's daily lives. In Mongolia, as in the world community, this is women's greatest contribution to development.

Oidov Enhtuya
Ulan Batur, Mongolia

'Perhaps that's what the twenty-first century has in store for us. The dismantling of the Big. Perhaps it will be the Century of Small Things.'

ARUNDHATI ROY, 'The Greater Common Good'

INTRODUCTION

Practising Theory Eye to Eye

Susan Perry and Celeste Schenck

This book was conceived as a development project, one that would enable us to rethink traditional development theory and foreground innovative development practices across the globe. In both content and form, the collection captures a transformative, transitional moment in women's lives as we remake development in our own image. The goal of our project is to promote the building of development communities that bridge theory and practice, the academy and the field. Thus, the book's contributors include a whole range of 'developing subjects': people writing about development from inside the process. Today development takes place in parliaments, factories, courts, banks, classrooms, roadside stalls, guilds, athletic fields, publishing houses, hospitals, movie theatres, community theatres, novels, and even in the home. By inviting the protagonists from all these stages to bear witness, we have sought to bring to life within these pages the lived experience of development.

In the development field, technical manuals on empowering women and academic books on development theory have replicated the dichotomy between academic treatises and how-to approaches, the split between theory and practice, often ignoring the impact of community on development, and failing to achieve a real dialogue with the grassroots sites where development occurs. We focus instead on the ways in which practice and theory interact. In our experience, the real-life solutions that women craft often navigate *between* theory and practice, the local and the global. To err too far in either direction – the imposition of a

feminist universal or the elaboration of a plethora of local practices —
would be to miss the richness and complexity of the development
experience. In fact, development as a process is most successful when
it mirrors the varied rhythms and cadences of the human condition. A
linear approach focused solely on measurable progress is limited in
comparison with the variety of views that make up this volume. The
differences in format throughout are deliberate: while some contributors have used academic constructs to discuss their views, others have
chosen personal narratives or even a short story in which to frame a
particular development practice.

The title of our volume, *Eye to Eye: Women Practising Development Across
Cultures*, attempts to capture the multiple viewpoints that women bring
to development as polyvalent theorists and practitioners. Our contributors may or may not see eye to eye on all issues, but they exchange
visions of development across disciplines and across cultures, and they
recognize the importance of sharing and comparing local practice.
Women who see eye to eye may also uphold differing interpretations
of the same practices. Some of our contributors participated in the
original conference that provided the occasion for this volume, 'Women,
Culture and Development Practices', an international symposium held
at the French Senate in November 1998. Both within individual chapters
and in the composition of the collection as a whole, we have created
a methodology that reflects the interactive dynamics of that Paris conference, and the international community it created.

For us, development feminism names this concern with the transformation of women's lives worldwide by means of dialogues across
cultures, capturing a dialectic that has always fuelled feminist theory:
feminism frames development ethically, and development brings global
feminism to the forefront of public policy, returning feminism to its
activist roots. Sparks at the interface are to be expected. One pungent
example of our contributors' eclectic backgrounds comes from the
chapter on female genital cutting (Chapter Five). Scholar Obioma
Nnaemeka is a Nigerian activist who lives and teaches in the United
States. Molly Melching is an American activist who has theorized on
development practice while living and working in Senegal for the past
twenty years. Linda Weil-Curiel is a member of the Paris Bar Association whose work on what she terms female genital mutilation limits
itself expressly to development work in France. The reciprocal, dynamic
exchanges in this book thus reflect the community-building process
itself, including the no-holds-barred dialogue and debate which is the
rising trend in development work today. Similarly, the ethos of develop-

ment feminism binds together players who are both Northern and Southern, both theorists and practitioners. In this spirit we have grouped fifteen development scholars and practitioners in six chapters featuring central development debates. Forming a pair of bookends to the collection, the Foreword by Oidov Enhtuya exhorts women to self-lead by taking development into their own hands, and the Epilogue/Short Story by Chinyere Okafor features characters who do exactly that.

The six chapters of *Eye to Eye* feature key development issues in the fields of economics, politics, education, peace mediation, culture and literature. Each contributor has exchanged her work with her co-authors, writing a short response or an addendum to the positions taken by her colleague(s). Assigning no hierarchy to the value of expressed ideas, this arrangement proposes a both/and approach to dialogue and debate. In several of the chapters where the contributors debate – such as the one on international development aid and the one on female genital mutilation – there are no clear winners. In other cases, such as the chapters on women's NGOs and on literature, the dialogue occurs across national and cultural – even generic – boundaries, and involves no opposition between the contributors.

Our first chapter pairs Sophie Bessis, an economist who theorizes the complexity of 'instrumental feminism' practised by international organizations such as the World Bank, with Aster Zaoudé and Joanne Sandler, high-ranking United Nations administrators, whose practice shows that this trend has had a beneficial impact on the lives of individual women in West Africa. Their exchange of rebuttals demonstrates that we must, as feminists, be attentive to the ways in which international institutions have jumped on the bandwagon of gender mainstreaming in order to further their own, often unacknowledged, policy aims. The far-reaching implications of such policies include the absorption of women into the informal economic sector as cogs in the machinery of global capitalism; nonetheless, practice demonstrates that women, far from being the dupes of such policies, have learned to manipulate these new cash flows to their own localist ends.

Chapter Two explores the politics of women's NGOs in three of the world's most densely populated countries: Bangladesh, India and China. Elora Shehabuddin highlights the tensions poor rural women face when they are caught between conservative religious forces on the one hand, and international NGOs and the Bangladeshi government on the other, as they struggle for control of the country's development resources. Jael Silliman explores the controversy surrounding the Narmada Dam project in India as an opportunity for local women's groups to influence the policy agenda. Susan Perry shows how China's continuing domination by the Communist Party has limited opportunities for women and restrained their political activity. Although China hosted the 1995 Beijing UN Conference on Women, the government remains profoundly ambivalent about the rise of an independent women's movement in that country. Despite the very different contexts of the essays in this chapter, all three authors bear witness to the remarkable ingenuity of women's organizations as their members manoeuvre to find operational space within difficult national circumstances.

Our third chapter contrasts two different African experiences in women's higher education. For Denise Newfield, one of the architects of the new educational practices in South Africa, the inclusion of black women in university graduate programmes is a means of empowerment, for which women are prepared to make great personal sacrifices. Her experience in designing teaching programmes for South Africa's future educators holds out the hope of realizing, via education, the dream of a fully multiracial, multicultural society. In Ghana, Vijitha Eyango has compiled empirical evidence demonstrating that gender-equity strategies in education are doomed to failure if they focus only on educational access for girls without adequately addressing the relevance and quality of the education received. Ghanaian girls make the rational economic decision to drop out of school to pursue the more lucrative opportunities of the marketplace, because education does not guarantee them subsequent viable employment. Addressing each other's analyses in their conclusions, both authors express concern for the future of formal education in Africa.

Chapter Four highlights the ongoing public debate on peace between Israeli and Palestinian members of the Jerusalem Link for Women. Gila Svirsky, former Israeli director of Bat Shalom, and Sumaya Farhat-Naser, a Professor of Sociology and Palestinian Director of the Jerusalem Center for Women, refer to themselves as practitioners, promoting peace in the Middle East as a development process. At the very heart of our book is an actual dialogue, taped during sessions in Jerusalem, in which they discuss their shared mission to build a sustainable quality of life in the Middle East for women and their families. They share a commitment to a rigorous peace process, to fight for an end to the Israeli occupation and the creation of a fully autonomous Palestinian state, and to create a support network between Jewish women and Palestinian women living within the state of Israel. One of their most successful practices for mediating disputes – the exchange of personal letters in which they write out what cannot be said – is reproduced in this book.

Investigating the politics of language around the issue of female circumcision, our fifth chapter turns upon the important differences implied by the deployment of terms such as excision, mutilation, cutting and circumcision. For Molly Melching, a practitioner with twenty-five years' experience working in Senegal, educational methods such as community theatre, role-playing sessions, and informal discussions encourage community members themselves to 'abandon' the practice of 'female genital cutting'. For Obioma Nnaemeka, 'female circumcision' is a multifaceted issue that cannot be approached without first examining the cultural framework in which its 'eradication' is being promoted. For French lawyer Linda Weil-Curiel, 'genital mutilation' is, quite simply, a crime. In her legal practice, Weil-Curiel relies upon existing French legislation to pursue and punish families who engage in the practice on French soil.

Chapter Six, 'Reading the Local and the Global', focuses on literary accounts of the development process, and foregrounds the ambivalences of participants in and witnesses to that process. In fact, literature and literary studies have recently played a central role in postcolonial debates on subject formation, subjection, and the politics of identity. Deirdre Gilfedder analyses autobiographical narratives by contemporary Indigenous women in Australia, members of the 'Stolen Generation' whose writings were in some cases commissioned by the Australian Human Rights Commission. Françoise Lionnet analyses the political economy of Mauritius's industrial zones, and ends with a reading of a contemporary novel, a fictional autobiography, which reinterprets current somatic symptoms in terms of a history of social and political events in her home country. Celeste Schenck reads a group of contemporary novels by Anglophone women authors that make powerful arguments against racism and social hierarchy by valorizing the cultural process of *métissage*. She suggests that recent changes in international publishing are fertile ground for development practice. In this chapter, literature brings to the fore the lived aspects of the development process and provides, given the increasing globalization of what we call 'literature in [e]nglish', an unexpected platform for the articulation of development ethics and policies.

This collection begins with a discussion of development policy as practised by international institutions and moves towards the cultural stages on which new, imaginative solutions may be played out. Recent alter-

native development theory has itself pointed the way. In a seminal essay
published elsewhere, 'The Myth of Development: A Critique of the
Eurocentric Discourse', Vincent Tucker traces the genealogy of development thinking from its inception as an extension of Western myths of
'civilization' and 'progress' to contemporary notions of modernity which
have the effect of reducing weaker societies to the status of objects.
Echoing Edward Said's call for a plurality of discourses, audiences and
terrains (Said 1985), Tucker insists upon the need to incorporate the
experience of other peoples, other perspectives and other cultures into
development discourse. In his essay, he demonstrates how 'the exclu-
siveness of the current discourses points to the need for open models
that emphasize process and dialogical exchange.... Inadequate conceptualizations of culture as somewhat closed wholes prevent us from seeing
the dynamism of cultural exchange and the power relations embedded
in it' (Tucker 1999: 22). We share with Tucker, as well as with recent
feminist theorists of development, a recognition of the importance of
decoupling Enlightenment narratives of progress from the real dramas
and dialogues of development today, and of dismantling Northern
universalism in the name of multiple voices, contradictory perspectives,
and competing visions of the truth (Marchand and Parpart 1995).[1] As
our collection attests, one of the most important challenges facing the
development field is the definitive abandonment of the North–South
divide. *Eye to Eye: Women Practising Development Across Cultures* inserts itself in
these debates by attempting to remap the terrain of the development
field, so that it might keep pace with the changing geocultural face of
the world we live in. All the contributors to this volume are 'developing
subjects', using our imaginations to reshape our own lives and the
various communities – virtual or otherwise – in which we live. In
every chapter of this collection, dreams, dialogue, novels, theatre and
community politics offer new ways of getting around preconceived
notions of women's potential as social, political and economic agents.
The last two chapters and the Epilogue foreground fictional and personal narratives as innovative sites where contradictions may be ex-
plored and new developments emerge.

 Our own experience as writers, scholars, practitioners and activists
has shown that the women who toil in the fields and factories and
various associations of the world we live in have indeed come to see
their lives increasingly as a kind of negotiation between what they can
imagine for themselves and what is possible within the limits of the
cultural. As anthropologist Arjun Appadurai sees it: 'the imagination has
now acquired a singular new power in social life.... More persons in

more parts of the world consider a wider set of possible lives than they ever did before' (Appadurai 1996: 53). Such an assertion, however, does not rest on a naive faith in happy endings. Instead, in the development experiences narrated in this book, a new set of creative solutions to difficult human problems are proposed. As Appadurai puts it: 'in the grinding of gears between unfolding lives and their imagined counterparts a variety of imagined communities is formed, communities that generate new kinds of politics, [and] new kinds of collective expression...' (Appadurai 1996: 54). The publishers, stall-vendors, teachers, community leaders, academics, factory workers, farmers, judges, politicians, novelists, mothers featured in this volume are such community activists, empowering themselves by building development communities within and across cultures. When Vincent Tucker documented the 'cultural turn in development', he encouraged us 'to leave behind the epistemological illusion of concreteness' provided by statistical and economic models, and to move towards integrating political economy and cultural analysis (Tucker 1997: 9). As the fuzzy ground of development theory and practice, culture figures differently in each context, and requires flexibility, creativity and imagination of those in the field. The women described in this collection, as well as those writing for it, have exploited the interstices of the cultures they inhabit to articulate new possibilities for sustainable personal and community development. The community we form shares a commitment to development feminism – an ethical vision and a practice that has set its sights for the twenty-first century upon the amelioration of women's status around the world, the quality of all of our lives, and that of the communities in which we live and work.

Note

1. This book charts new activist space at the juncture of the three fields placed in apposition in its title, and may be consulted for a fine overview and bibliography of the shifts that led from a liberal Women in Development (WID) perspective, through the more systemic analyses of a Woman and Development (WAD) approach, to the empowerment ethos of the more recent Gender and Development (GAD) debates. See also Martha Nussbaum's elaboration of feminist universals for reconceiving development (Nussbaum 2000).

References

Appadurai, A. (1996) *Modernity at Large: Cultural Dimensions of Globalization*, Public Worlds, vol. 1, Minneapolis: University of Minnesota Press.

Marchand, M. and J. Parpart (1995) *Feminism/Postmodernism/Development*, New York and London: Routledge.

Nussbaum, M. (2000) *Women and Human Development: The Capabilities Approach*, Cambridge: Cambridge University Press.

Said, E. (1985) 'Orientalism Reconsidered', *Race and Class*, vol. 27, no. 2.

Tucker, V. (1999) 'The Myth of Development: A Critique of the Eurocentric Discourse', in R. Munck and D. O'Hearn, eds, *Critical Development Theory: Contributions to a New Paradigm*, London: Zed Books.

CHAPTER ONE

The Feminism of International Institutions

The first chapter in this multidisciplinary collection focuses on the feminist politics of international institutions, placing the emphasis of development debate, as they do, on economic policies. Economist Sophie Bessis throws down the gauntlet, claiming that international institutions such as the World Bank manipulate gender-equality policies to their own economic ends. As a feminist, she poses a critical ethical question: whatever the benefits of making women into independent economic actors, do we ultimately want them to become agents in the exportation of global capitalism to the emerging economies of the world? Should development institutions whose mandate it is to assist the poor be promoting policies akin to those driving multinational corporations? Aster Zaoudé and Joanne Sandler, programme directors in the UN system, review what UNIFEM has accomplished to illustrate that gender mainstreaming is operative at every level of that institution as a central policy. Zaoudé and Sandler answer Bessis by demonstrating the extent to which encouraging women to become economic protagonists has a holistic effect on their overall quality of life. Bessis, responding, worries that the UN will increasingly become a forum for the exchange and containment of feminist ideas, while the banks and money funds actually retain control of the economic scene.

The World Bank and Women: 'Instrumental Feminism'

Sophie Bessis

For decades, the World Bank has presented itself as one of the principal laboratories in which dominant development theories are discovered and tested, without this really having been the case. For the last dozen years, the Bank has taken an interest in women's issues, an interest that it had never formerly shown. All its general policy documents and most of its reports[1] now refer to women, or gender. In addition, since the 1970s the Bank has consecrated virtually a hundred studies and monographs, of both a general and a very specific nature, to the subject of women. Such abundance of documentation reveals the central – and powerful – impact of this institution on the status of women in developing societies. In fact, the Bank remains the major multilateral funding institution for development in the world, and its policies have a profound influence on the political and social development of borrower nations. But even more important, these documents permit analysis of the reasons for the World Bank's decision to foreground women's issues at the current time. Why has gender suddenly inflected the World Bank's language? And what do women have to do with the usual subjects warranting the Bank's attention, such as the adjustment of Southern economies to global liberalism, and the insertion of those economies into today's global market?

Actually, these subjects are not so far from this Washington institution's understanding of the imperative of gender. Let us briefly recall the history behind the 'discovery' of women by World Bank experts. It is in fact rare for this institution to be in the avant-garde of debate on any important social subject, despite the image that the Bank tries to promote of itself. The Bank, in general, makes an issue its own only once that issue has acquired sufficient visibility. It looks as if the Bank was afraid of falling behind the pack on this newly important topic of debate, and of being overtaken by other institutions in a sector that had acquired the status of a key socioeconomic issue. In this respect, the case of women's issues resembles that of the environment. Although the Bank did not concern itself with the future of the planetary eco-system for decades, it focused on this issue at the exact moment when the environment became a central theme in the debate on economic growth and choice, and one of the new battlefields in the North–South conflict.

Taking Women into Account: Slow Progress

Thus the Bank began to discover women only in the mid-1970s, in response to the United Nations' request that it participate in the first international conference organized around this theme in Mexico City in 1975.[2] Once the United Nations proclaimed the years 1975 to 1985 the 'International Decade for Women', the second half of the 1970s witnes-sed the flourishing of 'women's integration in development' among the international funders. In 1977, the Bank participated in this trend by naming a token Women and Development Counsellor (who wielded neither power nor money); in 1979 it published its first document on the subject. During the first half of the 1980s, the Bank's interest in gender gradually increased, as is evident in the thirty-five case studies and evaluations published between 1979 and 1985. But no money was allocated. The financial commitment which would reinforce women's agency in the economy of developing countries was almost nonexist-ent. Even though the Bank was beginning to reflect on the timeliness of women's issues, the institution was not interested enough to devote the only thing that counted: money for project funding.

It is true that at this point in time the World Bank had other worries. The beginning of the 1980s marked both the apogee of the international debt crisis and the crucial period for setting up structural adjustment policies designed to bring indebted countries into line with economic and financial orthodoxy. While the IMF took over the task of restoring financial balance, the World Bank was assigned the mission of con-verting developing countries to an economic liberalism built upon the ebbing of the state sector and generalized competition among all national economies around the globe. Women could wait.

From 1985 onward, however, the Bank's interest in women picked up again, and has been maintained ever since. What happened in the interim to guarantee women an importance that was not just anecdotal in the eyes of the Washington experts? The response is simple: structural readjustment. During the painful years when the debtor nations of Africa, Latin America and Asia were subjected to drastic austerity cures, when the state could no longer recruit new employees, when unemployment grew, when the only money available was used to pay off the national debt to the detriment of health and social programmes, and when the mere mention of the term 'structural adjustment' shook the working-class neighbourhoods from Rio de Janeiro to Abidjan, women were suddenly no longer invisible. They were in the vanguard on every front: from the commercial market gardens of Sahelian Africa to community life in the Andes. Everywhere women were inventing survival strategies in order to get through the hard times, creating a social link among families weakened by the crises and the diminished stature of their men, who had been the first to suffer from the tidal wave that had hit the formal economic sector. Women's efforts were extremely impressive, and their toil probably prevented massive social upheaval, a surprisingly rare phenomenon in those countries subject to the shock treatment of the 1980s. They payed an exorbitant price, certainly, but this decade permitted women of the South to benefit from a level of visibility that they had never before experienced.

Women thus played a major role in adjusting to the vast changes that were imposed upon developing economies. What if, instead of simply adjusting to these changes, they were capable of accelerating the process? If, by increasing their interaction with local economies and augmenting their means, precious time could be gained in the project of converting the planet to a liberal market economy? These hypotheses, which were based on the discovery of women's capacity to manage crisis, indisputably changed the World Bank's mind about women – or, more precisely, finally led the Bank to take a look at them. The first consequence of this evolution in thinking – spurred by direct pressure brought to bear by women themselves, women who were fed up with being 'integrated' into the development process when they were already accomplishing the lion's share of the development task – was that the theme 'Women in Development' was rapidly converted into the notion of 'Gender and Development' founded on the analysis of the social relationship between the genders.

The World Bank was thus converted to gendered development, and in 1987 it began to place additional means at the disposal of the unit responsible for putting this evolution into action. From the late 1980s onward, a significant number of projects drawn up and financed by the Bank included a 'gender dimension'. For example, of the 4,955 projects financed between 1967 and 1993, most of the 615 World Bank projects approved between 1988 and 1991 had such a gender dimension.[3] Since then, the approval rhythm of 'gender projects' has stabilized. In 1994, the Bank's leadership promulgated a policy document entitled *Reinforcement of Women's Participation in Economic Development*, which had the official aim of modifying gender relations by articulating such objectives in the initial project goals. The 615 projects accepted between 1967 and 1993 represent 9.1 per cent of the Bank's financial commitments during this period, and 20 per cent of the International Development Association's allocations.[4] The greatest share of these went to human resources development (46 per cent) and agriculture (39 per cent). More than 40 per cent of the projects (251) concerned sub-Saharan Africa; slightly more than 15 per cent Southeast Asia (94); and slightly less than 15 per cent Latin America.

Women as Economic Agents and Vectors for Modernization

Above and beyond the clichés of official development discourse, what role has the Bank attributed to women in the modernization process of the South, and why did this institution decide to invest in women, however modestly? The answer is that the Bank discovered that the return on its investment in women's projects was far greater than had been imagined. In an attempt to justify its position, the Bank used a surfeit argument in all its documentation on this theme: that gender investment guarantees results. 'The economic and social return on educating the female population is high', insists the Bank in one such publication (Herz, Subbarao et al. 1993). It remains to be shown why there is such a great return on investing in women, and how precisely women promote the socioeconomic project of this Bretton Woods institution. The Bank affirms that the reinforcement of women's roles facilitates economic growth, improves family health and decreases fertility, according to a document prepared for the Fourth United Nations Conference on Women, held in Beijing in 1995 (World Bank 1995c). If we add to the list the fact that Bank administrators believe that this improvement is a key strategic element in the struggle against poverty, then we will have covered all the Bank's objectives in deciding to give gender a central place in its thinking, if not in its funding.

Protagonists in Demographic Transition

The decrease in fertility rates is, no doubt, a leading concern of the Bank. We know, in fact, that the demographic growth of the South constitutes, for both good and bad reasons, one of the main preoccupations of the richest nations, and what is referred to as 'the international community'. The rapid population growth of the past forty years has very evidently compromised chances for development in most of the countries of the South, since economic growth for the majority of these countries has been inferior to the demographic surge, at least until the beginning of the 1990s. The pressure on natural resources has also contributed to a dangerous degradation of the environment, which is difficult to maintain under any circumstances given the paucity of means available to these nations. Thus a variety of programmes became necessary to rein in population growth and effect the demographic transition to which virtually all Southern nations have long since subscribed. Clearly, the developed world has a lot at stake here: in comparison to the South's dynamism, the North's demographic decline has made it afraid of losing one of the fundamental elements of its power, as it rapidly becomes a minority player on the world's demographic chessboard. What is worse, in its own view, is that the pressure placed on the world's resources by this surplus population makes it unlikely that the North will be able to continue to do as it pleases. Developed nations will have to limit their predatory practices or, at the very least, share their short-term benefits with the world's demographic powers. Moreover, Western nations fear that strong demographic pressures may reinforce the migratory influxes that it is currently struggling to control. Any and all means are valid in neutralizing these threats.

Yet, although an ongoing and only partially successful battle has been fought for years against skyrocketing fertility rates in the South, progress in improving women's conditions has succeeded in reducing population growth in places where the most sophisticated population control policies have failed. Like UNICEF and the UNDP, the World Bank has carefully calculated the effects on fertility rates of educating girls. By reducing infant mortality and improving family health, education lessens the need for women to bear many children. Its next effect is to reduce by two simple means the number of children born: first, the farther a girl goes in her schooling, the later she tends to marry; second, educated daughters have easier access to salaried work, actively seek ways to decrease their domestic burden, and consequently convert to the idea of a smaller family. Educating girls pays, as the World Bank has recognized. But this policy also has other advantages.

Agents of Economic Innovation

Educating girls and women has a beneficial effect on their productivity. And since they make up the bulk of the workforce in strategic sectors such as agriculture or the informal urban economy, any increase in their productivity has a direct impact on the overall augmentation of production. Better yet, studies over the past twenty years all tend to show that, once they receive an education and professional training, women demonstrate a higher capacity than men to integrate innovation into their work (World Bank 1995d; Yunus 1999). Moreover, any increase in women's earnings has a direct impact on the community, because most women invest the major part of their earnings in spending which directly contributes to the family's improved quality of life, or in an upgrading of their income-generating activities, the profits of which will be similarly reinvested in the collective, and contribute to increasing social viability. Any similar such increase in men's earnings has had, in all the cases where studies have been done, a much more modest effect on household conditions. This type of economic behaviour and the sure returns on their activity give women the right to be considered the principal agents in the fight against poverty, one of the World Bank's professed goals; they must also be considered key agents in growth based on expansion of the private sector, especially since they benefited so little from the state's planning efforts at the time when the state was still in a position to direct economic development.

As the World Bank continued its search for the 'Homo economicus tropicalis', it seemed to discover an embodiment of this ideal species in the woman of the South. This surprise encounter was well worth a belated conversion to feminism. Having little to lose from the weakening of the rigid sociocultural conventions that inhibited their emancipation, women had become, in the Bank's eyes, the ideal propagating agents of a very pure form of popular capitalism incarnated by the informal sector in the underdeveloped countries. It is worth noting that the gender project 'success stories' invoked by the Bank to justify its actions nearly always tell of entrepreneurial women who made it thanks to their own inner strengths and resources, even the force of a raised fist ... and a timely bit of international financing. The absolute necessity – according to the Bank – of integrating women into the salaried work-force or the market sector was the real justification for including them in the decision-making process, and for modifying laws that inhibit their economic potential.

With this imperative in mind, the World Bank set itself two main goals, the first of which was to reduce women's domestic burden. The

IDA would henceforth target programmes designed to provide safe drinking water for villages, mechanize the transformation of basic grains, or set up community structures for childcare. The second goal was to encourage member states to modify their legislation in four key areas: property law – since women in most parts of the globe have been deprived of access to property, and have only limited access to land; labour law – the World Bank recommended greater flexibility in labour codes that forbade women certain jobs considered too 'dangerous' for them (Herz, Subbarao et al. 1993; Carolyn 1994); family law; and financial law (World Bank 1995a). But we must not be fooled. For the Bank, encouraging a more egalitarian evolution of the law stems less from ethical concern than from pragmatic interest. Utilitarianism wins out over principles in most cases. Several documents insist, for example, that it is best to create single-sex schools or classes, if single-sex education will make it easier for girls to attend school in conservative countries – a fairly acceptable position – or if it is proven that girls are more successful when they compete against girls only – an idea that must be considered cautiously (Herz, Subbarao et al. 1993). If women as women are considered apart from their economic utility, the World Bank experts have only a limited interest in their rights.

We will return to the Bank's utilitarian interest in women. First, let us recall that the World Bank, loath to give up its quasi-monopoly over the institutional study of poverty and development, judged it dangerous to show lack of interest in an issue which, until the second half of the 1980s, had been left to the United Nations. Second, women's rights also served to mobilize public opinion in countries of the South as well as the North. If feminism was going to leave the confines of the ideological margins, especially in the South, then it behove the World Bank to be a part of this process, since no development issue should escape its ascendancy. This change, of course, was made all the easier once the 1980s revealed the extent to which women could be a dynamic and wealth-accumulating factor in the traumatized societies of the South.

A Recognition of Their Roles
or Increased Burdens for Women? Discourse and Practice

Whatever its motivation, the World Bank's feminism seems to err on the side of common sense. How can one preach development while excluding half the population? How can one work to attain a general level of education that is both irreversible and a harbinger of progress when the divide between the sexes remains as wide as it is today in some countries of sub-Saharan Africa or South Asia? How can one work to modernize key economic sectors of the South if women, who represent the majority of the work force, are deprived of property ownership, access to the means of production, and an education? The World Bank followed the larger development agencies (timidly at first, but with increasing enthusiasm) in claiming that the slow pace of progress and the accumulated failures that had added up over forty years of development were due to the fact that governments, as well as mutilateral lending agencies, had simply forgotten women. Building women into the development process, removing the obstacles that prevent their full economic integration, taking their opinions and wishes into account in those areas where they are most present would allow for a renewal of growth, and render the modernization of social structures irreversible.

This, in fact, is what the World Bank is trying to do. But even if women have acquired a certain presence in the speeches of Bank administrators, their grassroots political position hardly reflects the attention paid to them in official discourse. Even such discourse remains cautious, and most documents exude caution as soon as the subject of women's emancipation is brought up, taking care 'to respect the autonomy of member nations on the sensitive subject of culture' (World Bank 1995b). Populations of member countries would most probably have preferred the Bank to be equally attentive to their traditions and cultures when it came to building huge dams or sharpening austerity programmes which often contributed to the disintegration of urban family ties.

Moreover, women are the main victims of the structural adjustment policies put in place under pressure from the Bretton Woods institutions. Generally speaking, the world has experienced a feminization of poverty since the beginning of the 1980s. Female unemployment has increased at a greater rate than male unemployment in those countries which base their growth on the development of manufacturing industries. The duration of unemployment is also longer for women than for men, and women make up the bulk of the long-term unemployed. As far as education is concerned, the combined phenomena of a decreasing budget for education and the impoverishment of the working class have diminished the numbers of girls in school in many countries; when a family cannot afford to send all its children to school, boys are considered a priority.[5] Furthermore, a major element of structural adjustment programmes everywhere is the emphasis on a culture of exportation, as the only way for a country to earn enough hard currency to pay off its debt. Yet according to the sexual division of labour existing in most countries of the South, rent-seeking activities are usually taken up by men, whereas women are responsible for meeting everyday needs. The priority given to the former has, in numerous cases, increased the already wide revenue gap between the sexes, and created further imbalances that are ultimately detrimental to women's economic worth in the household. In sum, within each social class taken separately, structural adjustment has penalized women far more than men in that it has systematically increased women's invisible, non-remunerated labour while simultaneously diminishing their share of paid employment. One of the principal consequences of the decrease in social investment in the countries of the South, and the overall concern with the profitability of social undertakings, is that a large proportion of public-sector responsibilities, such as health and childcare, have been transferred to the domestic sphere. This shift to free female labour in the household has allowed for considerable savings in terms of government investment and salaries in the structurally adjusted countries (Bessis 1996).

When the World Bank recognized the need to humanize structural adjustment at the end of the 1980s, women were among the 'target groups' which were to benefit from the 'social safety net' that the Bank began to put in place. To give us a better idea of the impact on women's lives of such institutional discourse, however, the Bank's proposals must be compared to the socioeconomic, grassroots reality created by the Bank itself in the first place over the past twenty years. Since the beginning of the 1990s, the Bank has nonetheless been active, especially in the area of schooling for girls – the institution is currently one of the main lenders for educational programmes in the South. According to the Bank, any apparent contradictions between discourse and reality should disappear in the future, because the institution's administrators have pledged to evaluate the impact of all projects on women's lives from the very outset. Yet many observers – even those most likely to support any effort to advance women's rights – are suspicious of the World Bank's relatively late championship of women.

A Dangerous Lure or a Useful Tool?

Do women, in the first instance, followed by the societies of the South, have anything to gain from the Bank's attention to gender in its policymaking, however relative? This question may appear absurd at first glance, but it deserves to be posed in the light of the damage caused by the successive certitudes of the Bretton Woods institutions. Many of the member countries, weakened by a lengthy, multifaceted crisis, certainly needed to clean house and attempt serious economic readjust- ment, but probably not according to the formula imposed by the inter- national lending institutions. While many women of the South are convinced of the need to accelerate their liberation and cast aside tra- ditions which restrict them to an inferior status, should they do so according to the guidelines proposed by the World Bank? The debate is a lively one in numerous countries of the South, particularly in Latin America, as women choose between an institutionalization of their associations, which would allow for greater funding opportunities by international organizations, and, at the same time, the preservation of their pugnacity and function as a space for speaking their minds (Falquet 1997). The World Bank's discourse can never be seen as neutral. The only arguments that the Bank puts forward to rationalize its interest in gender issues are generally of an economic order: investing in women is profitable, hence justified. Carried away by its focus on the economic, the Bank has undertaken econometric analyses in several areas on the rate of return on investment in programmes promoting women. In one instance, the Bank regrets that the 'actual success of awareness cam- paigns to educate girls cannot be analysed from an econometric point of view', wondering whether it is advisable to continue along this path when efficiency cannot be economically proven (Herz, Subbarao et al. 1993). The World Bank certainly resorts to moral argumentation from time to time and, in fact, sets forth two main reasons for its desire to integrate a gender dimension into Bank planning: economic efficiency and ethical justification. The term 'equity' appears time and again in the writings of the experts, but economic analysis continues to play a leading role in all cases. On the issues of domestic and sexual violence, for example, The Bank's *New Plan of Action for Women's Health and Nutrition* em- phasizes that 'the reduction in violence against women will contribute to a decrease in health expeditures and help bring an end to funda- mental human rights violations' (World Bank 1994a). One wonders what the Bank would do if economic and ethical opinions were on opposite sides of the fence, and the increased repression of women actually accelerated economic growth.

Fortunately, this is only a theoretical argument, and runs no risk of becoming reality; if we use it here, it is only to demonstrate the quasi- religious obsession with economics that has characterized the entire development field, as well as World Bank policies.[6] In fact, the Bank seems to regret that women's extraordinary energy and enormous capacity for work have in large part escaped the confines of the market sphere. Obviously the bulk of its programmes in this particular area consist of bringing women into salaried employment and introducing currency as the medium of exchange for their activities in the informal sector.

For these reasons, I would call the World Bank's feminism *instrumental*. If we understand its policies correctly, women's rights must evolve not because their condition is scandalously unacceptable from a legal perspective, but because this same condition thwarts the modernization model proposed by the Bank for the countries of the South, and is consequently counterproductive. As in the case of other similar issues, the Bank uses as examples only those countries where its hypothesis can be proven, making it impossible to contest the validity of its claim. Gender projects are most numerous in sub-Saharan Africa (see above), where the Bank congratulates itself on having contributed to giving gender its rightful place; it signals as noteworthy the study of poverty launched in 1993 under the Africa Special Assistance Programme, an intitiative which brings donors to the subcontinent together under the aegis of the United Nations.

The principal countries where the Bank has been active in gender programming during the past few years include the sub-Saharan nations, Pakistan, Indonesia, Bangladesh, Bolivia, India and Morocco. For each of these countries it is tempting to establish a cause-and-effect relationship between profoundly unequal gender relations, massive poverty and underdevelopment. Yet how obvious is this relationship? Sexual discrimination has always been an inherent and vital element in capitalist growth, even in those countries which have, until recently, been considered models of development for the whole world. The East Asian emerging economies owe the rapidity of their growth in large part to the unbridled exploitation of female labour, one of their 'comparative advantages' in the manufacturing sector during the 1960s and 1970s. The World Bank remains silent about such persistent inequality. Discussing the condition of women in Asia, the Bank mentions only the precocity and extent of the scholarization of South Korean girls as one of the reasons for that nation's economic take-off. Such an analysis is not wrong. But, like all World Bank analyses, it is simplistic and biased, and serves above all to legitimize the Bank's own claims. The World Bank's feminism appears to be no more than the latest tool in an attempt to confine poverty within the limits of what is politically 'acceptable'. The Bank's gender policies continue, in another mode, the very strategy of containment which has always been its trademark: unless, that is, the Bank, by joining the current revolution in gender relations, is unwittingly contributing to the inauguration of a new era in economics, one in which the idea of development takes priority over that of growth, and one which recognizes women's contribution to social and community needs is larger than that of men. But the World Bank's conversion does not seem to have gone that far.

Gender as an Alibi?

Once again, economic legitimacy serves to determine policy-making. The Bretton Woods institutions are masters at imposing Western policies on the rest of the world, particularly in the context of the ideological collapse of the socialist idea in the name of economic rationalism. The question here is not whether the structural adjustment programmes have been opportune, since the debate on this topic is far from over. What should be emphasized is that over the course of the past twenty-five years, the Bretton Woods institutions have remodelled the social and economic landscape of the adjusted countries, remade the state in their image, extinguished some productive activities to make way for others, and been indirectly responsible for the fall of many regimes or the survival of certain others, without ever engaging in politics. Such is the magic of economics.

In the past, technology overshadowed the political dimension of the development options chosen. Here I am obviously referring to the 'Green Revolution' of the 1960s. This technical revolution allowed for considerable expansion of cereal production in the large, heavily populated Asian countries; it was perfected and popularized with the intent of masking the social revolutions that would bring dangerous contagion to Asia at this moment of the Cold War. The augmentation of foodstuffs production and the creation of a rural bourgeoisie diminished the spectre of revolutionary calamity in those countries most likely to succumb. Despite the World Bank's important role in the spread of the Green Revolution,[7] that revolution was never described as a political act. Does the issue of gender, as it is currently used by the Bank, also serve as an alibi for a political agenda?

Two issues are elided if we pin the blame for the development failures and inequalities of the South on gender discrimination. The first concerns the lending institutions' fairly large share of responsibility for the vain efforts of the last few decades, if one agrees that their only error was that they did not measure the importance of the role that women were just waiting in the wings to play in the process of economic growth. The second is equally significant: placing the emphasis on gender depoliticizes searing questions of social inequality and conflict, and breaks down notions of solidarity founded less on gender than on social class.

Throughout the world – and not only in the South, which can hardly claim exclusivity in this matter – the struggle against sexual inequality has fortunately become one of the ethical imperatives of the new century. Inequality contributes to an increase in the poverty and distress of the female half of the world's population in many countries; the situation has worsened in recent years because the oppression of women also serves for some as a guarantee against the chaos of the times. Yet women cannot be the only explanation – after so many others – for the poverty and hardship many countries experience as a result of the development process. One of the Bank's timeworn strategies is to designate others as responsible for social inequality at the national level (the institution remains far more discreet on the subject of in-equality at the global level), rather than discuss the critical dysfunctions of the dominant economic system. The goal is to find other remedies for poverty than the redistribition and redefined use of the world's riches. As in the case of the Green Revolution – or, more recently, in the case of micro-credit, which has been hailed as a panacea in the struggle to end world poverty – women will find themselves assigned the role of increasing available wealth, and distributing that wealth to the poorest. Gender is an economical way to avoid analysis of the more complex issues of force and domination both at the heart of the soci-eties of the South and at the global level, where sexual inequalities will take their inevitable place as fundamental, but not exclusive.

The feminism of the World Bank is thus opportunistic and serves, first and foremost, the Bank's own aims. Must we, then, object to consequences of the Bank's policies which may very well be positive? This question summarizes a dilemma that women's movements have addressed from the outset: how to collaborate with dominant institutions without being manipulated by them, without serving as instruments for purposes other than women's true emancipation? This question has no general or definitive response, but must be negotiated – vigilantly – every day. Many women's organizations in the South have understood what a double-edged sword is the attempt to bargain with the World Bank in the name of their own best interests. Many have banded to-gether, forming an organization under the campaign banner – 'Women Targeting the World Bank' (Frade 1999) – with the goal of inducing this international institution to reduce the existing gap between its declarations and a real taking into account of gender issues in its pro-grammes. How to collaborate without being duped? That is the question.

Notes

1. From 1988 onward, the World Development Reports included a table entitled 'Women in Development'. In 1995 the title was changed to 'Gender Comparisons'. In the *Annual World Development Indicators*, which the Bank began publishing in 1997, several tables are devoted to comparisons according to gender. The 1993 *World Development Report*, which focused on health, devoted a good deal of space to women's issues.

2. For a history of the Bank's attention to gender issues, see *Gender Issues in World Bank Lending* (World Bank 1995b).

3. Structural Adjustment Loans are not included under the Projects heading.

4. The International Development Association, better known as the IDA, is a branch of the World Bank which lends to the poorest countries under less stringent conditions.

5. According to UNICEF, in Guinea and Benin (see documents on the situation of women and children published in 1997 and 1995, respectively, in these two countries), the disparities between boys and girls have increased in the past ten years. In Benin, the decrease in the literacy rate of ten- to fourteen-year-olds, which fell from 47.6 per cent to 46.5 per cent between 1979 and 1992, has mainly penalized the girls: in 1994, there was one girl for every three boys attending school. These two countries have been subjected to structural adjustment programmes.

6. George and Sabelli have virtually used a theological register in their work devoted to the World Bank; see their *Crédits sans frontières: la religion séculière de la Banque mondiale* (George and Sabelli 1994). In an article published in 1997, I myself resorted to the same tone, so compelling is the analogy. The Bank's dogmatism lends itself to such verbal flights. In the study cited above, *Let the Girls Learn* (Herz and Subbarao et al. 1993), the Bank insists yet again that 'economic reform will increase the financial productivity of women'. 'We can reasonably expect', it goes on, 'that when women's income increases their attitude toward their daughters' educations will change according to the measures adopted to deregulate the economy.' The causal link between these two phenomena seems evident only to the Bank.

7. The World Bank has been one of the principal funders of the Green Revolution, mainly in Asia. From India to Indonesia, irrigation projects have monopolized the majority of its funding. See *L'Arme alimentaire* (Bessis 1981).

References

Bessis, S. (1981) *L'Arme alimentaire*, Paris: Maspero.

Bessis, S. (1996) 'La féminisation de la pauvreté', in *Femmes du Sud chefs de famille*, Paris: Karthala.

Bessis, S. (1997) 'Les nouveaux enjeux et les nouveaux acteurs des débats internationaux dans les années 90', *Revue Tiers Monde*, no. 151.

Carolyn, W. (1994) *Mujeres trabajadoras en Latinoamerica: Brechas en la participación, remuneración y política pública*, Washington, DC: The World Bank, Region of Latin America and the Caribbean, Technical Department.

Falquet, J. (1997) 'Le débat du féminisme américain et des Caraïbes à propos des ONGs', *Cahiers du Gedisst*, no. 21.

Frade, L. (1999) 'La Banque mondiale, point de mire des femmes', *Contrôle citoyen*, no. 1.

George, S. and F. Sabelli (1994) *Crédits sans frontières: la religion séculière de la Banque mondiale*, Paris: La Découverte.

Herz, B., K. Subbarao et al. (1993) *Let the Girls Learn*, Summary Document 133F, Washington, DC: The World Bank.

World Bank (1994a) *New Plan of Action for Women's Health and Nutrition*, Washington, DC: The World Bank.

World Bank (1994b) *Reinforcement of Women's Participation in Development*, Washington, DC: The World Bank.

World Bank (1995a) *Advancing Gender Equality: From Concept to Action*, Washington, DC: The World Bank.

World Bank (1995b) *Gender Issues in World Bank Lending*, Washington, DC: The World Bank.

World Bank (1995c) *Toward Gender Equality: The Role of Public Policy*, Washington, DC: The World Bank.

World Bank (1995d) *World Development Report: Workers in an Integrating World*, Washington, DC: The World Bank.

World Bank (1988–1999) *World Development Report*, Washington, DC: The World Bank.

Yunus, M. (1999) *Banker to the Poor: Micro Lending in the Battle Against World Poverty*, London: Aurum Press.

International Organizations: Women's Rights and Gender Equality

Aster Zaoudé and Joanne Sandler

The Women Who Move Us

Like any other movement for social change, the global women's move-ment has its legends. Ela Bhatt of India, Wangari Mathai of Kenya, Alicia Villanueva of Peru, and Bella Abzug of the United States – each in her own way, and in her own country, has spearheaded a social movement that influenced the lives of millions of women and their families. Each of these movements ultimately challenged cultural norms and national legislation, and transformed the policies of international and multilateral institutions. These women engineered a significant shift in attitudes towards women's empowerment by bringing discrimination from the fringe of development discourse into the mainstream of development policy.

Indeed, organizing by the women's movement resulted in significant strides for gender equality long before the term *gender analysis* was promoted as a component of any sustainable development initiative. All the women mentioned in the paragraph above began their work before *gender mainstreaming* permeated the rhetoric of development policies and mission statements. None of these women had training in a rights-based framework. Yet their actions – undertaken more than twenty years ago – encompassed all the principles underpinning the numerous training courses, manuals, checklists and guidebooks that have been produced in the name of *gender awareness* in government agencies, multi-lateral and bilateral institutions, and large NGOs. These leaders' actions – and those of hundreds of thousands of women who were also organizing for gender justice and equality in countries worldwide – were instrumental in spurring the global consensus on women's empowerment that emerged from the UN world conferences of the 1990s.

The women's movement has broken through seemingly impenetrable boundaries by questioning prevailing paradigms, seizing opportunities, fashioning concrete responses to gender inequalities, mobilizing constituencies, providing alternative policy perspectives, and influencing decision-makers. Ela Bhatt organized unaffiliated street-vendors in India into a powerful union to claim economic rights and protection; Wangari Mathai mobilized the Green Belt Movement to challenge policies that threaten the environment and livelihoods of people in Kenya; Alicia Villanueva created a Peruvian artisan co-operative that sold to an international market and involved women in producing cloth sculptures portraying dignified figures living lives free from abuse and violence; Bella Abzug built women's caucuses on gender, the environment and development that influenced UN policy-making, and sent a clarion call to women everywhere to raise their voices.

Indisputably, there are many different feminisms. The arduous work that women like Ela Bhatt and Wangari Mathai have undertaken demonstrates the diversity of beliefs and local practices that characterize the global feminist movement. What remains constant throughout, however, is a deep-seated commitment to gender equality, justice and women's rights expressed through a constant search for broader spaces for women as agents of change. Their ambition is not limited to more women entering the mainstream but, rather, focused on changing the course of the mainstream with the new flow of empowered women.

The history of organizing in the last quarter of the twentieth century that led development organizations – such as the Bretton Woods institutions, United Nations agencies, and governments – to place gender equality and women's rights on their agendas is a story that is still being told. What started as a footnote indicating that women will benefit from these institutions' policies and programmes has become an international priority. The challenge ahead is to translate this commitment into tangible results, and hold the institutions accountable. The Fourth World Conference on Women (1995) produced the Beijing Platform for Action, a visionary roadmap on the path to gender equality. This is a consensus document agreed to by nearly two hundred countries, representing distinct and divergent cultures and, in some cases, nations engaged in protracted conflicts with each other.

We, as longtime administrators in the international development system, uphold the value of efforts to place gender equality on the global policy-making agenda, and discuss the ways in which it has yielded positive and concrete results for women, and their families and communities. We will highlight three changes affecting multilateral institutions that have the long-term potential to transform women's lives: first, the evolution of gender mainstreaming and women's empowerment as complementary strategies for achieving gender equality; second, the use of existing human rights machinery to promote equality and change institutions; and third, the growing co-operation and understanding within a critical mass of women – inside and outside development institutions – with the shared goal of moving the gender-equality agenda forward. Rather than follow any particular prescription for achieving gender equality, these changes demonstrate that the 'challenge is to spot the trends, identify the spaces where change is possible, make the most of productive alliances, and mobilize resources and arguments that can help at [any] particular moment' (Itzin and Newman 1995: 25).

Before beginning, we want to clarify the 'voice' in which this essay is being written. We are acutely aware of the privilege and responsibility that we have, as feminists who work in an outpost of the multilateral development community. The United Nations Development Fund for Women (UNIFEM) is an autonomous organization that works in close association with the United Nations Development Programme (UNDP). At the same time, UNIFEM is distinctly aware that it was created in response to demands on the UN by the global women's movement, and that it has a strong non-governmental constituency of women's advocates worldwide who will – and should – hold it accountable. On a personal level, working at UNIFEM, we link our lifetime commitment to the women's movement with our daily work in an organization that has the legitimacy to create a political space for women. UNIFEM is a *women's* fund that supports precisely the kind of organizing that Bhatt, Mathai, Villanueva and Abzug epitomize. We negotiate from a position of principle from within a bureaucracy that must fulfil its commitment to gender equality. While we recognize that bureaucratic procedures and principles are changing because of the pressure from within,[1] we also acknowledge that they remain quite distinct from the women's movement from which our work was born.

Putting Gender and Women's Equality on the Global Agenda

The growing interest in gender equality that emerged between the Third and Fourth World Conferences on Women (Nairobi in 1985 and Beijing in 1995) has been effective in chipping away at a number of entrenched paradigms. Gender has greater entrée as a form of analysis, and couches exploration of power relations in terms and methods that are far less threatening than the discourse on patriarchy or oppression. At the same time, it is crucial to make a strong case that a concentration on gender does not exclude an approach to development focused on women's empowerment. Rather, women's empowerment is both a strategy option and a prerequisite to gender mainstreaming. UNIFEM's programmes have demonstrated that women's empowerment and gender mainstreaming are both crucial and interlinked.

In West Africa, for example, UNIFEM has been instrumental in building women's political leadership skills to encourage more women to engage with confidence in the electoral process, to challenge the prevailing 'ethics' in electoral campaigns, and to create women's lobby groups, across party lines, when important issues are at stake. The case of the parliamentary debate led by women Members of Parliament on the law banning female genital mutilation in Senegal (discussed in Chapter Five of this volume) illustrates the power of a critical mass of women in multilateral institutions. The movement started with pioneer villages that abandoned female genital mutilation and ended in parliament with participation of village representatives who attended parliamentary debates for the first time ever. These village representatives – men and women, including religious leaders – are using the law to promote the adoption of public pledges to abandon the practice throughout the country, and in neighbouring countries that share a similar culture.

It was soon after the Third World Conference on Women in Nairobi (1985) that terms like 'gender analysis', 'gender-sensitive planning', and 'gender-differentiated statistics' began to enter the parlance of development institutions.[2] The use of gender analysis as a tool gave rise to the notion of 'gender mainstreaming'. This process for change used various tools to inform and sensitize policy-makers, to assist staff members in the implementation of gender-responsive programmes, and to raise the public awareness of both women and men. The debate on a precise definition of 'gender mainstreaming' rages on, with many valuable perspectives emerging in the discussions. For this essay, we find it useful to refer to Rounaq Jahan's definition, which highlights two approaches. First, Jahan identifies an 'integrationist' approach to gender mainstreaming, 'which builds gender issues within existing development paradigms; the overall development agenda is not transformed but each issue is adapted to take into account women and gender concerns' (Jahan 1995: 12–13). The second, an 'agenda-setting' approach to gender mainstreaming, 'implies transformation of the existing development agenda with a gender perspective.... It is not simply women as individuals, but a women's "agenda" that gets recognition from the mainstream' (Jahan 1995: 13). It can be argued that the first is a strategic step towards achieving the second, as long as it is clear from the outset that the objective is to transform the process and the results.

Writers of numerous studies, reports and papers have observed that the integrationist approach remains by far the most widely used in most international development agencies. And feminists continue to debate, as well, about whether the use of gender analysis and gender mainstreaming may not, in the long term, become an institutional tool that underpins the undoing of structures – gender units, gender focal points, gender teams – established to move the agenda for gender equality forward. Management in many organizations has attempted to determine whether mainstreaming has been accomplished, or contends that, with the establishment of a gender policy, there is no longer any need to support women-specific initiatives, or have special women's or gender units. Certainly, many organizations – from large NGOs like Oxfam International and the International Planned Parenthood Federation to UN and Bretton Woods institutions – are dismantling their gender units and replacing them with gender 'teams' that are more decentralized, and bring together those responsible for gender from different parts of the organization.

In addition to the two debates mentioned above – for example, what is gender mainstreaming? Will the promotion of 'gender' as a theoretical concept upon which to base programmes in support of equality ultimately be sustainable to ensure women's empowerment? – a third debate also underpins differing strategic approaches. This is the perceived dichotomy between 'gender' and 'women' as a strategic basis for programming. There is a widespread (mis)perception that if a women's empowerment strategy is used, then gender disappears as an organizing principle. We have many colleagues in multilateral and bilateral institutions, for instance, who would say that UNIFEM does not 'do' gender, and that it is concerned only with women's empowerment – this despite the fact that UNIFEM has been working on gender-mainstreaming strategies since its inception in 1976, long before the term came into popular use.

We have found, in fact, that the point at which concentration on women's empowerment and gender mainstreaming converge is precisely where transformation towards gender equality has the greatest potential to occur. This is true whether we are talking about internal organizational procedures – like promotions and work/family policies – or development programmes. There is a plethora of examples. One, from UNIFEM's experience, would be our work to mainstream gender into national development planning and political processes. We are supporting the Southern African Development Community (SADC), related to the Panchayat system in India, and to women's political participation in the South Pacific and West Africa, using both a gender mainstreaming and a women's empowerment approach. Each of these initiatives is based on a gender analysis that reveals different levels of access and control between men and women, and power relations that are exercised in a specific cultural context. Programme strategies respond to the need to build capacity and create political space for women – that is, provide opportunities for empowerment – with a view to achieving equal access to opportunities. Programme objectives are designed to achieve gender mainstreaming, with a focus on the 'agenda-setting' approach, rather than the integrationist approach.

Both approaches – gender mainstreaming and women's empowerment – are necessary, and mutually reinforcing. In UNIFEM's mainstreaming project in SADC countries, the signing, in 1997, of a Declaration on Gender and Development by SADC Heads of State at their annual meeting was a hard-sought gender-mainstreaming outcome that emerged after five years of work. The Declaration contributes to a policy framework that will enable resources to be allocated, government units to be created, and programmes to be implemented. But the statement alone would be far less effective without the five years of work involved training a cadre of internal and external advocates in gender-analysis skills, including the empowerment of women inside and outside of the bureaucracy through supporting their development of advocacy approaches that are useful for reaching decision-makers. At the end of the day, while the statement creates the political space, it is the empowerment of the advocates that is the essential element in ensuring that gains can be monitored and sustained.[3]

The debates taking place inside and outside international development institutions about 'women or gender', 'integration or transformation', 'mainstreaming or empowerment', often serve to distract us from the goals of gender equality and gender justice. The significant opportunity that we have, in this new century, is a mandate for both women's empowerment and gender mainstreaming. Through their endorsement of programmes of action from the International Conference on Population and Development and the Beijing Conference, governments have recognized the essential nature of both these approaches. Our challenge is to become 'ambidextrous' enough to identify where different strategies are most effective, and then to press for the resources and political space in which to use them:

> Gender advocates recognize the significance of collective action strategies in getting politicians, development agencies and bureaucrats to respond to gender demands. Indeed, a wide range of gender movements ... now exists in virtually every country in the world ... many of the gains which women have made in public policy owe more to the advocacy and mobilizational work of gender groups than to philanthropy or simple goodwill from men. (Bangura 1997: 26–7)

Rights-based Strategies

The effective coalition that has been forged by feminists and human rights activists in the past decade has the potential to transform both approaches and all outcomes of development. Powerful as the notion of gender was in the 1980s in stimulating a change in policies and practice, the notion of rights makes it possible to place on the agenda new issues that are critical to women's lives and livelihoods. Beyond the 'bilingualism' described by Naila Kabeer (Kabeer 1996), we now need a 'trilingualism' to work at the interface of women's empowerment, gender mainstreaming and women's rights.

The issue of gender-based violence illustrates most dramatically the ways in which the infiltration of rights-based programming has the power to change women's lives. As Secretary-General of the United Nations Kofi Annan has noted: 'Violence against women is perhaps the most shameful human rights violation. It knows no boundaries of geography, culture or wealth. As long as it continues, we cannot claim to be making real progress towards equality, development and peace' (Annan 1999). Work on eliminating gender-based violence has brought women's advocates together across boundaries of race, ethnicity, class and nationality. Throughout the early 1990s, the international development community still viewed violence against women – particularly domestic violence and violations of women's bodily integrity – as a *private* issue, and it was difficult to find a place for it on the development agenda. When UNIFEM published its position paper *Battered Dreams* in 1993, and increased funding available to groups working on issues of domestic violence at both local and national levels, there was little acceptance, or even discussion, of this issue in most multilateral organizations.

Women's rights activists have worked tirelessly at all levels to link movements, to create a new discourse – 'there are no human rights without women's human rights' – and to use the intergovernmental treaty bodies and conventions to create a mandate for change at the normative level. The appointment by the United Nations of a Special Rapporteur on Violence Against Women, the ratification of an Optional Protocol to the Convention on the Elimination of All Forms of Discrimination Against Women (CEDAW), and the infiltration of gender issues into discussions on the International Criminal Court, for instance, are direct results of the lobbying and advocacy undertaken by this movement.

What difference does it make in women's lives to work for gender equality? In UNIFEM's experience, the entry of discourse on gender-based violence into the development dialogue has been an extremely powerful vehicle for moving hearts, minds and – in increasing amounts – resource allocations to gender issues. UNIFEM's programming in 1998 is an example of this power:

- The work of transforming social values and creating a culture of respect for the human rights of women is a lengthy and critical process. Seizing opportunities presented by the fiftieth anniversary of the Universal Declaration of Human Rights, UNIFEM worked throughout 1998 to promote and protect women's human rights, and to eliminate violence against women.

- UNIFEM initiated global inter-agency campaigns, bringing together nine United Nations agencies to address the pandemic of gender-based violence. In Africa, Asia/Pacific, and Latin America and the Caribbean, the synergy and collaboration between the UN, leading women's NGOs and networks, the media, law-enforcement organizations, and government agencies created an unprecedented level of attention and activism around the critical need to eliminate violence against women.

- The overall campaign goals aimed to change attitudes and behaviours that perpetuate violence; motivate governments to develop or change policies, legislation, and practices to prevent violence against women and girls; strengthen the capacity of civil-society organizations effectively to advocate for and implement violence-prevention programmes; promote partnerships and co-ordination among UN agencies working on the issue of violence against women and girls.

- In all regions in which the campaign took place, concrete and significant results emerged in response to the powerful coalition of UN agencies, NGOs and government agencies. In the follow-up to African campaign activities, African governments have been pressured by their women's movements and human rights activists to review and adapt their national legislation taking CEDAW into account. Senegal and the Ivory Coast passed various laws that protect women and girls from domestic violence, rape, sexual harassment and female genital mutilation. Mauritanian women are pushing for the ratification of CEDAW, while Moroccan women are challenging their country's reservations to the convention. The African Charter on Human and People's Rights has a draft protocol on women's rights, and the African Commission on Human Rights has appointed a Special Rapporteur on Women's Rights.

- UNIFEM also launched a global electronic dialogue in 1998, called 'End-violence'. The End-violence list includes more than 1,600 people (30 per cent from the developing world) representing more than sixty countries who share strategies, experiences and concrete tools, such as legislation and campaign material, from their work on ending violence. The End-violence list was launched with support from the World Bank and the Global Knowledge for Development Partnership.[4]
- On 8 March 1999, the last International Women's Day of the twentieth century, UNIFEM co-ordinated a groundbreaking event, 'A World Free of Violence Against Women'. This global videoconference linked the UN General Assembly in New York to sites in New Delhi, Mexico City, Nairobi, and the European Parliament in Strasbourg, France. Human rights advocates, survivors of gender-based violence, UN decision-makers, and government leaders came together to highlight the achievements of and obstacles facing violence-prevention programmes. In addition to the 2,000-plus participants at the UN and those participating at the other four sites, viewing audiences from all over the world hooked up to the videoconference via satellite, the World Wide Web and videoconferencing technologies. Groups from Turkey to Fiji, universities throughout the United States, telecentres in Russia, and thousands of individuals at their personal computers listened and watched as government leaders and celebrities joined with the courageous survivors of gender-based violence; together they focused a global spotlight on what Secretary-General Kofi Annan calls, in the quotation above, 'the most shameful human rights violation'.
- The campaigns and the videoconference were both UN 'inter-agency' initiatives, which means that UNIFEM brought other UN organizations into the planning and implementation of these efforts. These initiatives have the power to be transformational with regard to the

United Nations' commitment and capacity to respond to violence against women as an obstacle to development. Organizations that participated in these activities reviewed their current programmes on this topic, developed internal working groups on gender-based violence, and, in some cases, committed new resources. Additionally, the legitimacy that the issue acquired through the holding of the videoconference in the General Assembly and the endorsement of the campaign by so many UN organizations and governments has other effects. Internal advocates and change agents are strengthened, through these efforts, to become more vocal and visible about the relationship of their work on gender-based violence to other development concerns. Subsequent changes need time to materialize, but there is no denying that the stage has been set for these changes.

The issue of gender-based violence has the potential to transcend organizational directives. It can attract powerful advocates who work as dedicated agents for change within their own organizations. While there is a long way to go and gains sustained to date are by no means assured, the institutional alliances and partnerships that have developed in confronting this global pandemic provide a model for agency in the field of gender and other thematic areas.

How Critical is the Critical Mass?
Building Alliances for Change

Anyone working on gender issues in international organizations has had the experience, in countless meetings and workshops with their colleagues, of being the lone voice in the room who is unceasingly compelled to correct, defend or lobby around gender and women's concerns. Likewise, we all know the feeling of relief and camaraderie when another voice enters the discussion; and we all rejoice when finally a male voice joins in, although we still have mixed feelings when he gets attention for raising the very issues that the woman has just presented so well. When the voices supporting women's concerns multiply to half of those in any given discussion, an entirely new organizing approach becomes possible. This is, in fact, happening increasingly in international organizations – a source of much pride and hope.

When we spend our time constantly defending a space for gender equality, there is very little opportunity for debate about different gender approaches, for analysis of good and bad practices, for honestly evaluating and sharing experiences in programmes. When that space becomes established and secure – whether at a meeting, within an organization, or in a country or community – the dialogue, experimentation and learning that influence the strategies we use to achieve gender equality can surface, and lead to programmatic innovations and change.

There is no doubt that a critical mass of women in key positions can make a difference, but the goal remains equal representation in all institutions. The notion of affirmative action or quotas is being debated as a means of bridging the gender gap in various institutions and democratic processes. In Senegal, the women's political lobby group got all the parties to agree to an allocation of seats for women candidates, and announced their initiative in the local press. It was an incentive for more women to test the political waters. But in practice, most women candidates were on the list of 'alternates', a peculiarity of political systems in France and Francophone Africa which provides a list of substitutes for all main candidates in the event of illness. Very few women were willing to play 'the dirty game of politics' under these circumstances and could not find a worthwhile campaign agenda on their parties' platform. Affirmative action may not be able to bridge gaps that require more than just numbers. Will greater numbers of women from different political parties (including conservative and extremist groups) make a difference in parliament, or should there be more concern about supporting candidates from the political parties that have gender equality on their political agenda? Will male-dominated political parties make a sustained commitment to gender equality without a critical mass of women *within their own parties* pushing the debate to the forefront?

Certainly, institutional representation is not just a question of numbers. But numbers *do* make a difference – probably a greater difference than can be made by the lone woman at the top. While the recent appointment of a number of women heads of agencies changes the face of the decision-making corpus of the UN, their effective advocacy of gender issues also requires support and allies. The extent to which their leadership fuels the transformation of the organizations of which they are in charge – as well as the UN Secretariat – will be one of the benchmarks by which their success will be judged by gender-equality advocates. To date, we are unaware of any analysis that explores the ways in which having an unprecedented number of UN women leading UN agencies has affected policy implementation and congruence.

As the UN moves through a reform process that promotes consultation and co-ordination, we would like to invoke a useful business example from John Naisbitt and Patricia Aburdene's *Reinventing the Corporation*:

> Significant change occurs when there is a confluence of changing values and economic necessity. Both the massive influx of women into the work force and the need for corporate restructuring constitute such a confluence, with each trend spurring, hastening and reinforcing each other. As companies reinvent themselves, they need to find new structures and values; those that learn from how women do things will have a head start. ... Women can transform the workplace by expressing, not by giving up, their personal values. (Aburdene and Naisbitt 1985: 204)

The expertise acquired in the women's movement is being recognized, and its protagonists are being recruited into international organizations – a process that has yielded some notable change. Like us, many women have left community or NGO organizing to become 'femocrats' in some cases, internal agents for change in others, or *both*, depending upon who is doing the naming.[5] In short, we used the pressure brought to bear by NGOs to force our own agencies to conform to public opinion on women. The world conferences of the 1990s – and the combination of an NGO forum with intergovernmental meetings – offered a good model for collaboration between internal and external gender advocates. Women in international institutions were able to create a political space in which those organizing on the outside could be heard and, in some cases, to generate support for their programmes.[6]

But roles have changed in the post-Beijing era. The multilateral system is going through significant reform; there are notable opportunities and threats from globalization, and infinite possibilities for connectedness through electronic networking. While NGO access to the UN is a subject of hot debate, the critical nature of working with civil society has been recognized. In fact, UNIFEM's history of working with NGOs, which at one time would have been viewed within the UN as an indication of UNIFEM's marginality, is now seen as a useful body of experience. Another example: in the Africa preparatory conference for the five-year review of the Beijing Platform for Action, greater efforts were devoted to promoting close collaboration between governments and NGOs in the national review process, and in forming delegations of NGO government representatives.

We now need powerful alliances to support implementation of Beijing conference recommendations. Such coalitions require collaboration on accountability strategies, on monitoring progress, on demands for transparency, on sharing best and worst programme practices, on linking gender-equality recommendations from all the world conferences to promote greater policy coherence. They also require collaboration on demands for increased resource allocations to gender-equality programmes, both within UN organizations and to NGOs through partnerships around common objectives. As Kathleen Staudt has observed:

> At the multilateral level, only one fleeting moment of the decades-long history of WID contained published (and therefore publicly accountable), precise and comparable categories and figures. Projects of exclusive concern to women were 5 per cent of all projects; projects designed to include women were 12 per cent of projects; projects affecting women with no provision for their participation were 56 per cent of projects, but 63 per cent of funding. A decade later, we have no published documentation to determine whether this has changed. (Staudt 1998: 180)

There is as yet untapped potential in seeking collaborative opportunities between NGO networks and multilateral networks. Electronic networking and years of experience have strengthened global, regional and national networks of women. Within multilateral agencies, a networking model is also being adopted. Within the United Nations, operational organizations have formed the United Nations Development Group (UNDG) Sub-group on Gender, which is chaired by UNIFEM and brings together members of gender units of all the funds and programmes. Another example is the gender unit within the UNDP, which regularly convenes gender focal points from all other departments to co-ordinate planning and policy advocacy. In the larger UN system, the Interagency Committee on Women and Gender Equality (IACWGE) meets annually and works on a task-force basis throughout the year to take on UN system-wide gender projects.

At the field level, the UN Resident Co-ordinator system often includes a gender thematic group, which brings together representatives of all UN organizations in the country to develop synergistic strategies for promoting gender equality. In many cases, where the new UN Development Assistance Framework (UNDAF) is being piloted, gender has been introduced as a crosscutting issue in all sectors and programmes of joint concern by the UN country teams, which includes the World Bank. In Senegal, UNIFEM chairs the donor group on gender, which extends to multilateral and bilateral donors, as well as international NGOs.

Some initial experiences of bringing these networks together illustrate their potential. It was the organizing strategies of regional and global women's human rights networks that stimulated the UN inter-agency campaigns on violence against women that UNIFEM convened. In many countries, the benefits from networking between UN and civil-society organizations included changes in legislation, vastly expanded media and public education around issues of gender-based violence, and breaking the silence on a previously invisible issue. Partnerships that bring NGO networks into collaboration with multilateral organizations focused on women's access to credit and on reproductive rights have also yielded important advances.

In preparation for the five-year review of Beijing, WomenWatch[7] was involved in a collaborative planning process with and provision of support to a network of nearly twelve alternative media networks from every region in the world. Working together, these networks were able to reach millions of people to support informed participation in the five-year review. Most importantly, the opportunities to generate and share accountability strategies have allowed for compliance with and implementation of commitments in ways that benefit women's lives.

Conclusion

Achieving gender equality is our challenge. The process of change will require the transformation of international institutions. And change, as Catherine Itzin reminds us, is 'not necessarily linear, deliberate and continuous, but sudden and built on potentials that have been latent or peripheral...' (Itzin and Newman 1995: 150). The addition of gender- and rights-based programming to WID empowerment perspectives stimulated latent potential in each, and built synergistically to expand and institutionalize support for gender equality.

We are certainly a long way, in practice, from achieving the equality we seek. At the same time, we have come a long way in establishing the potential and the policy framework. Strengthening protections available to women against previously invisible forms of violence, helping women to prepare themselves to expand their political influence, deepening women's understanding of and involvement in the economic decisions that affect their lives and communities – all these represent steps towards a greater goal. It is not an easy or a straight path, but a path that requires one step at a time, a vigilant holding of ground already achieved, and a clear vision of where we are going.

Notes

1. And from *without*, as recent pressure from NGOs and civil society worldwide demonstrates [Editors].

2. The Harvard gender-analysis framework (1985) became a classic reference on undertaking gender analysis; Maxine Molyneux injected notions of gendered practical and strategic needs as a way of understanding immediate and longer-term implications of mainstream initiatives (1985); Sara Longwe developed a theoretical framework and matrix widely used by UNICEF to guide analysis of projects from an empowerment perspective (1986); and Caroline Moser added the gender policy and planning dimension with IDS (1989). These and other concepts and tools became the basis for training courses which, by now, many thousands of programme staff in development and government agencies have attended, as a way of stimulating and improving gender-responsive programming.

3. The intrinsic necessity of managing both gender-mainstreaming and women's empowerment strategies simultaneously was articulated by UNIFEM's Executive Director, Noeleen Heyzer, in the 'Women's Development Agenda' the organization published in the lead-up to Beijing; the document was based on the priorities and principles articulated by women worldwide in the planning process leading up to the conference (Heyzer 1995: 11).

4. Which involves such international institutions as UNDP, UNICEF and the World Bank.

5. Karen Booth's article 'National Mother, Global Whore, and Transnational Femocrats: The Politics of AIDS and the Construction of Women at the World Health Organization' offers a provocative assessment of the way dialogue and debate in multilateral organizations compromise feminist values and goals, as well as the inside feminists who are negotiating their implementation (Booth 1998).

6. Examples are UNIFEM's financing of a gender adviser in the Secretariat of the United Nations Conference on Environment and Development, or the support provided by multilateral and bilateral agencies for global and regional networking activities.

7. An electronic gateway to information on gender produced by UN agencies and founded by UNIFEM, the Division for the Advancement of Women, and INSTRAW (United Nations International Research and Training Institute for the Advancement of Women).

References

Aburdene, P. and J. Naisbitt (1985) *Re-inventing the Corporation*, New York: Warner.
Annan, K. (1999) 'A World Free of Violence Against Women', address at the UN inter-agency global videoconference, 8 March.
Bangura, Y. (1997) *Policy Dialogue and Gendered Development: Institutional and Ideological Commitments*, Geneva: UNRISD, Discussion Paper No. 87, June.
Booth, K. (1998) 'National Mother, Global Whore, and Transnational Femocrats: The Politics of AIDS and the Construction of Women at the World Health Organization', *Feminist Studies*, vol. 24, no. 1.
Heyzer, N. (1995) *Women's Development Agenda*, New York: United Nations Development Fund for Women.

Itzin, C. and J. Newman (1995) *Gender, Culture, and Organizational Change: Putting Theory into Practice*, New York: Routledge.

Jahan, R. (1995) *The Elusive Agenda: Mainstreaming Women in Development*, London: Zed Books.

Kabeer, N. (1996) *Focus on Integrating Gender into the Politics of Development*, UNRISD, no. 2.

Staudt, K. (1998) *Policy, Politics and Gender*, Hartford, CT: Kumarian Press.

Response to Sophie Bessis

Aster Zaoudé

Sophie Bessis begins her essay with a very important statement on the role of the World Bank. It is indeed a major source of funding for development and a powerful lending instrument, compared to other multilateral institutions: it has the capacity to orient borrowers' policy-making through conditionalities attached to its lending policies. It is therefore important to analyse the Bank's commitment to gender equity in the light of its mandate and of its unique capacity to influence policy changes at the highest levels.

In dealing with women's marginalization, many development institutions were hoping to bridge the gap by bringing more women into the mainstream economic framework. African women are a good example. Rural women are fully involved in the production, processing, conservation and marketing of food commodities. Even when they play a major role in cash-earning agriculture, their inputs are not accounted for. They have limited – and often no – right to land, no access to credit, to training and to technologies that could have helped them improve their economic contribution. They are not considered as economic operators because the analytical framework is not equipped to register small, informal, indigenous activities, despite the impressive cumulative volume of income generated by the informal sector.

There is general agreement that agriculture is the backbone of African economies, and women have shown that agricultural processing is perhaps where indigenous industries have a good chance to develop. This reality is not translated into a potential for the development of most African economies that have turned their backs on the food sector in favour of export-oriented cash crops and the export of raw materials. Processing food and raw materials in developing countries has not been privileged for historical reasons, and not much has changed since the end of colonial times.

Gender analysis is an instrument that would inform economists on the potential of women's work in the food sector. Gender analysis is a framework through which women's economic contributions can be brought to light, valued and accounted for. Gender mainstreaming is not a simple arithmetic operation. It is not the simple addition of women's labour-force and productive activities to those of men, because in development 2 plus 2 can add up to 5 or 6. Investing in women is investing in communities. Social services provided freely by women in terms of their reproductive role, their informal activities and their role in educating, healing, feeding and ensuring social cohesion are not given a monetary value. When the same services are charged for by insurance companies, health services, and entertainment and educational institutions, when food is bought and water and fuel are distributed by big companies, they have a monetary value that women's backs do not have.

According to Sophie Bessis, the World Bank has jumped on the gender 'bandwagon', and she believes that it is mainly because the Bank did not want to be left out of the gender 'fad'. Bessis also believes that the Bank has an 'instrumentalist' approach to gender mainstreaming: if more women can help move the Bank's economic agenda forward, then the Bank will not mind being feminist.

I am not sure that the World Bank needs to be in fashion, nor if it is a concern for the Bank to be part of the feminist movement. However, considering its critical role in the development community, it can only be welcome to the gender discourse. The international women's movement has brought the development community to understand that gender equity is not just the business of women but the responsibility of all those who aspire to build a better world for everyone. The World Bank may have realized the economic weight and potential of women through an assessment of the failed structural adjustment programmes it strongly supported. What is important is that the Bank has developed a gender policy, and that its president has committed the institution to integrate gender issues in all its programmes and policies. This does not mean that the Bank has become – or will become – a 'feminist' institution. I am not sure that such a transformation should be expected of the Bank.

Bessis is right to say that it is not enough to take this first step, especially if the purpose is to add more hands to make the old machine continue to grind out more of the same failed models. Recognizing the value of the informal sector is one thing. Trying to bring it into the formal sector through a range of prohibitive procedures and endless red tape that gets compounded with gender discrimination is definitely not the answer. Most mainstream institutions have not yet taken the bold next step: to conduct a critical review of their policy and programme frameworks using gender mainstreaming as a process towards radical change and transformation. Transformation through the search for gender equity is a necessary, inevitable and healthy process, because development is about people, and more than half of the six billion people of the world are women. They have their own needs, their own experiences, their own contribution to make to the future of their communities as economic agents, as social agents and as citizens in their own right.

The World Bank has a very important mandate and a powerful position in the development community. It has made progress in its approach to economic development with increasing concern for human dimensions and social impact, and more and more attention to gender issues, even if this is still very limited, and aims at efficiency rather than equity. If the World Bank has made a move in the right direction, feminist economists should take advantage of their opportunity as experts in the field to provide the kind of gender-based economic research and alternative frameworks that will push for a new vision.

In this world of shifting paradigms we are encouraged, as we begin a new millennium, by the achievements of the international women's movement. Gender is on the agenda, and gender issues are taken seriously by major development institutions. Even if the space offered by the World Bank for mainstreaming gender issues is limited, even if feminist economists – if any – are too few and far between within the Bank, the challenge is to widen this space. We must introduce the best macro-economic analysis and policy framework in order to bring the Bank and economists worldwide to understand the value of gender analysis. There are lessons that economists can draw from the realities of people's lives (men and women) to show how much human resource is wasted because of gender discrimination. The indicators of success of growth-driven economies should be revisited in order to capture their impact on the lives of women and men. Sustainability of economic growth should be examined in the light of adequate investment in men and women as producers and as beneficiaries of the returns. There is a tremendous momentum for broadening the macro-economic discourse to address issues of good governance, issues of human rights and the free movement of people, capital and goods. The gender gap is not an option that one can choose to ignore in any serious consideration of any development issue. If economists can agree that the simple fact that women constitute half the population of the world is worth their attention, this will be an important step forward. It is not enough. We should continue to move from gender equality to gender equity. Only then can we make a qualitative leap forward. Calculators and standard measures are confining and inadequate. Transforming analytical tools is an imperative if we aspire to capture development in all its dimensions, and if our vision is to build a world of inclusion and opportunities for both men and women.

Response to Aster Zaoudé
and Joanne Sandler

Sophie Bessis

Not long ago, I was sent to West Africa by an important international human rights association to write a report on the situation in one of the nations of that region. When I discussed with a UN representative my intention to devote part of my report to women, he told me point blank that I had got my priorities wrong.

As a regular participant in major development conferences – such as the 1993 Vienna Conference on Human Rights, or the 1995 Social Development Summit in Copenhagen – I remember very well the disorientation of the governmental delegations and the larger NGOs when they were confronted by the offensive launched by the women's associations. These associations had decided to seize the initiative and to make their voices heard on all manner of subjects that had been judged too serious to be handed over to them. I was also invited to participate during the 1990s in informal discussion groups made up of intellectuals from the Arab world and Israel. At one of these meetings, I was the only women among twenty men – men with the best humanist intentions, but men who could not really understand why I demanded that there be more women present to speak of peace.

Most of us are familiar with this sort of tokenism in which just a select few are invited to participate in a collective debate, on the condition that they implicitly promise not to 'gender' the discussion. In other words, women promise to remain silent regarding the place which has been allotted to them in the management of human affairs, since there are now specific venues, organizations and conferences for the discussion of their condition. Apart from these spaces reserved for them, their presence remains marginal in any arena of global dimension where the world's 'real' problems are addressed.

The international system is hardly an exception in this respect. Imagine a fully representational general assembly of the International Monetary Fund or the World Bank, a World Trade Organization conference on international trade, or a high-level meeting on disarmament. I am not sterotyping these international bodies, alas, but describing a reality of which everyone is only too well aware.

It is important to recognize, however, that the United Nations has played an essential role in the global unveiling of women's issues for the last quarter of a century. Thanks, in part, to women's activism, these issues can no longer be ignored without a fair hearing. Aster Zaoudé and Joanne Sandler's rich and stimulating article, which traces the history of this unveiling, seems to me to err on the side of naivety. In subsequent paragraphs I will temper their optimism with several arguments that should not be overlooked.

The first concerns the question of shared tasks within the galaxy of international organizations. Although they theoretically belong to the same group, everyone knows that the United Nations and its agencies, and the Bretton Woods organizations, grew out of extremely different historical imperatives. The mission of the former consists of concretizing the Universal Declaration on Human Rights, which was, to a certain extent, its founding principle. The UN's duty is to put an end to all forms of discrimination, including discrimination against women, as specified by the 1979 International Convention. Part of its *raison d'être* is to include gender in the formulation of development strategies. The intent is to reinforce the presence of women in all areas, and to defend their rights, in much the same way as the UN protects all other constituencies in the articles which make up the Universal Declaration on Human Rights. By these standards, although we may believe that the United Nations has made progress in certain areas, change occurs very slowly at the heart of a system known for its inertia.

The Bretton Woods organizations have benefited from the financial and economic prerogatives bestowed upon them by their founding fathers, the Allies. These dominating interests were – and remain – totally disconnected from the social sphere. The World Bank first addressed the question of women very differently from the UN. Obviously the rising feminist awareness of the 1970s did have an effect on the Bank, although women's rights issues remain secondary for an institution which perceives women, first, as a new type of economic actor and, second, as possible agents for a social stability that is increasingly difficult to achieve under current global circumstances. I have called this positioning of women by these institutions 'instrumental feminism', because the promotion of women is not an end in itself but, rather, an instrument of policies promoting economic growth and trying to reduce poverty. For the moment, the World Bank's proclaimed feminism has not borne fruit to the extent that we might have wished. It is up to women to be on their guard, and to use the Bank's current goodwill and financial resources without being manipulated.

If women are not careful, this task-sharing at the heart of the international system could lead to an even greater split between the financial and the social organizations. The 'serious' organizations will increasingly dominate world affairs, while the United Nations will slowly become a forum for the world's marginalized and excluded – from women to indigenous peoples to social movements – where they will be heard without having any real say concerning the fate of the planet. The non-strategic part of the UN will evolve towards a certain pluralism, which will have the effect of sealing off those places where real power continues to be exercised. In order to prevent such a danger from occurring – and this is the second point in my argument – I believe that the UN has to be far more alert and aggressive than it is at the moment. Clearly, UNIFEM and the other agencies accomplish remarkable work by furnishing millions of women with the practical tools for their own liberation. But the triumph of the gender approach – so commonly used as to have become an integral part of official UN-speak – may actually mask resistance within the international system to the struggle for women's equal rights and the diversification of their roles. For the moment, despite the nomination of several women to important positions within the UN, mainstreaming demonstrates only the mincing steps and timidity which have overtaken the necessity to act. The term 'gender' itself depoliticizes and neutralizes the impact of feminist demands. The United Nations, on the whole, busies itself only with non-issues. The organization refuses to do sufficient politicking, since cultural relativism often wreaks havoc, since almost anything may be defended in the name of national identity, and since geopolitics essentially ignores women. Today, the task of the women of the United Nations is to impose on this ungainly machine both a change in rhythm and a clarification of the language used to define women's rights. Women must do this in order to avoid becoming no more than a cog in the machine, as well as to prevent the marginalization of an institution that the world's big interests would like to reduce to a sideshow.

CHAPTER TWO

The Politics of Women's NGOs in India, Bangladesh and China

Turning from international institutions to grassroots activism, this chapter focuses on three specific geopolitical examples of how women organize at the local level. Women's activism in these countries is generally constrained by ambivalent government policy, restrictive laws, and discriminatory religious and ideological practices. Elora Shehabuddin suggests that Bangladeshi women have learned to navigate skilfully between the exigencies of development programmes and Islamic tradition. Jael Silliman describes the polemic surrounding the Narmada Dam project in India, focusing on the way in which that project served as a catalyst to women's grassroots organizing and environmental consciousness. Finally, Susan Perry compares these two examples with the very different case of women's activism in China, where the restrictions of one-party rule reduce the space available for independent, non-governmental activity. All three authors explore the adaptive strategies of real women in real development settings as they manoeuvre within the constraints of politics, religion and social policies.

Gender and the Politics of Fatwas in Bangladesh

Elora Shehabuddin

In the spring of 1995, shortly before a scheduled trip by US First Lady Hillary Clinton to visit some of Bangladesh's renowned indigenous non-governmental organizations, or NGOs, the enmity between groups for and against NGOs spilled out on to the streets of the capital city, Dhaka.[1] Members of the NGO community had applied to the government for permission to hold a 'national conference' on 31 March on Manik Miah Avenue, a wide boulevard that runs in front of the national parliament building. This conference would have comprised 'those villagers who are trying to stand on their own two feet' with NGO assistance (Samad 1995). The government did not grant that permission. According to Maulana Mufti Fazlul Huq Amini, secretary of the Shommilito Shangram Parishad (United Action Council or UAC),[2] NGOs had intended to use the rally to demonstrate their own power: 'That rally would have been a direct challenge to Bangladesh and Islam. However, as a result of objections from vigilant members of the public, this rally was forced to be postponed. The NGOs should know that at no point in any of the twelve months will they be allowed to hold such a meeting. They will be hindered by all means' (*Inqilab*, 24 March 1995).[3] Amini called on all concerned citizens to attend instead an anti-NGO rally scheduled for 31 March on Manik Miah Avenue – the same day and the same venue originally proposed by the NGOs. The government denied permission for this rally, too; nonetheless, by the afternoon hundreds of UAC activists had broken through the police cordon and assembled on the site.[4] Over the course of several hours, various speakers proceeded to attack foreign-funded NGOs operating in Bangladesh, the government for allowing NGOs into the country, and rural women for becoming involved with NGOs.

In this essay I explore attempts by rural women in Bangladesh to negotiate between competing visions of development as they struggle to carve out a better life for themselves. An examination of public political discourse in Bangladesh reveals two competing visions of 'development' and 'modernity' that vary primarily on issues surrounding the role of religion and women in society, and are crystallized in deliberations over the appropriate role of NGOs. Not surprisingly, these national debates have repercussions for the lives of ordinary rural women; they help to structure the environment in which women must make decisions about joining NGOs in their area. Today millions of women throughout the country are NGO members, and it is on their views regarding religious practice, NGOs and development that I focus here. In the absence of viable alternatives, women are increasingly compelled to turn to NGOs; this very often entails ignoring or over-coming the objections of members of their families and communities. The charges of Islamists and the expectations of secularists notwith-standing, women who join NGOs do not see themselves as rejecting religion and tradition, or as becoming 'bad Muslims', in the process. Much as both Islamists and secularists insist on the incompatibility of Islam with what each side understands to be modern or Western, this is not a distinction that is ultimately relevant to a rural woman trying to decide whether she should join an NGO.

I begin with a brief introduction to the NGO scene in Bangladesh, then outline the different positions vis-à-vis Western-funded NGOs – that of the state, the secularists and the Islamists. These positions reflect each side's vision of development, progress, and the future of Bangla-desh and its women. I conclude by examining the experiences and views of the targets of these measures – impoverished rural women – and their attempts to negotiate the seemingly competing demands of religion and survival, as represented by the need to observe purdah and the need to earn a living with NGO assistance.[5]

Bangladesh's National Report to the 1995 Beijing Conference on Women begins with a vehement affirmation of Bangladesh's participation in 'the worldwide movement for the emancipation of women and their full participation in policy and decision-making at all levels' (GoB 1995a: 1). It closes with a pledge of Bangladesh's commitment to:

> the upliftment of women's status backed by adequate allocation of resources to implement policy decisions and an integrated and holistic multisectoral

> approach to women's development where they can play a central role as
> agents of change in their own right as well as beneficiaries of economic
> growth and social and political development. The vision of Bangladesh is of
> an ideal society where men and women are equal as human beings and are
> entitled to equal access to opportunities for the realization of the goals of
> Equality, Development and Peace. (GoB 1995a: 41)

The state has voiced commitment to women's issues since the earliest
days of the nation's independent existence, but one could argue that its
efforts over the years, while always very visible, have often been less
than adequate, at times even misplaced (Ahmed 1985; Goetz 1998; Jahan
1995). While it has had a fair degree of success with some recent
programmes targeting women, it is NGOs rather than the state that
tend to be seen as the primary actors in the struggle to improve the
lives of poor women, the majority of whom live in rural Bangladesh.
In any case, NGO programmes are even more likely to be at the centre
of controversy than similar state-sponsored programmes.

It is important to point out that while NGOs are indeed providing
valuable services in rural Bangladesh, I am by no means suggesting that
they are destined to become a parallel state, or that the state risks being
'privatized'. Such a scenario is both unlikely and undesirable. First,
despite the vast numbers of NGOs in the country, their operations are
not well co-ordinated; there is considerable inefficiency and replication
of services. Thus some parts of the country, particularly those within
easy driving distance of a major metropolitan area, host several NGOs,
all offering roughly the same services, while some more remote corners
remain untouched by NGO activity. Second, the experience of the last
two decades has shown that NGO involvement in any issue is circumscribed by donor interest in that issue. Thus NGO provision cannot be
substituted for long-term planning in crucial sectors like education.
Third, while successive governments have not been fully accountable to
their citizens, NGOs are even less so; a future run by NGOs would not
necessarily be characterized by greater participation. In the foreseeable
future, then, the two must coexist. For all their external funding, NGOs
remain dependent on the state's goodwill to continue to function; after
all, their activities are subject to the supervision of the NGO Affairs
Bureau. The government, for its part, has found itself increasingly
compelled to acknowledge the role played by NGOs. This has been the
case particularly since the mid-1990s, which saw a private visit to
Bangladesh by a US First Lady, motivated by admiration for the Bangladesh Rural Advancement Committee (BRAC) and the Grameen Bank, as
well as international summits that showered praise on Bangladeshi NGOs.

Moreover, the state itself remains heavily dependent on foreign aid, and donors, too, are increasingly requiring greater co-operation between the government and NGOs.

NGOs first appeared in war-shattered Bangladesh around the time of independence in 1971; although their numbers expanded during the famine and floods of 1974, initially they remained largely 'restricted to relief and rehabilitation' (Hashemi 1995: 123; Wood 1994). Over time they moved into community development interventions, on the assumption that prosperous communities would produce prosperous individuals within those communities. As they realized that benefits did not automatically trickle down to those at the bottom of the pile, they adopted target-group strategies − that is, targeting groups normally left out of top-down development processes (Hashemi 1995; Smillie 1997).[6] The number of NGOs registered with the NGO Affairs Bureau (NAB) has risen rapidly: according to Qazi Faruque Ahmed, chairperson of the Association of Development Agencies in Bangladesh (ADAB), by 1995 NGOs in Bangladesh reached about 3.5 million poor households (*Daily Star*, 30 December 1995).[7] The Grameen Bank, for instance, has disbursed small loans to over 2.1 million poor village women (*Grameen Dialogue*, January 1998). The NGO Proshika now has over 650,000 members, of whom half are women, in over 5,000 villages; according to its own estimates, about four million people have benefited from its activities.[8] NGOs are involved in a variety of issues, including the establishment of effective democratic institutions at the local level, poverty alleviation, women's rights, education, health and family planning, and the environment (Rahman and Mustafa 1995).

The largest and most prominent NGOs in Bangladesh are indigenous organizations like the Grameen Bank and the BRAC, which have no formal links to any religious groups. Others can be characterized as explicitly 'Christian', such as Caritas, or 'Islamic', such as the International Islamic Relief Organization and Muslim Aid; Islamic NGOs, however, tend not to be perceived as NGOs (see Naher 1996). It is possible that this stems from a general acceptance of a dichotomy between Islam on the one hand, and development and Westernization on the other − of the prevalence of what Jo Rowlands describes as a 'particular view of "development-as-Westernization"' (Rowlands 1998: 12; see also Hours 1993). Indeed, although Islamist groups in Bangladesh attempt to propound an alternative and distinct vision of development, they find themselves unable to compete with the large NGOs in terms of sheer presence and numbers on the ground. In the end, the activities of Muslim organizations tend to be oriented more towards charity and disaster relief; thus, even if they are recognized as 'do-gooders', they are not considered to be NGOs in quite the same way.[9] In keeping with common practice, then, I do not include Islamic non-governmental organizations when I use the term 'NGO'.

In Bangladesh today, women serve as positive markers of time-honoured tradition for some, negative markers of backwardness for others. This excerpt from the Bangladesh Country Paper prepared for the World Summit for Social Development in Copenhagen in March 1995 illustrates the state's preoccupation with 'developing women' and with linking development to women's dress, in particular their shedding of the *burqa*, an ankle-length garment that covers the entire head and body, and may also cover the face:

> A generation ago, it would be difficult to find a woman in a college or a university without a Burqa. Now not only in the universities and colleges, but the streets of Dhaka and even in *mofussil* towns [smaller district towns] women are not only found without Burqa and dressed in traditional *sarees* but also one finds scores of women in [the] latest fashionable modern dress in the educational institutions, offices and work places. This is a change which was unthinkable for the previous generation. ... Women are developing fast and are increasingly participating in every walk of life. (GoB 1995b: 18)

One NGO devotes a chapter in its textbook *Adult Education Lessons to Raise Consciousness* (vol. 1), to the subject of purdah and discusses it in the following terms: 'Because of *purdah*, we are unable to work [outside the home]. That is why we are unable to earn money. That is why we cannot improve our situation' (Saptagram n.d.(a): 8). The accompanying *Teachers' Guide* advises the instructor to tell the story about a woman who was kept in the strictest purdah and then died in childbirth because her father refused to summon a doctor to see her (Saptagram n.d.(b): 26–7). It continues: 'The *purdah* is an obstacle in the path of women's freedom and development. We are suppressed through being kept locked away behind *purdah* in the name of religion and unless we break free from such superstitions, we shall never be able to obtain our rights' (Saptagram n.d.(b): 27).

While NGOs and secularists generally see the shedding of purdah as a positive development, for Islamists the transformation reflects a serious threat to indigenous culture. The state, for its part, often finds itself caught between competing secularist and Islamist visions as it strives to avoid alienating donors supporting either position, or the country's predominantly Muslim population. Indeed, although no ruling party to date has sought to establish an Islamic state, all parties have made concessions to Islamist forces in their policy-making, particularly in matters pertaining to women. At the same time, however, they have all ratified international conventions and established government agencies dedicated to women's issues (see Feldman 1998; Kabeer 1988).[10]

The secularist approach calls for the abolition of religion from the public domain. In this camp are to be found Western donors and aid agencies, NGOs who receive funding from these sources, and intellectuals and public figures who wish to restore Bangladesh to its secularist roots.[11] While they are critical of certain features of NGO activity, secularists laud NGOs for stepping in where the state has failed in order to provide essential services to the rural majority, and to promote women's rights. They hold women responsible for the nation's present 'backwardness', both social and economic, insisting that women retard development with their dismal illiteracy and ignorance (the two are often read as synonymous), unfettered fertility, and blind adherence to religion, superstition and old traditions. The secularists espouse an understanding of gender relations that accords with international agreements like CEDAW, and believe that NGOs are well-suited to rescue women from their present plight. At the same time, on a positive note, secularists see these same women as open to outside influences – to what development planners regard as more progressive views on such matters as gender relations, family planning and legal awareness.

Islamists, on the other hand, regard NGOs as a threat to the Islam-based culture of Bangladesh. The Islamist model is also espoused, imposed and funded by international donors – albeit, of course, a different set, based primarily in the oil-rich Arab countries. A small number of organizations use the funds to promote a polity, a society and gender relations governed by Islamic rules as they understand them. The Islamist vision of society does not encompass large numbers of women joining NGO programmes, and throughout the country local religious leaders have condemned women's involvement with NGOs, calling it un-Islamic and the women, by extension, bad Muslims. In contrast to the secularists, Islamists interpret women's 'openness' to new ideas as a sign of weakness; in other words, women represent the chink in the nation's cultural armour – they are the most vulnerable to undesirable, un-Islamic, alien ideas and practices. For Islamists, women have a valuable role to play in society as repositories and transmitters of venerable traditions; it is women's responsibility to inculcate the next generation with the appropriate customs and manners. They insist that an Islamic state would solve the problems of the country's poor, and allow women to fulfil their natural roles.

Secularists and Islamists alike generally recognize NGOs' valuable contribution to the national development effort, but both groups also find a great deal to criticize in NGO activity. It is in the matter of NGOs' impact on rural women that the two groups part company: secularists believe that this impact has been largely positive, whereas Islamists believe that it has been un-Islamic, and thus negative. A grievance that both sides often air is that of NGOs' lack of financial accountability to anyone other than their foreign donors. Related issues include agenda-setting, national sovereignty and participatory decision-making. For instance, who decides what programmes should be undertaken – the donors, the NGO directors, or the NGO members, ordinary men and women? Both secularist and Islamist groups raise pertinent questions about the motives underlying NGOs' policy choices, accusing them of basing their decisions on the wishes of foreign donors rather than on local needs (see Hashemi 1995). Critics charge that, as a result, many NGOs have no deep attachment to the issues on which they work; rather they switch focus in accordance with donor priorities – one writer characterizes this practice as 'the "flavour of the month" approach to development' (Chowdhury 1995). Thus, today, almost all NGOs operating in rural Bangladesh provide micro-credit, because that is where donor interest lies. While one cannot ignore the many useful programmes that have been initiated and supported by donors, such as non-formal education and infant immunization, the problem remains that as soon as the donors lose interest in the issue, the programme grinds to a halt; such was the fate of adult literacy programmes. To quote Syed Hashemi: 'donor dependence creates a situation in which NGOs end up reprioritizing their own agendas' (Hashemi 1995: 130). As for the target groups themselves, at no point in the decision-making process are they consulted.

In the opinion of some secular nationalists, NGOs are merely the tools of Western imperialism (see, for example, Umar 1996). Such comments are quite reminiscent of those of some Islamist leaders, as I show below. But while the Islamist leaders are concerned that Western interests are endangering the very basis of Islam in Bangladesh, secular nationalists believe that the NGOs pose a threat to the ancient Bengali culture of the region. According to Dhaka University professor Ahmed Sharif, the government has 'leased the country to NGOs' which represent the interests not of Bangladesh but of the foreign powers who funded them (*Bhorer Kagoj*, 23 July 1995). Many observers question the extent to which NGOs actually help the poor, or make more efficient use of resources. On the basis of her research on NGO activity on the ground, Kirsten Westergaard argues that most NGOs have not really succeeded in making the rural poor independent – that impoverished villagers are simply transferring dependency from the wealthier villagers to NGOs. There are, of course, exceptions: some NGOs are 'withdrawing direct supervision and support with the objective of creating self-reliant organizations' (Westergaard 1996: 53).

In response to claims that NGOs necessarily make better use of the resources at their disposal, Syed Hashemi and Sidney Schuler (1992) point out that there is no empirical evidence that NGO provision of social services is cheaper than public provision. Hashemi concedes, however, that NGO workers are probably more effective than government workers simply because they are more accessible to ordinary people (Hashemi 1995: 128) – in the sense that they maintain a presence at village level, and their doors are usually open to villagers. On the other hand, the fragmented nature of NGO provision means that not all areas of the country are equally covered. Although it is clearly inappropriate to think of the NGO community as a substitute for the state, this has not precluded occasional hostility from various levels of government – from bureaucrats, for example, who are anxious 'that voluntary organizations are stripping away their conventional realm of power' (Rashid-uzzaman 1997: 240). The government was particularly displeased that the first visit to Bangladesh by a US First Lady was motivated by an interest in successful NGOs rather than by some more official purpose. Nasreen Khundker quickly reminded the government that NGOs have by no means met all needs at the grassroots, and that there is still ample opportunity for the government to participate in the process: 'Institutions such as the Grameen Bank have so far limited their credit operations to the functionally landless.... This leaves the government with unlimited terrain in which to show their effectiveness. Unfortunately, this has not happened' (Khundker 1995). Mahfuz Anam responds to criticisms about NGOs seeking to 'impose a Western model of development on Bangladesh' by pointing out that 'the free market model has been adopted by practically all governments, including our own. As for dependence on donor money, why blame the NGOs alone? Is our government any less dependent?' (Anam 1995). I contend that differences exist. First, while it is certainly true that the state is hostage to policy packages dictated by major donors such as the World Bank and the IMF, it is important to remember that – at least in theory – the government – and in particular the two recent democratically elected governments – is ultimately accountable to the people. NGOs have no such responsibilities. Second, while the Jamaat-i Islami, perhaps the most articulate proponent of an 'Islamic development' in Bangladesh, does appear to support privatization and liberalization, it also does claim at least to present an alternative model of development.

Islamist critiques of NGOs also stem from concerns about national sovereignty and cultural autonomy; in addition, however, they display a particular concern with what they see as the negative impact of NGOs on the women of the country. During the anti-NGO rally of March 1995, Allama Mufti Ahmed Shafi, who presided over the event, called on God-fearing Muslims to promote alternative development-oriented institutions, so that 'the poor would no longer have to run after NGOs'. To that end, he urged the imams of the 250,000 mosques in Bangladesh to set up relief funds in order to collect money. It was not enough simply to make long speeches against NGOs, he pointed out; rather, it was necessary to inform the public about the NGOs' inappropriate activities, and build up public opinion against them. The East India Company, he reminded his audience, entered this region on the pretext of engaging in trade, but then took over the country; it was the *'ulama* who finally kicked out the British, and brought about independence. Today, these enemies had put on new sarees and returned in the guise of NGOs to transform the local people yet again into their servants. Once again, it was up to the *'ulama* to play a part in rescuing the country from their clutches. He noted that in Chittagong, illiterate destitute village women were being given loans only after they secretly converted to Christianity. He referred to incidents in which, upon dying, some women were given a proper Muslim burial, only to be exhumed shortly thereafter by NGO workers who insisted that they were actually Christians, and then reinterred them with Christian services.

Amini then stressed that the rally was being held for Islam, for an Islamic state in Bangladesh, and for the destruction of NGO strongholds in Bangladesh. Those who wished to transform this country into a Christian state, he continued, were the very same people who had tried to prevent them from holding this rally. He warned that God would not support a government that wished to root out Islam and put NGOs in power for much longer. He explained that the NGOs had wanted to convene a meeting in order to destroy Islam, the Quran, and the traditional family structure, but God did not allow that meeting to be held. Addressing Hillary Clinton, who was scheduled to arrive two days later, he entreated: 'Please do not come. Your NGOs are working against the Quran and against Islam in this country.... God is the greatest power. God destroyed Russia. Can God not destroy America?' (*Inqilab*, 1 April 1995).

Another speaker, Maulana Mohiuddin Khan, announced: 'The devout people will not welcome [Hillary Clinton] if she comes to Bangladesh to see only the NGO projects' (*Daily Star*, 1 April 1995). At a regional meeting later that month, Amini attacked the government for support-ing 'atheist, apostate, and anti-Islam forces [that] are working to destroy this country's sovereignty and independence'. He believed that NGOs were 'engaged in a campaign to completely expunge Islamic culture' from Bengali society, and threatened to issue a fatwa 'calling for the destruction of all centers of NGO activity' unless the government itself took steps to put an end to NGO activities (*Ittefaq*, 29 April 1995). According to Abdur Rahman Siddiqi, national development and social care were not the true objectives of these NGOs. Rather, he argued, the NGOs were no more than a Trojan Horse left inside the country by Western imperialists to attack 'our education, culture, religion in the homes of the weakest members of our society' (*Inqilab*, 9 August 1995).

And what do the more Islam-oriented groups consider to be 'accept-able' development? At a meeting of women representatives from the major political parties arranged by the Dhaka-based research organization Women for Women, members of the Jamaat Islamist organization laid out very clearly what their party saw as areas in need of change. At the root of Jamaat ideology regarding development and gender relations is the notion – based entirely on Quranic precepts, the representatives declared – that men and women are equal and complementary. In other words, they argued, although men and women have the same status in the eyes of God, 'there is a distinct difference in their spheres of work ... based on the difference in their physical abilities' (Women for Women 1995: 29). They insisted that women in Bangladesh would not be able to enjoy fully the rights granted to them by God until true Islamic law were established in the country.[12] On the subject of wom-en's employment, the Jamaat members pointed out that Islam had spared women the burden of earning a livelihood and providing for their families; women's primary responsibilities lay elsewhere – as wives and mothers. This did not mean, of course, that women could not or should not work: they were free to pursue professional careers – within 'the bounds of the *shari'a*' (Women for Women 1995: 30). Islamists did not, however, support jobs that permitted or encouraged women to discard purdah or work with men (Shehabuddin 1999a).

In interviews conducted shortly after a series of attacks on NGOs in 1995 – when NGO schools were set on fire, and mulberry trees planted by NGO women members were chopped down – Nurul Alam asked rural religious leaders what they understood by development. His respondents emphasized that development should reflect Islamic values and be in accordance with shari'a; the country should draw on its own resources rather than be dependent on foreign aid; one way of raising money domestically would be to co-ordinate the collection and distribution of zakat (the annual alms tax compulsory for every financially secure Muslim); special attention should be given to tackling illiteracy and unemployment; there should be increased support of madrasas (religious schools) and Quranic teaching; the banking system, and all loans, should be interest-free; men should play the primary role in development activities (Alam 1996: 15). The religious leaders listed the following reasons for their hostility to NGOs: women's involvement in activities 'outside the home boundary'; training sessions for women in distant places; overreliance on foreign money, especially funds seen to be coming from Christian or Jewish sources; limited involvement of men; no provision for Islamic education; concerns about conversion from Islam to Christianity; high interest rates charged by the providers of micro-credit (Alam 1996: 19). All these points were iterated again and again in anti-NGO speeches at the national level. Rural elites, also, accused NGOs of violating local norms and attacking Islam – for instance, by encouraging women to work outside the home, by enrolling pregnant women in prenatal programmes, by vaccinating infants, by providing un-Islamic education (in terms of curricular content) in an un-Islamic setting (coeducational) and by disrupting divinely ordained harmonious relations between husband and wife (Shehabuddin 1999b).

The main tools used by development programmes to 'empower' women are perhaps education and micro-credit. The assumption is that education can open up more employment opportunities for women, and that the ability to earn an income can improve women's bargaining position and decision-making power within the family. Employment opportunities for women are limited, however, and what opportunities are available are not deemed desirable by all women or their families. In the last two decades, thousands of women in Bangladesh have entered the formal and visible labour force, with most of them working in the export-oriented garment factories in Dhaka and Chittagong. Between 1976 and 1985, the number of garment factories in these two cities grew from about four or five to sixty (The Economist, 23 September 1989: 46), while between 1980 and 1989 the number of female garment workers increased from 50,000 to 225,000, creating 'a first-generation female industrial work-force' (Kabeer 1994: 181). As has been the case with the first cohorts of female factory workers elsewhere in the world (see, for example, Stansell 1986), such women tend to be regarded as loose and immoral, and not as appropriate role models. Moreover, lack of adequate childcare facilities and discrimination against older and married women mean that factory work is simply not an option for all women. Basic literacy requirements by many employers also exclude a large part of the female population (Kabeer 1994: 169–70).

Consequently, many women prefer to work at home, surrounded by family members who can help them keep an eye on their children. And therein lies one of the greatest attractions of micro-credit, which has permitted large numbers of women of all ages throughout the country to start small businesses out of their own homes. Today, Bangladesh is synonymous in international development circles with micro-credit and the Grameen or Rural Bank. Micro-credit is being hailed as the solution to both mass poverty and the population problem. Pioneered and popularized by Dr Mohammad Yunus, a US-trained Bangladeshi economist who continues to head the vast Grameen Bank, micro-credit has been adopted by the state's development programmes as well as most NGOs, both large and small. At the international level, even the World Bank, traditionally more drawn to big dams, bridges and roads, has turned its attention to these tiny loans without collateral to individual men and women, and is supporting their use throughout the world.

But micro-credit has its share of critics – a group that would make strange bedfellows indeed. Feminists, for instance, argue that micro-credit programmes tend to confine women to low-yield enterprises such as making handicrafts or poultry-raising rather than encouraging them to engage in alternative modes of income generation. Furthermore, micro-credit alone cannot help women to improve their lives. This is borne out by studies which show that women who receive these loans do not always maintain control over them. I found that sometimes male relatives seize the money from them, and use it for personal or family needs.[13] One solution is to offer loans alongside legal and basic literacy classes. At other times, the women themselves choose to hand the money to their male kin to invest in more profitable ventures than those open to them as women. From the Left come charges that micro-credit, by facilitating the entry of individuals into the capitalist nexus and focusing on individual profit, prevents the development of the class consciousness that is necessary to bring about much-needed major structural changes. In other words, the situation of individuals may improve somewhat, but the lives of the majority remain unchanged, if they do not actually deteriorate.

Islamists, for their part, approve of loans in that they enable women to work within the home, within purdah; they point out, however, that the charging of interest itself is contrary to Islam, and propose the provision of interest-free loans. Also, they object to the fact that in order to receive loans, women have to attend weekly meetings, shout slogans and often do physical drill – all under the supervision of male NGO officers, and in violation of their understanding of purdah. Many also object to the training sessions in legal and other rights mandated by some NGOs alongside their micro-credit programmes.

While there are thousands of poverty-alleviation programmes in the private sector, Islamists have been particularly critical of the larger indigenous organizations that receive funds from abroad. At the local level, many people – men and women, Islamist or not – have asked why organizations like the Grameen Bank prefer to give loans to women, when it would make more sense to invest in male borrowers (Shehabuddin 1992: 114). Indeed, given that 'many NGOs themselves (the Grameen Bank in particular) are mostly run by men, it certainly makes no sense to tell the rural people that their women need to be empowered' (Naher 1996: 39). According to one religious leader in Sarail interviewed by Alam's study team in 1995: 'If a man asks for a loan, [NGOs] show indifference. There are millions of unemployed youths who deserve credit but on the contrary they give these [sic] to women. When men are capable to work [sic], there is no justification to advance [sic] loans to women' (Alam 1995: 15). A madrasa school-teacher complained: 'Our women are going out of the house at the instigation of NGOs. They are doing whatever they like. They are going to town for training. We must stop all these objectionable acts in the country' (Alam 1995: 20).

Poor rural women have a less negative perception of NGOs, which, for many, represent a 'potential sector of employment' (Naher 1996: 34). When I asked rural women what they considered to be the main job of an NGO, they proffered a variety of answers: giving loans; teaching poor men and women how to make marketable handicrafts; providing adult and health education; providing free legal services; providing training in fish-, poultry- and cattle-farming; eradicating poverty; helping the poor to improve their lives; 'getting money for us from overseas'; and 'making women independent'. Given the climate of hostility towards NGOs, women's decision to join them – to take credit, to join literacy programmes – is not an easy one. During interviews, rural women described the objections they encountered when they first joined an NGO programme. Local people tried to dissuade them from joining in the first place by telling them that they would lose their religion, their money, would be forced to raise pigs, and would be

denied a *janaja* (proper Muslim funeral); they also told them that they
would not allow their husbands in the mosque, and would expel their
families from the *samaj* (community). The following quotations echo
comments heard all over the country:

> Our *murobbi* [elders] said that the NGOs were giving out *haram* [unlawful in
> Islam] money and I shouldn't touch it. (Azizan, 32, Sylhet)

> Other villagers told me that this was Christian money, that it would be a sin
> to take this money. (Salma, 45, Sylhet)

> The village *matbor-morol* [traditional village elite] said that I'd become Chris-
> tian, that I shouldn't be given water and that nobody could eat my cooking.
> (Shahar Banu, 35, Jessore)

> People in the village said: 'Why should you, a woman, go out of the house?
> Your purdah will be destroyed, you will lose your faith!' (Firoza, 35, Jessore)

> People in the village said that we would become Christian, that NGOs would
> take us off to their country, that we would no longer be able to practise
> Islam. (Fuljaan, 45, Madaripur)

> The village *matbors* said that my religion would be destroyed if I joined an
> NGO, that I would be trafficked overseas. (Pakhi, 24, Dinajpur)

> The village *huzur* [religious leader] and my father-in-law said that I would
> become *be-parda* [without purdah] and my faith would be destroyed. (Malatun,
> 25, Dinajpur)

Despite such obstacles, these women and numerous others went on to
become involved with NGOs. Shefali of Jessore explained: 'I don't pay
attention to their objections; if there's no food in my belly, will they
give me food to eat?' Similarly, Rahima of Dinajpur said: 'I didn't believe
what they had to say. They just talk. They never help us. So, I went
ahead and joined the *samity* [group].' For Sakhina of Jessore, the choice
was a clear one: 'I didn't pay any attention to anyone. I didn't want to
die of starvation, I wanted to work, I wanted food.' Women who have
joined NGOs say that they have benefited not only financially but also
from the general experience; for instance, they admit that they are
more articulate and self-confident as a result of having to participate in
– and even run – meetings, talk with strangers, and manage their micro-
enterprises.

At the same time, it ought to be kept in mind that despite the
overwhelming poverty of rural Bangladesh and the limited alternatives
available to women, large numbers of poor rural women have *not* joined
NGOs. In interviews, it emerged that these women were among the
poorest of the poor, and their decision not to join was influenced less
by Islamist decrees against NGO involvement and more by the opposition

of their families and husbands, and by fears that they would be unable to pay the weekly instalment on the loan. For instance, of the women interviewed who were not involved with NGOs, just under a third cited objections from their husband as the reason they had not joined. Although many lending organizations such as the Grameen Bank target the 'poorest of the poor', they are not always successful. I found that very often the poorest women hesitate to take out loans because they are afraid they may be unable to make the weekly payments. Many of the women who do receive credit have the security of an additional source of income within the family. Tohura, a 45–year-old widow in Dinajpur, said she didn't join because 'I don't have enough money to join a *samity*.' Similarly, 19–year-old Parveen of Sylhet explained, 'I don't have the means to pay the *kisti* [loan repayment instalments].' Clearly, it is not the poorest women in the village who actually take advantage of credit opportunities.

Following the discussion above, it is possible to identify three categories of poor rural women according to their relationship to NGOs. At the very bottom of the economic ladder lie the 'poorest of the poor' – those who are ostensibly the targets of NGOs, but consider themselves too poor even to join an NGO. Next come those who are somewhat better off, and are confident enough of their ability to pay off loans (usually with the assistance of a male breadwinner in the family) to be willing to risk social censure initially. Finally, there are those who have sufficient income not to need even to consider joining an NGO. It is members of this group who support Islamist critiques of NGOs; while they certainly cannot compete in wealth and status with the local landowner, the importance they attach to purdah and their eagerness to question the morality of those who are unable to uphold social norms of seclusion reveal a desire for acceptance by the rural elite as one of 'them'.

Although both local and national critics of NGOs have been quick to accuse NGO women of breaking norms of purdah, these women do not easily accept the charge. The Islamist understanding of purdah – as articulated by the Jamaat, for instance – calls for the wearing of the *burqa* or a similar garment. Given the amount of fabric and the elaborate stitching required, the final product is beyond the means of most poor women. In interviews with almost five hundred men and women, only 16 per cent understood purdah to mean wearing a *burqa*. Others cited the importance of covering the head and body (i.e. with the sarees they were already wearing, rather than purchasing an additional piece of clothing), keeping away from men, avoiding public roads and pathways, and simply conducting oneself with decency and propriety. For some, purdah represented a state of mind, a purity of thought. According to 28-year-old Sultana Begum, a teacher at the village school (and thus not a prospective member of an NGO): 'The purdah of the mind [internal purdah] is the real thing.' Many landless women, such as Selina of Rajshahi, explained that they do not observe purdah because they are too poor to do so: 'I am poor. It isn't possible for me to observe purdah. Purdah means not going out.'

Thus NGO women counter the objections of Islamist groups by pointing out that they feel that they do observe purdah in their own way – although they cannot afford to buy the burqa which, many Islamists believe, demonstrates true adherence to purdah. While they cannot afford to ignore the opportunities offered by NGOs, at least by working in their homes, they minimize contact with achena purush (male strangers); they are certainly less exposed than they might have been on a factory floor. Interestingly enough, among the unexpected consequences of NGO involvement is that, contrary to the expectations of development workers and policy-makers, many women use their new incomes to observe better purdah: they may buy burqas, or build a higher wall around their homes for greater privacy. The ability of a family to keep its women in purdah has long been a sign of status in South Asia – the message being that such a family can afford not to have its women work; thus it makes sense that many women would spend their new-found income on demonstrating their new status in society. Evidence suggests that most women take advantage of what limited opportunities are available to them; contrary to the claims of secular development workers or Islamists, they do not do so merely as 'dupes' of the other side. In the end, it appears that neither the secularists nor the Islamists truly take into account the realities, the needs and the concerns of the poor women they claim to represent. While the former falsely assume that women would want to discard purdah given half a chance, the latter wish to impose on the women an interpretation of Islam that limits the options available to them.

In this essay I have tried to show that different understandings of 'development' and 'modernity' coexist in rural Bangladesh today – especially in matters pertaining to women: the hegemonic model espoused by the major international donors like the World Bank and the UN and their dependants – states and NGOs; a counter-hegemonic model, such as the one proposed by Islamist organizations like the Jamaat, premissed on a very different conception of gender roles in society; and, finally, the perspective of poor women themselves, and how they understand the policies and programmes currently targeting them from all quarters. Poor women try to take the best of the options available to them, and, contrary to the complaints and expectations of both secularist and Islamist elites, they are not constantly hoodwinked by the other side. My research shows that impoverished rural women's decision to join an NGO should not be read as a rejection of religion – to be lamented by some and celebrated by others. They see no contradiction between being good Muslims and working for *unnoti* (positive change) in their households; given the limited employment opportunities available to rural women, the latter is often possible only through involvement with NGOs. I cite the important example of purdah – when women join an NGO, local people threaten that they are violating purdah and will lose their religion; when they have saved up some money, many women spend it on buying a nicer, fancier *burqa*. This confounds Islamists who are apprehensive that NGOs are ruining the tradition of purdah, as well as secularists who hope that women involved with NGOs will shake off the shackles of traditions like purdah and embrace a secularist understanding of modernity. Struggling within formidable constraints, both material and cultural, impoverished rural women in Bangladesh fashion their own understanding of development and modernity.

Notes

An earlier version of this essay appeared in E. Shehabuddin 1999b. It also draws on an argument I present in greater detail in E. Shehabuddin 2000.

1. Despite the recent proliferation of NGOs throughout the world and, subsequently, of literature on NGOs in political science and other fields, no one clear definition of the term 'NGO' has emerged (Clarke 1998). Strictly speaking, NGO, as the term suggests, refers to any non-governmental organization. Thus it can include neighbourhood soccer clubs as well as vast organizations like the Bangladesh Rural Advancement Committee (BRAC), which, by 1997, had over 1.8 million members in 54,000 villages (Smillie 1997: 9). According to Richard Holloway, it is apparent what NGOs are *not* – they are *neither* government, *nor* for profit. He posits that 'in common parlance in Bangladesh, [NGOs] refer to organizations started in Bangladesh, or brought in from overseas, that claim to do development work, and usually do this with foreign money' (Holloway 1998: 19). Some see the main tasks of NGOs as 'help[ing] the government' and 'do[ing] things the government cannot do or does not do well' (Holloway 1998: 20).

2. A coalition of various Islamist organizations that came together with the stated goal of having all NGOs shut down (Rashiduzzaman 1994: 983).

3. A national convention of the poor was finally held on Manik Miah Avenue on 1 January 1996. Over 100,000 poor men and women from all parts of the country converged on the avenue in front of parliament. The gathering adopted a declaration calling for greater attention by the government to issues of poverty alleviation, the environment and gender issues (*Daily Star*, 2 January 1996). Unless otherwise noted, all translations from Bengali are my own.

4. NGOs and intellectuals immediately charged the government with double standards, and with – at least passively – supporting the anti-NGO rally (*Daily Star*, 2 April 1995).

5. Purdah, which literally means curtain, refers to rules governing interaction between women and not only men but sometimes also non-kin women. It has implications for dress, architecture and behaviour. Generally speaking, observing purdah means conducting oneself so as to avoid interaction with non-kin men, though as I show below, rural women subscribe to a wide variety of interpretations of the term.

6. Smillie focuses on the BRAC experience; however, BRAC, as the oldest and largest indigenous NGO, reflects the changing priorities of the NGO community in Bangladesh. See also Chen 1983.

7. According to a 1995 government estimate, there were approximately six million landless and functionally landless (0.5 acres of land or less) households in Bangladesh (GoB 1995a: 21).

8. Proshika calculates that by 1995 it had planted 50 million trees, constructed 30,000 new homes, installed 10,000 tubewells and 76,000 latrines, and set up 300 non-formal schools. By the end of 1993, it had disbursed 46,431 loans amounting to Taka 895 million (US$22,375,000), an average of Taka 19,276 (US$482) (Ahmed 1995).

9. Most of the Islamic NGOs currently operating in Bangladesh concentrate on charity, relief and rehabilitation work. Muslim Aid, for example, has provided humanitarian assistance not only in Bangladesh following numerous devastating floods and cyclones but also in war-torn regions of the world such as Rwanda, Bosnia and Afghanistan. Others – like the Islami Samaj Kalyan Samity (Islamic Social Welfare Association), Dhaka – run orphanages, adult literacy classes and medical clinics (Hours 1993: 72–6). While these organizations clearly provide invaluable services, they do not purport to encourage their beneficiaries to question the status quo, or transform society. In contrast, organizations such as the Bangladesh Masjid Samaj (Society of Mosques), Bangladesh Masjid Mission (Mosque Mission), and the state-run Islamic Foundation have grander objectives. According to Hours, they seek to enhance 'the social and religious role of mosques' by training imams to participate in the task of economic and social development within an Islamic framework (Hours 1993: 76–8). Members of these organizations believe that the moral reform and development of individuals must precede any societal development; that social justice will follow only after virtue and peace have been established in society. They understand 'welfare' not as 'material prosperity and well-being' but as 'an intimate harmony between individuals and nature, a gift from God' which in turn generates a respect for the teachings of Islam (Hours 1993: 78).

10. Meghna Guhathakurta provides a telling example of the contradictory

pressures upon the state. In its bid to modernize, President Ziaur Rahman's government not only introduced women traffic police but even required them to wear shirts and trousers like the male police – instead of sarees. Before long, however, they were withdrawn from the streets to duty inside various checkpoints or traffic booths. According to Guhathakurta, there had been pressure from the Saudi government to remove women from such public gaze. Having women traffic wardens out on the streets 'did not quite tally with the values being cultivated by an aspiring Islamic state' (Guhathakurta 1985: 86).

11. Bangladesh's first constitution, promulgated in December 1972, enshrined secularism as one of its four directive principles. This clause was later removed under military rule.

12. For a discussion of the Jamaat's position on poverty alleviation, see E. Shehabuddin 1999a.

13. Women in one village recounted the story of one woman whose husband actively encouraged her to join the Grameen Bank; when she brought the money home, he would take it from her, but leave her with the responsibility for weekly payments. Finally, the woman decided that she had had enough, and refused to take any more loans from the bank. She arrived at the next meeting battered and bruised – her husband had sent her to collect her new loan. Interview, Chittagong, 19 February 1996.

References

Ahmed, I. (1995) 'A Quiet Revolution: Changing Social Structures in Rural Bangladesh', *Daily Star*, 30 December.

Ahmed, R. (1985) 'Women's Movement in Bangladesh and the Left's Understanding of the Woman Question', *Journal of Social Studies* 30.

Alam, S.M. Nurul (1995) 'NGOs Under Attack: A Study of Socio-cultural and Political Dynamics of NGO Operations in Bangladesh', unpublished paper.

Alam, S.M. Nurul (1996) 'Understanding NGO Operations in Bangladesh: Views from the Field', unpublished paper.

Anam, M. (1995) 'Where the World Emulates Us', *Daily Star*, 30 December.

Chen, M. (1983) *A Quiet Revolution: Women in Transition in Rural Bangladesh*, Cambridge, MA: Schenckman.

Chowdhury, N. (1995) 'What's the Flavour of the Month?', *Daily Star*, 17 April.

Clarke, G. (1998) *The Politics of NGOs in South-East Asia: Participation and Protest in the Philippines*, New York: Routledge.

Feldman, S. (1998) '(Re)presenting Islam: Manipulating Gender, Shifting State Practices, and Class Frustrations in Bangladesh', in P. Jeffery and A. Basu, eds, *Appropriating Gender: Women's Activism and Politicized Religion in South Asia*, London: Routledge.

Goetz, A.M. (1998) 'Mainstreaming Gender Equity in National Development Planning', in C. Miller and S. Razavi, eds, *Missionaries and Mandarins: Feminist Engagements with Development Institutions*, London: Intermediate Technology Publications/United Nations Research Institute for Social Development.

Government of Bangladesh (GoB) (1995a) 'Women in Bangladesh: Equality,

Development and Peace – National Report to the Fourth World Conference on Women, Beijing 1995', Dhaka: Ministry of Women and Children's Affairs.

Government of Bangladesh (GoB) (1995b) *Country Paper – Bangladesh, Prepared for World Summit for Social Development, Copenhagen, Denmark, March 1995*. Dhaka: GoB.

Guhathakurta, M. (1985) 'Gender Violence in Bangladesh: The Role of the State', *Journal of Social Studies* 30.

Hashemi, S.M. (1995) 'NGO Accountability in Bangladesh: Beneficiaries, Donors, and the State', in M. Edwards and D. Hulme, eds, *Beyond the Magic Bullet: NGO Performance and Accountability in the Post-Cold War World*, West Hartford, CT: Kumarian Press.

Hashemi, S.M. and S. Schuler (1992) *State and NGO Support Networks in Rural Bangladesh: Concepts and Coalitions for Control*, Copenhagen: Centre for Development Research.

Holloway, R. (1998) *Supporting Citizens' Initiatives: Bangladesh's NGOs and Society*, London: Intermediate Technology Publications.

Hours, B. (1993) *Islam et Développement au Bangladesh* [Islam and Development in Bangladesh], Paris: L'Harmattan.

Jahan, R. (1995) 'Men in Seclusion, Women in Public: Rokeya's Dream and Women's Struggles in Bangladesh', in A. Basu, ed., *The Challenge of Local Feminisms: Women's Movements in Global Perspective*, Boulder, CO: Westview Press.

Kabeer, N. (1988) 'Subordination and Struggle: Women in Bangladesh', *New Left Review* 168.

Kabeer, N. (1994) 'Women's Labour in the Bangladesh Garment Industry: Choice and Constraints', in C. el-Solh and J. Mabro, eds, *Muslim Women's Choice: Religious Belief and Social Reality*, Oxford: Berg.

Khundker, N. (1995) 'Agents of Change: GO or NGOs?', *Daily Star*, 31 March.

Naher, A. (1996) 'Gender, Religion and Rural Development in Bangladesh', MA thesis, University of Sussex.

Rahman, A. and S. Mustafa (1995) 'Governance and Participation: The NGO Experience in Bangladesh', *Morning Sun*, 15 March.

Rashiduzzaman, M. (1994) 'The Liberals and the Religious Right in Bangladesh', *Asian Survey*, vol. 34, no. 11.

Rashiduzzaman, M. (1997) 'The Dichotomy of Islam and Development: NGOs, Women's Development and Fatawa in Bangladesh', *Contemporary South Asia*, vol. 6, no. 3.

Rowlands, J. (1998) 'A Word of the Times, but What Does it Mean? Empowerment in the Discourse and Practice of Development', in H. Afshar, ed., *Women and Empowerment: Illustrations from the Third World*, New York: St. Martin's Press.

Samad, A. (1995) 'Cold War Between Government and NGOs', *Holiday*, 31 March.

Saptagram (n.d.)(a) *Adult Education Lessons to Raise Consciousness*, Vol. 1, Dhaka: Saptagram.

Saptagram (n.d.)(b) *A Guide to Enhanced Awareness, Adult Education Lessons to Raise Consciousness*, Vol. 1: *A Teacher's Guide*, Dhaka: Saptagram.

Shehabuddin, E. (1999a) 'Beware the Bed of Fire: Gender, Democracy, and the Jama'at-i Islami in Bangladesh', *Journal of Women's History*, vol. 10, no. 4.

Shehabuddin, E. (1999b) 'Contesting the Illicit: Gender and the Politics of *Fatwas* in Bangladesh', *Signs*, vol. 24, no. 4.

Shehabuddin, E. (2000) 'Encounters with the State: Gender and Islam in Rural Bangladesh', Ph.D. dissertation, Princeton University.

Shehabuddin, R. (1992) *Empowering Rural Women: The Impact of Grameen Bank in Bangladesh*, Dhaka: Grameen Bank.

Smillie, I. (1997) *Words and Deeds: BRAC at 25*, Dhaka: BRAC Centre.

Stansell, C. (1986) *City of Women: Sex and Class in New York, 1789–1860*, New York: Knopf.

Umar, B. (1996) 'On the Subject of NGOs', *Ajker Kagoj*, 26 April.

Westergaard, K. (1996) 'People's Empowerment in Bangladesh: NGO Strategies', *Journal of Social Studies 72*.

Women for Women (1995) *Women and Politics: Orientation of Four Political Parties on Women's Empowerment Issues*, Dhaka: Women for Women.

Wood, G.D. (1994) *Bangladesh: Whose Ideas, Whose Interests?*, Dhaka: University Press.

Gender Silences in the Narmada Valley

Jael Silliman

Women's human rights, and their access to environmental goods and resources, are a sensitive issue in India. Women have only recently begun to mobilize in order to challenge development projects on ecological grounds, buttressed by issues of cultural survival and human rights. In calling for an end to the violence of development, the Narmada Bachao Andolan (NBA), a grassroots movement that has opposed the construction of the Sardar Sarovar Dam, has been precedent-setting. Sardar Sarovar, which has been called 'the world's biggest planned environmental disaster' (Esteva and Prakash 1992: 47), will flood sixty thousand acres of forest and very productive agricultural land, lead to a loss of biodiversity and species, and also disrupt downstream fisheries. The NBA is a vanguard people's movement that has worked successfully at both local and transnational levels to enrich environmental discourses and activism regarding the construction of the dam. Consequently, local communities' traditional rights and access to resources are increasingly being incorporated into environmental policy and decision-making.

Although the NBA has mobilized women in the Valley, it has not highlighted gender inequities. Yet women will be particularly and severely affected by the dam's construction. Their unequal treatment is perpetuated by the development establishment, as well as by state and local government policies and programmes regarding displacement and resettlement in the Narmada Valley. In this essay, I examine the varied roles played by women of the NBA in their quest for a sustainable development; I also analyse the constraints they face in addressing gender inequality in a political context where the NBA has to maintain unity

among a diverse group of constituencies held together by their opposition to the dam.[1] The political representation of women in local
governments, by the authority of the seventy-third amendment to the
national constitution which reserves places for women on the local
panchayat (village council), has created a momentum for greater attention
to women's political participation and representation. These outside
factors, together with pressure from within the NBA, places the organization at a crossroads regarding its position on gender issues.

The Narmada Case

The Sardar Sarovar, the largest dam in a series of dams scheduled for
construction, has been the flashpoint for opposition to this elaborate
dam network that is being put in place in the Narmada Valley. The NBA
has used it as a symbol for the violence of development. The Sardar
Sarovar has been opposed because of the damage it will do to the
environment; the inadequate resettlement and compensation earmarked
for displaced persons (referred to in government documents as 'oustees');
the disruption it will cause in tribal lives and lifestyles; and the abrogation
of the right to full information for people affected by the project (referred
to as 'project-affected persons' or 'PAPs' in government records). The
Narmada Bachao Andolan argues that water will not reach the
Saurashhtra/Kutch area, even though much of the emotive appeal of the
dam is that it will provide drinking water to these drought-prone regions.
The NBA goes beyond the specifics of the dam, and critiques the
Narmada project as an example of 'maldevelopment'. It advocates an
alternative development path that incorporates the needs of people,
such as the *adivasi*, or tribal peoples. This alternative also calls for valuing
the environment not only on economic but on social and cultural
grounds as well.

   The Narmada resistance, in many respects, illustrates the coming-of-
age of the environmental movement. It has forced the various state
governments (Gujarat, Maharashtra and Madhya Pradesh), the Government of India (GoI), and the World Bank to revise the ways in which
they examine and develop public policy on resettlement issues, tribal
(*adivasi*) rights, human rights and environmental impact assessments.
The NBA has led the World Bank to expand its environmental staff and
reorient its lending procedures to take environmental and resettlement
issues more seriously into account. Governments outside India, too,
have been made to rethink the ways in which they design and assess
large-scale projects. The NBA has been able to orchestrate a transnational

campaign that has had significant repercussions around the world in the setting of new environmental and resettlement standards for major development projects.

Although numerous and extensive official and technical studies have been conducted to support or oppose the building of this network of dams, only a handful of scholars and activists (Baviskar 1995; Bhatia 1997; Kapur 1993; O'Bannon 1994) discuss the ramifications of the project for the different groups of women who live in the Valley. This silence occurs despite a rich feminist movement within India, and almost three decades of scholarship demonstrating how development interventions have differing impacts based on gender, and that gender-blind interventions further impoverish women. The NBA – although it is led by Medha Patkar, a charismatic woman leader, and has many women in key leadership positions – has not organized women as a constituency; nor has it articulated the practical needs or strategic interests of women.[2] I will elaborate the gender implications of each of the key issues raised by the Narmada campaign, then go on to discuss the implications of these gender silences for women's lives.

Displacement, Resettlement and Rehabilitation: Land Rights

The resettlement policies in the case of the Sardar Sarovar Project (SSP) have evolved over a decade in response to pressures from opponents of the dam. Joshi argues that as the resettlement policies stand today, they are the most liberal rehabilitation policies in the Third World (Joshi 1997: 177). Yet while issues of resettlement and compensation for 'oustees' have been at the core of the Narmada struggle, the gender bias implicit in these policies and awards has not been challenged. Thus, while these may represent the most forward-looking resettlement policies, they discriminate against women, and undermine women's rights (Basu 1992: 9).

For those to be displaced by the Sardar Sarovar reservoir, the award of the Narmada Water Disputes Tribunal laid down certain guidelines for rehabilitation in 1978. The three states announced their policies subsequently. The definition of a 'family' as laid down in the Tribunal Award includes 'husband, wife and minor children and other persons dependent upon the head of the family, e.g., widowed mother'. The Award specifies that every major son will be treated as a separate family; women are considered as mere dependants. The states of Madhya Pradesh and Maharashtra treat the widow as dependent on the head of the family. Many widows, however, are not taken care of by their sons or other relatives (Bhatia 1997: 293). Nevertheless, a widow's right to the allotted land ceases to exist, since the alternative land is allotted to the head of the family (i.e. her adult son). According to local tribal custom, however, it is the youngest son who looks after his widowed mother. If the son is under 24, neither he nor his mother is entitled to compensation. In 1990 the Gujarat government decided to recognize a woman who became a widow after 1980 as entitled to a separate package (Dhagamwar, Thukral and Singh 1995: 272). Despite this improvement, many widows in the submergence areas and the resettlement sites have been further marginalized and dispossessed as a result of the resettlement process (Bhatia 1997: 292). Bhatia discusses some of the widows' attempts to resist these policies.

The various unequal settlement packages adopted and modified by the three states all treat the household as a unitary category. Central to this definition is the notion that the household is governed by altruism.[3] It is assumed that there is a shared harmony of interests among household members. Research shows that, especially in places like rural India, females have much less access to household resources than do males (Agarwal 1994; Bagwe 1995; Rao 1996). The Tribunal Award ignores the inequalities that exist between family members, as well as the reality and needs of households headed by women. Yet we know that female-headed households are common throughout the region. In this patriarchal model there is no acknowledgement of the needs, or even the existence, of deserted or unmarried women – it is assumed that all women are married or widowed. Basu records the importance of land titles to women who are insecure without property titles in their name: 'Babu, it is well and good to give *puttas* [land titles] to our husbands. But if they leave us we become propertyless again' (Basu 1992: 63). As of 1993, the Maharashtra government did revoke its earlier decision whereby daughters of oustees were not to be considered as separate families to entitle 'adult daughters of project affected persons' who were unmarried on 1 January 1987 to receive one hectare of land (Dhagamwar et al. 1995: 278–9).

In the official framework, then, only those women who fit within dominant patriarchal discourses – daughters, wives and widows – are bestowed with some, albeit unequal, rights to land. Conversely, single – and, by extension, divorced or deserted – women who do not adhere to these norms, or violate them, have their rights to land forfeited. Yet informal estimates made by voluntary organizations indicate that a third of all women between the ages of 18 and 30 (in rural India) are either deserted by their husbands or choose to leave them. Nevertheless, because of the immense social pressures on women to be married, these once-married women pretend to be married to men who live and work in the cities (Rao 1996: 7–8).

The Tribunal's policy, through its stereotypical representations of women, disadvantages women and intensifies the dependence of single women and female-headed households on male recipients, exacerbating gender inequalities (Rao 1996: 7–8). The tunnel vision of states, and their inability to work except with modular schemes, is well documented in development literature. Even the problematic and undifferentiated household is invisible in the NBA scheme, which is organized on the basis of adversely affected communities. Both these conceptualizations of women as part of undifferentiated households or communities stand in the way of framing them as a constituency. What is particularly disturbing is that the Narmada is a precedent-setting case which is establishing standards and policies that are being watched in India and elsewhere. A sensitivity to gender inequities here would have far-reaching consequences. Nonetheless, these discriminatory practices have not been criticized by environmental organizations (national or international), the NBA, or the Independent Review – even as they have highlighted environmental concerns, the special needs and rights of indigenous people, and other human rights violations in their critiques of the Project (O'Bannon 1994: 259).[4] Nor has the Indian women's movement pressed this point, though in general there is an increasing awareness in the literature, and in sections of the movement, of the importance of land rights for women.

The absence of an outcry against the handing of land rights to male members only is particularly disturbing given the importance of land rights for women on the subcontinent (Agarwal 1994). Land is the single most important asset – landownership determines economic well-being, social status and political power in rural South Asia. Agarwal, in her book *A Field of One's Own*, cogently argues that women's lack of effective property rights, especially land, explains their social, economic and political subordination. She concludes that women's struggle for their legitimate share in landed property may be the most critical entry point for their empowerment in South Asia (Agarwal 1994). The Tribunal's stipulation to make this crucial and scarce resource available only to male heads of household denies independent land rights to women in the Valley. It thereby impedes the chances for establishing more equal gender relations both within and outside the household. Women's independent land rights – or, at least, joint titles to land – are forfeited by the failure to raise this critical women's rights issue.

Agarwal suggests why the issue of land rights for women has not been raised by political and social movements: 'acknowledging the varying and sometimes conflicting preference[s] and interests and access to resources among family members means admitting new contenders for a share in this scarce and highly valuable resource ... [bringing the conflict over land] into the family's innermost courtyard' (Agarwal 1994: 3). Political and social movements like the NBA have deliberately side-stepped this issue because of its politically charged nature. Yet experience from the Jharkhand movement, where the issue of separate allotments of land was raised by women, demonstrates that

> The demand of land for women cannot be taken up in isolation, nor can it be won by women alone. Such a demand has to be part of the movement to stop the process of alienation of *adivasi* lands, integrated into the Jharkhand movement for political, economic and other favorable conditions for the advance of Jharkhand. It is also necessary that the men realize that the demand is not such as will disrupt and destroy whatever is left of the community. (Kelkar and Nathan 1991: 108)

Thus, women's rights cannot be treated as residual – as issues to be dealt with at a later and more opportune moment (see Seager 1993: 171).

Gender bias is even more pervasive in the official Indian and inter-national development discourses about women in the Narmada Valley. Women are treated not as individuals with rights, but as dependants. Kapur points out how the World Bank, in its paper on relocation, grouped women and the elderly together while discussing the stress that 'compulsory removal' could cause them, noting that '[t]he grouping of women who are so economically and socially central to tribal (and non-tribal) societies with the elderly ... is disturbing and inadequate since it devalues women as well as the elderly' (Kapur 1993: 61).

Extending Economic and Political Dependency

There is an ungendered understanding of the negative consequences of displacement, which include

> the dismantling of production systems, desecration of ancestral sacred zones or graves and temples, scattering of kinship groups and family systems, disorganization of informal social networks that provide mutual support, disruption of trade and market links, etc. Essentially, what is established in the accumulated evidence in the country suggests that ... forced displace-ment has resulted in a 'spiral of impoverishment' ... trade links between producers and their customer base (and systems of exchange and barter) are interrupted and local labor markets are disrupted. Additionally, there is

also a loss of complex social relationships which provided avenues of representation, mediation and conflict resolution. (Kothrari, Pratap and Visvanathan, 1995: S. 12)

The particular impact of displacement on women is not clearly articulated. However, a number of studies have scattered references to the fact that women experience displacement differently. For example, a series of changes have been observed in the lives of women now living in the resettlement sites in Maharashtra. Whereas these women were once agriculturists, and did not have to leave their villages for wage-labour, they are now engaged in wage-labour at the resettlement sites. They have needed this additional income to meet their consumption needs. They must make up for their losses, 'as activities relating to tending cattle have declined and the collection of forest produce has disappeared' (Tata Institute of Social Sciences 1997: 207). Preliminary research indicates that certain types of housework are less onerous in the resettlement sites, as water can be pumped closer to home and women have easier access to some technologies, such as a grain grinder. Yet no rigorous studies have been undertaken to evaluate ways in which displacement will have an impact on women who have gender-specific relations to production systems, play different roles in kinship groups, rely heavily on social networks, and have specific market roles. A gendered analysis that takes into consideration the complexities of women's lives, and incorporates an understanding of the various roles played by women, would provide the baseline data (which do not currently exist) for an assessment of the particular impact displacement will have on women. Only with these data could some of the positive and negative effects upon women be factored into the creation of a social and economic cost–benefit analysis for determining the value of such a mega-project.

There is no breakdown of the differential employment impacts for men and women in the arguments put forth by pro-dam proponents with regard to the increased employment opportunities the Sardar Sarovar Dam will generate. This ignores the data that do exist, which point to the growing rate of unemployment among women in this region. Data compiled by the International Labour Organization (ILO) indicate that in the 1980s unemployment among women rose by 5 per cent relative to unemployment among men. Even if women's labour-force participation were to increase, it would need to be understood in relation to the growing number of women searching for work. The large number of unemployed women would depress the wages for employment generated by the dam (O'Bannon 1994: 260). ILO data on male and female employment in seven sectors of the modern economy showed that men and women are not integrated into the workforce in a 'single and linear, cumulative fashion' (O'Bannon 1994: 257). Rather, researchers found that women made no advances, or actually lost ground to men, and made significant gains only in those sectors that extended their traditional domestic roles. Thus, although government estimates state that the dam may create employment for one million workers, the prognosis for women looks bad. Women will be, for the most part, employed in the poorly remunerated, unskilled or semi-skilled positions generated by the construction of the Sardar Sarovar, unless special policies are implemented to counter this trend. Since women's demands have not been identified, there are no policies or programmes designed to give them the skills and training they would need to improve their employment prospects.

NBA activists do have an understanding of the particular impact that displacement has on tribal women.[5] For example, there is an awareness of the relative freedoms that tribal women enjoy in comparison to other rural women. The emotional and economic support provided by a woman's parents throughout her marriage, and the dependence on the 'free goods' of the forest and easy access to the river for daily chores, will be severely disrupted through displacement. From the women's point of view, displacement gives rise to problems connected with fuel and fodder. Women play an important role in maintaining the ecological balance (Patkar 1992: 289). Although women constitute a large proportion of the displaced, 'little attention, if any, is paid to them by the concerned authorities and the males in their own families' (Dhamgawar et al. 1995: 278). Scholars note that women's opinions are rarely sought, and that women are rarely informed of dam-related developments.

Damage to the Environment

Although there is general information on how dwindling ecological resources make women work harder, walk further, eat and prepare less nourishing foods, and generally endure greater hardships, we know less about how this affects their

> life-views, self-images, coping strategies, choices and consciousness and, consequently, their ability, potential and willingness to organize as a group and struggle for social change.... Theorizing the concept of non-renewable ecological resources ... from a feminist perspective is therefore a crucial step in understanding these complex and dialectical interrelationships between objective and subjective conditions for rural women's protests. (Rao 1996: 7-9)

The considerable damage done to the environment by large-scale development projects is only now being factored into cost–benefit analyses of the development establishment. Critics argue that there is growing evidence from all over India that

> the concentration of large numbers of people on the increasingly fragile ecosystems most often leads to the further unsustainability of resources. All this leads to increasing economic marginalization and cultural insecurity which compel most of the displaced to seek desperate means of survival – cultivating increasingly fragile lands, migration, bondage, contract, crime, even prostitution. (Kothrari, Pratap and Visvanathan, 1995: S. 11)

What is rarely factored into the discussion of the negative environmental impacts is the particular and differential impacts that environmental loss and displacements will have on women. There is an understanding of the fact that both tribal men and women are dependent on the forests for fodder, fuel, fibre, fruit, house-building material, medicines and edible gums. Women's roles in managing natural resources and their dependence on the natural resource base differ from those of men, because of the gendered division of labour. Much evidence explains how and why women must depend on and use the river and forests to prepare and provide food and water for their families. Collecting food, fuel and water is a considerable and time-consuming task for women. Their use of the river and forests for medicinal and religious purposes also differs from that of their male counterparts. Yet while the rights and access of *adivasis* to the forest are presented as a reason for opposing the dam, the differential environmental impacts on men and women are not articulated.

Women will be particularly disadvantaged through the loss of place-based knowledge of social and natural resources. Very little attention is given to the fact that women depend on these local networks and resources for social and economic information, income and cash, as well as non-cash assistance in providing for their families (Ahlawat 1995). Women often tend to rely more on such networks than men, and they cannot be replicated in resettlement sites. Disruption of these networks reduces their household bargaining power, and their well-being.

Tribal Lifestyle Changes

Opponents of the dam have argued that displacement deprives tribal communities of their history, religion and culture. The specific impact on tribal women, however, has not been discussed. When tribal women are resettled in the plains area, they will be placed in communities that practise purdah (the seclusion of women), and will experience social tensions in their new settings (Kapur 1993). For example, hill *adivasis* enjoy considerable autonomy in their choice of partner, and elopement and abduction are socially sanctioned:

> The festival of Bhagoria in February–March, when *adivasis* gather together in the *haats* to select their partners, celebrates that freedom of choice. Marriages are sealed by the payment of brideprice to the woman's father; they are broken when she leaves her husband, who then tries to get his money back. The ease of divorce also sets the hill *adivasis* apart from the people of the plains. Finally, the notion of the gift of a virgin appears ludicrous in a society that does not place a high value on the chastity of unmarried women. Sexual liaisons are easily acknowledged and people live together before wedding rites are performed. All of which is quite contrary to the Hindu norm. (Baviskar 1995: 96)

Baviskar discusses how, in the process of Hinduization, through settling in caste communities that have traditionally looked down on tribal ways and lifestyles, *adivasis* have become ashamed of their social customs, and gradually seek to alter them. In addition to feeling shame in the resettlement areas, tribal women will most probably face new restrictions on their movements. The greater mobility and freedom that *adivasis* enjoy in their social interactions have led plains people to label tribal women 'deviant' or 'loose'. In other areas where *adivasis* have been displaced, the lack of employment opportunities, combined with this social stigma, has led many tribal women into prostitution. The documented case of Ukai, which shows that tribal women displaced by the projects were regularly soliciting truck drivers on the national highway from Baroda to Ahmedabad, is no exception (Kothrari, Pratap and Visvanathan 1995: 11). It is also likely that tribal women in the resettled areas will be targets for sexual assault. Finally, tribal women in the resettlement sites will also have to adjust to living far from their parental homes. Living in close proximity to their parents is a source of emotional and financial support. Tribal women typically remain in close touch with their families even after they move to the husband's village (Baviskar 1995: 111–12). When they seek to leave their husbands, *adivasi* women in tribal areas seek refuge in the homes of their parents.

Discussion with NBA activists revealed how *adivasi* women are finding that their workload increases considerably in the resettlement sites. While *adivasi* women who tended livestock used to let their flocks loose to graze and get water by the riverbank, in the resettlement areas they find themselves pumping water to feed their livestock. Increased workloads and changes in lifestyle, diets and cooking styles (due to reliance on different sources or quantities of fuel) will most probably have negative health consequences. For example, Baviskar mentions how livestock – cattle, goats and hens – and people share the large and airy tribal homes. Being near the river, they have easy access to water for the livestock, and the fish caught in the river are also an important source of protein in their diets in the summer months. She noted that people catch and eat more than twenty-five varieties of fish: 'Access to forest and river resources enables the people of Anjanvara to hold their own economically. What is classified in government terminology as "minor forest" produce is an integral part of what they live on' (Baviskar 1995: 142). The fact that women will not have access to these 'free goods', coupled with the lack of landownership in the resettled areas, further impoverishes and marginalizes tribal women in the new sites.

Whereas a great deal of attention has been paid to the special ways in which *adivasis* interact with the environment, there has been no scrutiny of local tribal traditions that may disadvantage women. This lack of recognition of gender inequality by the NBA, as it simultaneously tries to validate and uphold tribal culture, is disconcerting. We know from studies of other social movements in tribal areas – such as the Shramik Sti Mukti Sanghatana (SSMS) in Dhulia district of Maharashtra – that tribal women do face sexual inequality in their home environment. Issues of inequality that were raised in Dhulia 'ranged from sexual harassment to the patriarchal character of Bhil ritual and superstition, women's lack of control over their own bodies, and the unequal division of labor within the home' (Basu 1992: 89). Alcoholism was also a key issue for women in Dhulia, because *adivasi* men were heavy drinkers, and the commercialization of agriculture had disrupted traditional social relations, leading to increased alcohol use (Basu 1992: 87). The SSMS also saw several disadvantages for women in terms of *adivasi* customary law in the area of polygamy, custody rights over children upon divorce, the institution of bride price and women's representation in the *panchayat* (Basu 1992: 87). These inequalities have not been raised publicly by the NBA, although patrilineal descent and patrilocal residence arrangements within an overarching patriarchal context are defining social features among *adivasis* in the Narmada Valley.

Rights to Information

The NBA has challenged the government on its failure to disclose information about the dam to the people who will be affected. However, the NBA has not highlighted the fact that rural and tribal women do not have the same access to information as men. Enabling women to obtain information would require not only an understanding of prevailing customs and social norms but also a knowledge of women's daily work and family demands, and the physical spaces most suitable for women to exchange and receive information. The NBA tries to include women in its meetings, and often does this by holding meetings at night, when some are able to attend. Still, younger women would not be able to leave their homes in the evenings, especially in more conservative communities in the plains area. Organizing meetings and gatherings around women's lives takes commitment, but it can be done. The Anti-Price Rise Movement in Maharashtra mobilized vast numbers of women. Contrary to conventional wisdom, Mrinal Gore, a leader in the APRM, stated: 'Housewives are the most well placed to participate in politics because they have flexible hours and a lot of spare time in the afternoon' (Gandhi 1996: 56). Through adjusting the times and locations of their meetings to the rhythms of women's daily lives, the movement was very successful in mobilizing women. There has been no official recognition by the opposition, critics of the project, or the authorities of the special needs of women in terms of unequal access to information.

Neither tribal nor plains women will have access to information, even were the government to make it available, unless special mechanisms are put in place. Their greater illiteracy rates further disadvantage them from obtaining public/government information. Culturally, it is husbands who are expected to gather information for the family. Information is power; therefore the lack of special arrangements for women to get access to information means that women are further disempowered.

Alternative Development Policy

[L]arge scale displacement is inbuilt in the patterns of economic development which themselves are incompatible with social justice and long-term environmental sustainability. (Kothrari, Pratap and Visvanathan 1995: 11)

The NBA is calling for an alternative development paradigm premissed upon a deep respect for local culture and knowledge, a concern for the environment, a critical stance towards established scientific discourses that have directed mainstream development thinking and practice, and a focus on democratic participation. It is challenging the government's callous invocation of 'development by displacement'. This cynical slogan informs oustees that they will have access to schools and other public services that are currently unavailable in most tribal areas in the

Valley. The NBA argues forcefully that *adivasis* should have rights and access to these public services where they currently reside, and should not be displaced in order to receive them. They have highlighted the point that national development strategies consistently bypass tribal people.

The NBA is not, however, taking its argument a step further to advocate a development that explicitly sets out to meet the needs of all tribal people, including tribal women, whose needs and priorities may, in some cases, conflict with those of men. In other parts of India (both tribal and mainstream), the conflict between women's and men's priorities based on the gendered division of labour and the unequal access to resources has been documented. Similarly, in advocating on behalf of the plains people for continued access to irrigated land, the NBA does not raise issues of gender discrimination against women in the Nimar plains. There are several customary practices in this area that are particularly oppressive to women, but have not been challenged or been reconsidered by the NBA in their envisioning of an alternative development path. In the final analysis, the NBA does not think it is their role to catalyse the transformation of gender inequalities in the Valley.

Gender Silences within the NBA

There is a keen awareness of gender inequities among several of the NBA activists who have been associated with, and are familiar with, other leftist social movements that have addressed issues of gender inequality. Since the Chandwad conference of the Shetkari Sanghatana in 1986, activists (men and women) working within mass organizations of tribal peoples, peasants and workers have become sensitive to women's issues, and have made conscious efforts to raise women's issues along with class issues. Also, a deliberate attempt to encourage women leaders at the local level within several organizations has been noted (Datar 1995: 27).

Activists in the NBA argue that women's interests are being addressed by the Andolan. This reflects an ongoing debate within the women's movement on what issues can be termed women's issues, and whether they should be defined narrowly to address specific women's issues, or defined more broadly.[6] Despite these claims and debates, and admiration for their work on alternative development, Datar states that the NBA 'has not yet made serious efforts to connect women's issues with alternative development policies' (Datar 1995: 35). I concur, and contend

that the NBA has not articulated or addressed strategic gender interests
in its public documents or statements. As the NBA has focused its attention on halting the construction of the dam – and has done so amid
great opposition – it has most probably seen that women's issues could
be too divisive for the movement to take on. According to Kapur, this
failure has reduced opposition to the dam 'to a solely male discourse
which operates within the logic of the system that it is trying to oppose' (Kapur 1993: 61). Feminism, as articulated by the various streams
of the women's movement in India, was not part of the NBA's ideological base. Medha Patkar, the charismatic leader of the NBA, is clearly
familiar with struggles that incorporated a gender perspective, and
several important women's movements emerged from her home state
of Maharashtra to take on issues of gender inequality and patriarchy.
Nevertheless, in the opposition to the Sardar Sarovar, women have not
been organized as a constituency around their special needs. Patkar
explains her approach to organizing tribal women as follows:

> When I started working in tribal villages, tribal women were not at the
> forefront. I have never insisted that women be dragged into it from the
> beginning. I have been criticized for this – why women are never seen at
> my rallies, etc.... I think it does not make sense to insist that women must
> attend our rallies, only for the sake of appearance, [and be] included in
> decision-making structures. We go to their homes and they give us some-
> thing to eat and that is how the process starts. To begin with, they take part
> in only the major programmes. Here I am first talking about the tribal
> areas.... Women got some exposure as they began to attend our big rallies.
> At the village level, we tried to include women as much as we could. Things
> have changed a lot since those early days. We were conscious of this but we
> were never for enforcing it somehow or other.... Women now know about
> the fight and gradually their participation is increasing. (Patkar 1992: 289)

Since women were not made central to the movement, or seen as
a key constituency in its formative period, they have not played a role
in setting its priorities and agendas. Rather, women contributed to and
joined the movement after the broad contours and framework for the
NBA had been established. Thus, women's issues and their participation
were considered secondary from the outset, and their role was deemed
a supportive one. Patkar explains how the NBA was too busy to dedi-
cate time to organizing women:

> [We were] ... organizing people, carrying out dialogues, finding docu-
> ments, establishing a network, explaining things from one point of view to
> the human rights activists, and from another point of view to the environ-
> mentalists as well as worrying about the forest dwellers. In the process,

there was literally not a single moment to arrange separate meetings with the village women. If you want to deal with both men and women, you need special manpower for that, a special approach, different strategies. We didn't have the time to do any of this. (Patkar 1992: 290)

Rather than working specifically on women's concerns, which are deemed too 'time-consuming', the NBA's priority is to unite *adivasis* with people from the plains who will also be affected, together with urban supporters in India and elsewhere. Thus in this struggle they have given priority to *adivasi* rights and biodiversity. Gender issues, besides being 'too time-consuming', may have proved too divisive, as Agarwal has suggested in her discussion of land rights. However, NBA activists also justify their political stance regarding women by stating that the NBA does not set priorities and directives but follows the lead of the communities within which it works. They have worked largely with the men in the community, who have not determined women's issues a priority. Rather than questioning who is speaking on behalf of the community, and why men should do so, the NBA enables men to continue in these roles. As men are considered the authoritative voice, and do not raise gender concerns, the NBA feels that if it were to advocate on behalf of women, it would be imposing its own agenda on the movement.[7]

Although the NBA has not organized around specific gender interests, some encouraging ties are being forged between the NBA and women's movements that can galvanize a consciousness and mobilization around women's issues in the Valley. Over the last two years, in the NBA's organizing around the Maheshwar Dam, a woman's wing, the Narmada Shakti Dal, has been formed. Furthermore, the NBA is reaching out more formally to women's organizations and women's movements. For example, the National Commission for Women (NCW), the highest body in the country dealing with women's issues, has been invited to public hearings on the Maheshwar Hydel Dam Project. At these large gatherings women who are affected by the Maheshwar Project testified against cash compensation in return for displacement. Women's groups from other parts of the country have also lent their support to the movement. For example, women's groups from Bombay produced a report on state violence directed at the NBA and its supporters. These alliances, together with the greater concentration on women's partici-pation in politics through women's representation in *panchayat*, will bring attention to women's interests.

I believe that the NBA will be able to respond to women's interests because it is decentralized, loosely structured, and not affiliated to any political party. It has provided a space for women to come together and speak both with men and against them, giving women greater agency as decision-makers within the family, the community and the movement. Thus, although the NBA has not overtly addressed the strategic interests of women, it has given women greater political visibility, and become a source of support that women can approach in times of stress. Furthermore, by mobilizing men in the community and exposing them to an alternative and democratic politics, 'a necessary precondition for women's mobilization' has been attained (Kishwar 1988: 2754).

These positive developments – together with the fact that the NBA does not have an overarching ideology to contain the scope of women's activism and their struggle – are promising. The NBA's democratic structure enables its base to raise issues of concern, and expand the movement's agenda to question the status quo and represent the interests of the vulnerable. I believe that the NBA has a foundation from which it can respond effectively to the pressures both from within the movement and from the political environment to enable a liberating, transformative potential for women to emerge from the Valley.

Notes

1. I appreciate the many lively discussions, penetrating insights and numerous suggestions that Pratyusha Basu, a graduate student at the University of Iowa, has provided through her research and field experience in the Narmada Valley.

2. Maxine Molyneux (1985) makes a distinction between practical and strategic interests. These practical interests can be addressed by improving women's access to income via income-generating skills or the use of mechanization to reduce women's labour. The entire family benefits from these improvements. It is much more difficult to address the strategic needs of women. Attempts to organize around strategic interests that would encompass challenging gender roles, the gendered division of labour and male privilege are resisted by males and those in authority, whose privilege is threatened as a consequence.

3. For a further overview, and discussion of the problems associated with viewing the household in this manner, see 'Benevolent Dictators, Maternal Altruists and Patriarchal Contracts: Gender and Household Economics', in Naila Kabeer (1995) *Reversed Realities*, New Delhi: Kali Press for Women, pp. 95–136.

4. A long time ago the NBA decided not to work towards attaining better resettlement policies, but it is calling for a complete halt to the building of the Sardar Sarovar Dam. It believes that the problems are far deeper than the issue of a just settlement, which it had originally struggled hard to obtain.

5. I had the good fortune to spend almost five days with Sylvie, one of the activists from the NBA, on a study tour. She demonstrated a keen awareness of these issues, and was quick to point them out to me when I revealed my interest.

6. There are those in the women's movement who argue that 'feminist' concerns are too narrowly defined, and insist that women's issues cannot be addressed without addressing broader social inequities and injustices. While I agree that women's issues should be broadly defined, and go beyond immediate concerns, it is equally important that the special interests of women be an integral part of the agenda, as must be a recognition and commitment to challenge the gendered character of inequality and justice.

7. In keeping with its political position on women, the NBA has partnered environmental and labour organizations in opposing the dam, but has established no systematic links to the women's movements in India. Until very recently, not only have women in the Valley been effectively excluded from having a voice in this struggle, but so has the women's movement. Few Indian feminists have written on this subject, and it is not a case that is discussed even in the environmental literature of the Indian women's movement. Rather, one finds a handful of piecemeal and rather disparate articles and isolated references to women in the vast literature on the Narmada controversy. Most of these papers and commentaries are produced by Indian feminists living overseas.

References

Agarwal, B. (1994) *A Field of One's Own: Gender and Land Rights in South Asia*, Cambridge: Cambridge University Press.

Ahlawat, N. (1995) *Women's Organizations and Social Networks*, New Delhi: Rawat.

Antrobus, P., J. Ross-Frankson and K. Alleyne (eds) (1994) *DAWN Informs*, Barbados: DAWN.

Bagwe, A. (1995) *Of Woman Caste: The Experience of Gender in Rural India*, London: Zed Books.

Banerjee, S. (1995) 'Hindu Nationalism and the Construction of Woman: The Shiv Sena Organizes Women in Bombay', in T. Sarkar and U. Butalia, eds, *Women and Right Wing Movements*, London: Zed Books.

Basu, A. (1992) *Two Faces of Protest*, Berkeley: University of California Press.

Basu, A. (1995) 'Feminism Inverted: The Gendered Imagery and Real Women of Hindu Nationalism', in T. Sarkar and U. Butalia, eds, *Women and Right Wing Movements*, London: Zed Books.

Basu, A. and J. Silliman (2000) 'Red and Green Not Saffron: Gender and the Politics of Resistance in the Narmada Valley', in C. Chappell, A. Sharma and M. Tucker, eds, *Hinduism and Ecology*, Cambridge, MA: Harvard University Press.

Baviskar, A. (1995) *In the Belly of the River: Tribal Conflicts over Development in the Narmada Valley*, Delhi: Oxford University Press.

Bhatia, B. (1997) 'Forced Evictions in the Narmada Valley', in J. Drèze, M. Samson and S. Singh, eds, *The Dam and the Nation*, Delhi: Oxford University Press.

Datar, C., ed. (1995) *The Struggle Against Violence*, Calcutta: Stree.

Datta, B., ed. (1998) *And Who Will Make the Chapatis? A Study of All-Women Panchayats in Maharashtra*, Calcutta: Stree.

Dhagamwar, V., E.G. Thukral and M. Singh (1995) 'The Sarda Saroval Project: A

Study in Sustainable Development?' in W.F. Fisher, ed., *Toward Sustainable Development? Struggling Over India's Narmada River*, New York: Sharpe.

Escobar, A. (1995) *Encountering Development: The Making and Unmaking of the Third World*. Princeton, NJ: Princeton University Press.

Esteva, G. and M.S. Prakash (1992) 'Grassroots Resistance to Sustainable Development: Lessons from the Banks of the Narmada', *The Ecologist* 22.

Fisher, W.F., ed. (1995) *Toward Sustainable Development? Struggling Over India's Narmada River*, New York: Sharpe.

Flavia, A. (1995) 'Redefining the Agenda of the Women's Movement within a Secular Framework', in T. Sarkar and U. Butalia, eds, 'Women and Right Wing Movements, London: Zed Books.

Gandhi, N. (1996) *When the Rolling Pins Hit the Streets: Women in the Anti-Price Rise Movements in Maharashtra*, New Delhi: Kali Press for Women.

Joshi, V. (1997) 'Rehabilitation in the Narmada Valley: Human Rights and National Policy Issues', in J. Drèze, M. Samson and S. Singh, eds, *The Dam and the Nation*, Delhi: Oxford University Press.

Kapur, R. (1993) 'Damming Women's Rights: Gender and the Narmada Valley Projects', *Canadian Women's Studies*, vol. 13, no. 3.

Kardam, N. (1990) 'The Adaptability of International Development Agencies: The Response of the World Bank to Women in Development', in K. Staudt, ed., *Women International Development and Politics*, Philadelphia, PA: Temple University Press.

Kelkar, G. and D. Nathan (1991) *Gender and Tribe: Women, Land and Forests in Jharkhand*, New Delhi: Kali Press for Women.

Kishwar, M. (1988) 'Nature of Women's Mobilization in Rural India', *Economic and Political Weekly*, 24–31 December.

Kothari, S., V. Pratap and S. Visvanathan, eds (1995) *Lokayan Bulletin*, Delhi, vol. 11, no. 5.

Kumar, R. (1993) *The History of Doing*, London: Verso.

Molyneux, M. (1985) in D. Slater, ed., *New Social Movements and the State in Latin America*, CEDLA.

O'Bannon, B. (1994) 'The Narmada River Project: Toward a Feminist Model of Women in Development', *Policy Sciences*, vol. 27, nos 2–3.

Patkar, M., in conversation with D. Roy and G. Sen (1992) 'The Strength of a People's Movement', in G. Sen, ed., *Indigenous Vision: Peoples of India, Attitudes to the Environment*. New Delhi: Sage.

Rao, B. (1996) *Dry Wells and Deserted Women: Gender, Ecology and Agency in Rural India*, New Delhi: Indian Social Institute.

Sarkar, T. and U. Butalia, eds (1995) *Women and Right Wing Movements: Indian Experiences*, London: Zed Books.

Seager, J. (1993) *Earth Follies: Coming to Feminist Terms with the Global Environmental Crisis*, New York: Routledge.

Tata Institute of Social Sciences (1997) 'Experiences with Resettlement and Rehabilitation in Maharashtra', in J. Drèze, M. Samson and S. Singh, eds, *The Dam and the Nation*, Delhi: Oxford University Press.

Between a Rock and a Hard Place: Women's Organizations in China

Susan H. Perry

Bright light filters through an open window into the room where Yi Nianhua is seated at a bamboo table, a writing brush suspended in her hand as she pauses for a moment to appraise the sharp, slender strokes of her own calligraphy. An expression of deep-seated satisfaction flits across her 80-year old features. She dips her brush again in the dark ink and continues writing the secret Nu Shu script, character by character, line by line, across the face of a white paper fan. This is her autobiography, a tale of unending woe that she has retrieved in bits and pieces from the recesses of her memory. A little girl gets up from the floor where she has been playing to watch her grandmother write. They exchange a brief moment of complicity before Yi turns her attention to the bitter verses of testimony that fill up the blank spaces of her fan.[1]

Yi Nianhua was one of the last surviving members of a Nu Shu sisterhood. The sisterhoods flourished along with the secret script in a remote, mountainous area of China's Hunan Province before the advent of the Communist revolution in 1949. Throughout history women have developed survival strategies designed to make their daily lives more bearable, and Chinese women have obviously been no exception. Their ancient civilization is rich with examples of women's associative behaviour, ranging from archaic clan rituals to early industrial-sector union activities. In imperial China, females were relegated to second-row status, with their position in the social hierarchy entirely determined by their reproductive role, and the clout wielded by their husbands and sons.

China has always been a patrilineal and patriarchal society (Chan, Liu and Zhang 1998; Johnson 1983; Rai 1994; Stacey 1983; Wolf 1985).[2] Nu Shu helped women to maintain links with their natal family and village, a protective and nurturing connection for young women when they 'married out' into their husband's village (Perry 1991). Informal or secret associations, such as the Nu Shu sisterhoods, also granted women a form of self-expression and self-valorization that were difficult to obtain within the confines of traditional patriarchal culture.

With the modernization of Chinese society and the 1949 Communist Liberation, women moved out of the home and into farming and factory production, and into the professional spheres traditionally reserved for men. Yet, like their female counterparts the world over, Chinese women have continued to face subtle and overt forms of discrimination (see Chan et al. 1998; Honig and Hershatter 1988; Stacey 1983; Wolf 1985). Today, governmental and quasi-non-governmental associations allow rural and urban women alike to defend themselves, promote their interests and, above all, define a new space for themselves within the parameters of a single-party state. As Jael Silliman has pointed out in her essay, however, contrary to official proclamations of the importance of bettering the status of women and reducing gender inequalities, the improvement of women's lives by governments and development agencies often remains a marginal endeavour. The Beijing leadership, in fact, is very ambivalent regarding Chinese women's potential to organize.

For the past fifty years, Chinese law has made it illegal for women to associate independently of the state. Under the auspices of the one-party state, women are encouraged to join one of the eight officially sponsored organizations for the masses, each organization with a membership running well into the tens of millions. These mammoth entities not only assist those who join in navigating their way through the one-party system, they also carefully monitor individual behaviour and ensure that all members adhere to central government policy. Consequently, according to the women interviewed for this essay,[3] most Chinese women today avoid joining government-sponsored women's organizations altogether. Those who do join are faced with the dilemma of conforming to national policy as dictated to their organization, or subtly seeking to reform their offically sponsored NGO from within. A few intrepid souls have formed independent organizations that operate either underground, or in the twilight zone of associations receiving foreign funding. Yet according to our interviewees, none of these choices is entirely satisfactory.

This essay will explore the limited but growing margin for manoeuvre experienced by women organizing in today's China.[4] Official
and quasi-official NGOs operating under Chinese national law, foreign
NGOs and twilight organizations comprise an unusual mix of possibilities. At the present time, the extensive economic reforms and decentral-
ization promoted by the Beijing government for the past twenty years
have led to a rapid shift towards horizontal relations, rather than the
usual vertical hierarchy imposed from above by the Chinese Communist
Party. As China's economy has opened up to the outside world, new
ideas with far-reaching social impact have infiltrated traditional society
and Marxist ideology. Centralized political control has lost ground to a
plethora of local business and social activities. Moreover, as sponsor to
the 1995 Fourth United Nations Conference on Women, the Beijing
government inadvertently promoted a watershed event that allowed for
broad exposure to international feminism and encouraged the growth
of government-affiliated and independent NGOs (Perry 1998).

The current spate of women's official and quasi-official NGOs, and
the complementary movement for Women's Studies in many universities,
are an outgrowth of the UN conference. Fifty years of dominance by
the Party-sponsored All-China Women's Federation is now being challenged: some women appear to be returning to more traditional patterns
of associative behaviour, such as sisterhoods or religious affiliations;
while others are exploring newer organizational structures that resemble NGOs the world over. The diversification of organizations that
negotiate women's concerns between the government and society at
large in China is an important trend. As the women's movement gains
momentum, the nation's leaders have been reluctant to permit a real
burgeoning of women's associative behaviour, threatened by the possibility of a legitimate challenge to the Communist Party's control over
China's political landscape.

The Law

According to administrative regulations, all non-profit social organizations formed in China must register with the local and national authorities under the auspices of an official sponsor. These regulations
were first promulgated in the 1980s, reinforced following the Tiananmen
protest movement of 1989, and further refined in October of 1998 in
an attempt to monitor independent civil activity in China closely.[5]
Ironically, China also expressed its intent to sign the International
Covenant on Civil and Political Rights in October 1998 and, as a

signatory, will be required to permit unlimited civil and political activity within its borders, as long as that activity does not constitute a threat to national security. Beijing has chosen to interpret 'national security' in a far-reaching manner by promulgating legislation that constitutes outright interference in the creation and management of non-profit organizations. These new regulations increase the number of legal, financial and administrative hurdles that must be overcome if such organizations are to remain within the strict confines of the law.

First and foremost, all persons wishing to associate as a non-profit 'social' organization (shehui tuanti) in China must first pre-register with the Ministry of Civil Affairs. The rules state clearly that any non-profit organization that begins activities before the registration process is completed will be considered illegal, and risk severe penalties. The actual registration process begins with the search for an offical sponsor, preferably one of the 'big eight' Communist Party organizations for the masses which include the All-China Women's Federation. The sponsoring unit (guakao danwei) must agree to be responsible for the political orientation of the candidate; obviously, these government-funded organizations for the masses choose their protégés with care. Once a candidate has managed to find an offical sponsor, it must then prove that it has 'legitimate' sources of financing: from 30,000 yuan for a small, local organization up to 100,000 yuan for a group hoping to operate on a national scale.[6] The use of the word 'legitimate' allows the Chinese government a wide margin for manoeuvre in its interpretation of this particular clause. Moreover, these financial imperatives appear excessive compared to the annual GNP per capita income of less than $3,000 per year. Finally, the candidate must prove that its administrative officers are in full possession of their civic rights (faren) – an impossibility for former prisoners of conscience, for example. The declared purpose of any non-profit social organization wishing to register officially must be to adhere to the basic principles of Chinese law and the dictates of the Communist Party. Furthermore, the overlap of more than one group within a specific domain is strictly forbidden – a provision which severely limits pluralistic debate within a particular field (Woodman 1999).

The vagueness of the language used in the clauses of the new regulations, combined with the number of administrative steps necessary to procure official permission to operate, render the development of any real non-governmental activity in China all but impossible. According to one account, many individuals have been detained by the authorities over the past few years, and even sent to labour camps, simply because they attempted to register an NGO (Woodman 1999). So far as the Chinese government is concerned, however, this law has helped to weed out undesirable elements. The 1989 regulations resulted in the closing of some 30,000 groups. Under a clean-up campaign launched by the Communist Party in 1997, another 13,995 existing NGOs were banned, although 8,357 new groups were also registered within the same year (Woodman 1999: 17). According to one Chinese academic, the deciding factor in granting operational status to these new groups was the pressure of connections, or *guanxi*, that could be exercised on local or national Communist Party officials by those organizers who knew people in important Party positions (anonymous, July 2000). For those who do not benefit from an extensive *guanxi* network, the Chinese government seems determined to 'use the laws to govern the country' (*yi fa zhi guo*) – an approach that considerably narrows the space in which women may find political and cultural expression without endangering their personal well-being and that of their families.

The All-China Women's Federation

The All-China Women's Federation, founded on 3 April 1949, is the mother of all Chinese women's NGOs, a monolithic organization designed to mobilize women to contribute to socialist construction under the banner of the Chinese Communist Party.[7] Because Marxism emphasizes class as the agent for change, women have been encouraged since the 1949 revolution to enter the workforce to gain their liberation, rather than fight for gender equality (Chan et al. 1998; Honig and Hershatter 1988; Stacey 1983; Wolf 1985). Even today, the State Council's Programme for the Development of Chinese Women, promulgated in July 1995 on the eve of the Fourth UN Conference on Women, states in no uncertain terms that the programme is to be carried out in the context of 'Deng Xiaoping's theory of building socialism with Chinese characteristics' (ACWF 1995: 3). The All-China Women's Federation has, since its inception, been a mouthpiece for Party propaganda and has been associated with both positive and negative government policies, such as the promotion of more liberal marriage laws versus the draconian measures used to enforce the One-Child Campaign, designed to limit each couple to only one child. Yet, there is increasing evidence that the ACWF is currently undergoing a subtle transformation; as women intellectuals and activists began agitating under the influence of the preparations for the 1995 UN Conference on Women, the ACWF appeared to realign its priorities more firmly alongside those of its constituents.

A glance through the current 'official' Directory of Chinese Women's NGOs reveals that every single entry is affiliated in one way or another with the government or, more specifically, with the ACWF. More importantly, many of the organizations listed were founded in the 1990s as part of the Federation's push to modernize its structure and answer the demands of its members. Among the entries with earlier start-up dates, propaganda tools such as *Family Magazine* (*Jiating zazhi*), which advocates 'socialist spiritual civilization in the field of marriage and family', or *Chinese Women's Magazine* (*Zhongguo funu zazhi*), which 'pounds at traditional perspectives on gender roles, advocates equality between men and women, and establishes new concepts on women's value', demonstrate the range of critical possibilities open to women who operate within the government-sponsored framework (*ACWF Directory* 2000: 129, 99). While virtually all the *Directory* entries listed under the rubric of Women's Studies Programmes are recently established and affiliated with academic institutions, two stand out. The first is the China Family Planning Association. Founded in May 1980 to supervise the national government's One Child policy, the organization has one million branch associations at all levels nationwide, surely the largest political machine ever put in place to control women's reproductive behaviour. The second organization is the newly founded China-AIDS Network. Since 1994, the Network's seven volunteer workers have nonetheless managed to compile five brochures on AIDS consultation and one looseleaf pamphlet, plus a series of seminars and training classes, such as those organized for 'long distance transportation drivers and service people in the roadside stores of Shandong [eastern China] and Guangxi Zhuang Autonomous Region [southwestern China]' (*ACWF Directory* 2000: 61–2).

Despite the fact that the All-China Women's Federation's interests clearly mirror the official Communist Party line on topics such as AIDS (which is ignored) and birth control (which is promoted), various sources attest to an awakening of the Federation from within. Certain Federation members, such as Xie Lihua, editor of *Rural Women Knowing All* (*Nongjia nu baishi tong*), suggest that the debate is not about whether the ACWF is or is not a proper non-governmental organization, but whether the Federation can move away from 'administration from above' towards 'a horizontally linked women's network' and, more importantly, improve its links with the market economy (Xie 1999). One businesswoman interviewed for this essay pointed out that if the ACWF were to offer workshops on how to set up and manage a private business venture or, at the very least, provide a networking forum for business-women, then many professional women might be interested in joining. She also proposed private funding for the ACWF in order to guarantee greater financial independence from the central government in Beijing (anonymous May 2000). Researchers and activists working with the Federation point out that the key to future success is 'specialized women's work that is closer to women's needs in the community', including support groups for single mothers, protecting older women's rights and interests, helping unemployed women to re-enter the workforce, and support for migrant women workers (Han 1999). Federation-sponsored efforts such as the locally managed Spring Bud programme, designed to increase the number of rural girls in school, or the Pioneers Project, which offers professional retraining for nearly half a million unemployed urban women every year, attest to the fact that the Chinese government has successfully mimicked international development trends in its attempt to head off social unrest among the undereducated and unemployed (Perry 1998).

Scholar Jude Howell emphasizes that the main constraint on the pace and extent of change within the ACWF is its complex relationship with the Chinese Communist Party (Howell 1999). As local branches of the Federation gain autonomy, much effort is spent on avoiding tasks that are viewed as an exercise in 'collecting resources for the top' (Jin 1999). A great deal of local – particularly rural – resistance to the ACWF is due to its crucial logistical role in the promotion and implementation of the One-Child policy campaign. As indicated above, this long-standing campaign has attempted to reduce China's galloping population growth by restricting couples to only one child. Since 1984–85, the government has tried in numerous regions to overcome rural discontent by officially sanctioning the birth of a second child in cases where the first child is female. Well-documented human rights abuses have been committed in the name of this campaign.[8] Even the ACWF has condemned family violence against women because of the birth of un-wanted baby girls, the use of ultrasound to 'select' a child's sex, and female infanticide (Perry 1998). The majority of the peasant women interviewed in Southwestern Hunan's Jiangyong County, for example, definitely felt that their support for all things communist had slackened due to the exigencies of the campaign, and the use of forced abortion and sterilization to ensure county and township quotas.[9] More research needs to be done on the impact of the One-Child policy on women's support for the Communist Party and the ACWF, particularly in rural areas.

Religious Organizations

Another area of women's associative behaviour closely tied to the state is that of religious affiliation. Unlike the dichotomy described by Elora Shehabuddin in her essay on Bangladesh above, there is little overt opposition between the Chinese state and the network of religious organizations in China. Yet, although the 1982 national constitution guarantees freedom of religion, the central government controls all religious activity through state-sponsored groups such as the Islamic Association of China or the Chinese Catholic Church, to which all religious leaders and mosque or church managers must belong. Any independent religious or quasi-religious activity in China is duly quashed, as the continuing crackdown on the Protestant China Fancheng Church or the Falungong movement amply demonstrates.

China is unusual in that the approximately one million Muslim women of the Hui minority pray in 'women's mosques' managed by a female *shetou* and operating under the tutelage of a female *ahong*, who leads her congregation in prayer. In the city of Kaifeng alone, there are nine female *ahong* for thirteen males, a situation that is unique in the Muslim world (Allès 1999: 221). These women are often following a family tradition of male or female *ahong* and *shetou*, and find that in the restricted world of Islam the status of religious leader is often the only way for a woman to broaden her horizons.[10] While the women of Bangladesh are caught between the constraints of locally interpreted Islam and the more liberal expectations of international NGOs and the national government, Hui women must negotiate the narrower space defined by local Islamic culture and the Chinese state in order to maintain the right to pray in the women's mosques. They are apparently quite successful. One comparative study found that Muslim women showed 'a tendency for self-initiative' in setting up and developing organizations for women (Shui 1999). This tendency was matched by members of the Christian faith in the same region of Central China. While women's organizations in both religions attach great importance to religious education, Christian women's groups feature flexible and active forms of organization, constantly expanding in response to given projects. Muslim women's groups, on the contrary, have reformed their local organizations in order to sustain tradition – a finding that seems ironic in light of their unusual status as religious leaders in the Islamic world (Shui 1999). The growing body of scholarship on Hui and Protestant women in China[11] indicates that one area requiring further study is the international funding of religious movements in this country, and the way in which that funding is spent. Although the Chinese government controls the Islamic and Christian faith movements in theory, in practice the increase in international funds for religious organizations has long been an issue in the Xinjiang area of China, and is on the rise among Christian populations as well.

Independent Activity: Foreign and Local NGOs

The impact of foreign NGOs in China is a double-edged sword for the Beijing government. While international NGOs working with women bring much-needed income to China's development strategies and programmes, they have also introduced new ideas and expectations. First and foremost, their presence during the preparations for the Fourth UN Conference on Women and NGO Forum allowed for a well-funded, in-depth exploration of the women's movement on the mainland, and offered a model for independent NGO activity. The Ford Foundation, for example, published *Reflections and Resonance*, a poignant collection of narratives by Chinese women involved in international preparatory activities leading up to the 1995 conference (Wong 1995). Funded by the Foundation and other international doners, over one hundred women travelled abroad to attend the many preparatory conferences that preceded Beijing. The naive expectations and apparent awakening of these Chinese participants illustrate the extent to which international NGO donors served as a catalyst to the current spate of women's organizational activity in China. The Asia Foundation's China Programme Director in Beijing points out that the NGO movement in China has been pioneered by women. 'New concepts, such as gender perspectives, advocacy and empowerment, and the process of networking among NGOs', have allowed women to break out of the 'isolationism of traditional Marxism', and to encourage legislators and Party cadres to rethink and redraft policy to guarantee women's rights (Zhang 1998: 3–4). Local – along with international – prompting resulted in the publication of a government White Paper on Chinese Women's Status in 1994, the first time the Chinese leadership directly addressed issues such as violence against women (Government of China 1994). This does not mean that these women are necessarily involved in the building of a 'civil society' in China. Most of them are simply seeking a margin for manoeuvre within the confines of the one-party state.

But women may have moved farther afield than intended. This is amply demonstrated in the variety of 'women's societies' and 'women's friendship associations' that have followed the Beijing conference. These organizations operate within the twilight zone of permitted associative behaviour, and are tolerated so long as they remain small. Horizontal networks operating in collaboration with or beyond the reach of the All-China Women's Federation include the East Meets West Feminist Translation Group, the Shaanxi Women's Theories, Marriage and Family Research Society, and the Lesbian and Gay Comrades Beeper Hotline. Since homosexuality is not yet fully accepted either by the Communist *nomenklatura* or by society at large, the beeper hotline operates via donations from foreign residents living in Beijing, and uses a beeper rather than a telephone line, because 'a beeper is able to maintain secrets better than a telephone [line] and [is] not easily suspended' (He 1999).

Women academics have also become extremely active in promoting women's studies and advocacy in China. New and very interesting fields of research have emerged as scholars attempt to change the system within the confines set for them by the Party. Since – as mentioned above – the Chinese government seems determined to 'use the laws to govern the country' (*yi fa zhi guo*), women's legal services centres, hotlines and publications on divorce, domestic violence and the sale of women may take extraordinary liberties in criticizing gender discrimination in China, because they are claiming to uphold the 1992 Law on the Protection of the Rights and Interests of Women, which provides a systematic and full-scale regime for protecting women's equality. The 1999 Thousand Oaks series of papers on *Violence Against Women*, for example, focuses its case on the growing body of Chinese laws and regulations which guarantee gender equality, and sharply critiques administrative incompetence in effectively applying the law. More important, however, is the networking that preceded the birth of this series: the linking of mainland and Hong Kong scholars (Meng and Chan 1999), and the cooperation between academics and rural practitioners. Law professor Chen Mingxia and activist Wang Shuzhen, for instance, base their analyses on a shared experience as leaders of the Qianxi County Women's Federation in Hebei Province, where they continue to collaborate on a range of programmes designed to deliver practical assistance to women (Chen 1999; Wang 1999). Grassroots activism of this kind is not only tolerated but encouraged by the government as a means of reinforcing the nation's failing social welfare system through locally funded programmes in micro-credit, healthcare and assistance for the elderly. And in demanding greater efficiency in carrying out the law, these women also bolster the legitimacy of Communist Party rule in China.

All the women interviewed for this essay were very much involved in using formal and informal organizations to assist women in difficulty. Yet their solidarity with other women did not blind them to the irony of their situation. By using the law as a vehicle to criticize gender inequality in China, they were recognizing the legitimacy of the Party and assisting the Party in extending its control over society at grassroots level. As one woman argued, however, by 'using the laws to govern the country', the Party could no longer place itself above the law. Moreover, by increasing its reliance on local women's groups to improve access to social welfare, the Party was inadvertently empowering women's networks throughout China (anonymous November 1999). These women were willing to be patient, betting that they could outwit the government in their bid for a more flexible civil society in China.

Organizations as varied as the timeless sisterhoods based on the secret Nu Shu script, or the nineteenth-century Canton textile workers' women's hostels and early-twentieth-century Shanghai women's unions, demonstrate that women have always sought the ways and means to meet, and to promote their collective interests. What is most striking, in fact, about the recent spate of women's acitvity in China is the relative lack of reference to historical precedents. Contemporary Chinese feminists hurry to quote Simone de Beauvoir or Betty Friedan (anonymous March 2000; Zheng 1997, n. 19), but are only just beginning to explore what is on their own doorstep. The idea of 'sisterhood' is ever-present in the history of Chinese women's associative behaviour. Whether women spontaneously formed organizations to protect themselves against the Green Gang in Shanghai of the 1930s (Honig 1986), or refused marriage in order to join dormitory groups that would provide for them in old age throughout the Pearl River Delta in the nineteenth century (Stockard 1989), the act of swearing allegiance to a group of women was common in both rural and urban areas. The protective and nurturing role played by sisterhoods has all but died out under the forced co-operation of the official women's movement under communism. Yet the consciousness-raising experience of the 1995 Beijing conference may mark the return to local associative behaviour as the nucleus for the empowerment of women across communities. Chinese women are increasingly aware that they owe their liberation not to the Chinese Communist Party, but to themselves.

Conclusion

In their essays on Bangladesh and India, Shehabuddin and Silliman make a fundamental assumption about the role of the state in development policy and planning which simply does not hold true for China. On the Indian subcontinent, the government is – in theory – democratically elected; hence development is a subject that is open to debate. The plethora of local and international NGO activity in both India and Bangladesh creates a climate where differing theories, policies, models and programmes contend with one another in an effort to secure the loyalties of a constituency, often at the expense of an entrenched religious or social hierarchy. The ruling elite in China is not yet answerable to an electorate. As this essay has demonstrated, most NGO activity in the People's Republic of China is carefully controlled and subject to stringent regulation and the complex mechanisms of *guanxi*, or personal networks, that are the backbone of Chinese politics. Government leaders have been particularly astute in allowing foreign NGOs to spend money on developing the country, while curtailing their capacity to reach local populations through careful containment of their projects. For the moment, there is no adequate public forum for a free discussion of development policy, religion, union activity, or any other associative behaviour that could threaten the supremacy of the one-party state.

Chinese women are cautiously exploring the options available to them, often creating a quixotic blend of compromises that allows them to manoeuvre within the confines of the law and the one-party system. All the women interviewed for this essay considered the Chinese Communist Party's dictatorship beneficial in that it can mobilize impressive resources to support a women's rights agenda, and threatening in that it can snuff out any unauthorized organizational activity overnight. Yet development, in all its myriad forms, is proceeding at breakneck pace in China. Whether one is discussing an annual economic growth of approximately 8 per cent over the past decade, or new laws protecting women from violence, the People's Republic of China is squarely on the road to its own form of modernization. Reform efforts have touched every sector of society, including women's rights. From a Western theoretical perspective, however, China is a development anomaly, a nation where democracy has not accompanied economic and social reform. Chinese women must therefore seek their own way, borrowing ideas from abroad, seeking out forgotten episodes of past activism, in order to construct their own strategies for coping in the here and now.

Notes

1. This scene is taken from the video documentary *Nu Shu: Women Poets of Hunan*, produced and directed by the author and screened at UNESCO.
2. As many scholars have pointed out, these patriarchal concepts are evident

even in the Chinese language. For example, the chinese character for a woman (fu nu) shows a woman cleaning with a broom (Meng and Chan 1999).

3. Of the eight Chinese women interviewed for this essay, only four consider themselves activists, while all eight describe themselves as feminists. They work in sectors as varied as law, academia, government administration, NGO management, medicine, journalism and publishing. Extensive interviews were conducted in person and by e-mail, over a two-year period (1999–2000). All eight have preferred to remain anonymous.

4. I would like to thank the following individuals for their assistance with this essay. Nicola Macbean, my co-director at the Programme for Political Participation in Asia and Europe (Asia–Europe Centre, Institut d'Etudes politiques), has offered excellent advice and invaluable contacts throughout. Dr Cecilia Milwertz at the Nordic Institute of Asian Studies very generously sent me the abstracts for her own volume on *Women Activists in Contemporary China* (working title), edited by Ping-Chun Hsiung, Maria Jaschok and Cecilia Milwertz (forthcoming 2001). Zhang Ye, the China Programme Director in Beijing for the Asia Foundation, has been extremely helpful concerning the activities of foreign NGOs operating in China. Finally, I am grateful to the eight Chinese women who agreed to be interviewed.

5. Both the 1989 regulations and the 1998 amended version are referred to as the *Shehui tuanti dengji guanli tiaoli* (Ordinance for the Registration and Management of Social Groups); the 1998 amended version was promulgated by the State Council on 25 October 1998, as Decree No. 43.

6. Approximately $3,750 to $12,500 with the exchange rate at eight yuan to the US dollar as this book went to press.

7. An interesting comparison can be made with Kenya (Aubrey 1997).

8. The Laogai Foundation and Asia Watch have been particularly active in monitoring the One-Child Campaign human rights abuses in China.

9. Informal interviews conducted by the author in 1986 and 1987 in Jiangyong County, Hunan Province, China.

10. According to one *ahong* from Kaifeng: 'at the age of ten we could no longer leave home unaccompanied, and the Mosque was the only place where we were authorized to go' (Allès 1999: 221).

11. In addition to the Allès and Shui articles cited above, see Jaschok and Jingjun 2000.

References

All-China Women's Federation (ACWF) State Council (1995) *Programme for the Development of Chinese Women*, Beijing: All-China Women's Federation Press (published in English and Chinese).

All-China Women's Federation (2000) *Directory of Chinese Women's NGOs*, Beijing: All-China Women's Federation Press.

Allès, E. (1999) 'Des oulémas femmes: le cas des mosquées féminines en Chine', *Revue des mondes musulmans et de la Méditerranée*, nos 85–86, Aix-en-Provence.

Aubrey, L. (1997) *The Politics of Development Cooperation: NGOs, Gender and Partnership in Kenya*, New York: Routledge.

Chan, C.L.W., M. Liu and Y. Zhang (1998) 'End of Women's Emancipation?', in J. Cheng, ed., China in the Post-Deng Era, Hong Kong: Chinese University Press.

Chen M. (1999) 'From Legal to Substantive Equality', symposium on Violence Against Women, Thousand Oaks, CA, December.

Government of China (1994) 'White Paper on Chinese Women's Status', published in the People's Daily, 3 June.

Han, H. (1999) 'Network; Reputation and Professional Approach: A Case Study of the Chongwen Women's Federation', abstract for workshop on 'Women Organizing in China', Oxford University, 12–16 July.

He, X. (1999) 'Chinese Queer Women (rongzhi) Organizing in the 1990s', abstract for workshop on 'Women Organizing in China', Oxford University, 12–16 July.

Honig, E. (1986) Sisters and Strangers: Women in the Shaghai Cotton Mills 1919–1949, Stanford, CA: Stanford University Press.

Honig, E. and G. Herschatter (1988) Personal Voices: Chinese Women in the 1980s, Stanford: Stanford University Press.

Howell, J. (1999) 'Rethinking The State and Gender: Challenges from Below', abstract for workshop on 'Women Organizing in China', Oxford University, 12–16 July.

Hsiung, P.C., M. Jaschok and C. Milwertz (2001) Women Organizing in China, Oxford: Berg.

Hsiung, P.C. and R. Wong (1998) 'Jie Gui – Connecting the Tracks: Chinese Women's Activism Surrounding the 1995 World Conference on Women in Beijing', Gender and History, vol. 10, no. 3.

Jaschok, M. and J. Shui (2000) The History of Women's Mosques in Chinese Islam: A Mosque of Their Own, Richmond: Curzon Press.

Jin, Y. (1999) 'The Women's Federation: Today's Challenges and Tomorrow's Moves', abstract for workshop on 'Women Organizing in China', Oxford University, 12–16 July.

Johnson, K. (1983) Women, the Family and the Peasant Revolution in China, Chicago: University of Chicago Press.

Meng, L. and C. Chan (1999) 'Enduring Violence and Staying in Marriage', symposium on Violence Against Women, vol. 5, no. 12, December.

Milwertz, C. (2000) 'Organising Rural Migrant Women in Beijing', in J. Drake, S. Ledwith and R. Woods, eds, Women and the City: Visibility and Voice in Urban Space, London: Macmillan.

Perry, S. (1991) Nu Shu: les poétesses du Hunan, unpublished thesis for the Diplôme d'études approfondies (Master's degree), University of Paris.

Perry, S. (1998) 'Holding Up Half the Sky', Current History, vol. 97, no. 620.

Rai, S. (1994) 'Gender Issues in China: A Survey', China Report, no. 30.

Republic of China (1989 and 1998) Shehui tuanti dengji guanli tiaoli (Ordinance for the Registration and Management of Social Groups), promulgated and amended by the State Council of the People's Republic of China.

Shui J. (1999) 'In Search of a Religious Women's Organization', abstract for workshop on 'Women Organizing in China', Oxford University, 12–16 July.

Stacey, J. (1983) Patriarchy and Socialist Revolution in China, Berkeley: University of California Press.

Stockard, J. (1989) *Daughters of the Canton Delta: Marriage Patterns and Economic Strategies in South China, 1860–1930*, Stanford, CA: Stanford University Press.

Wang, S. (1999) 'New Perspectives on Rural Women's Enterprises', symposium on *Violence Against Women*, Thousand Oaks, CA, December.

Wang, Z. (1997) 'Maoism, Feminism and the U.N. Conference on Women: Women's Studies Research in Contemporary China', *Journal of Women's History*, vol. 8, no. 4.

Wong, Y.L. (1995) *Reflections and Resonance: Stories of Chinese Women Involved in the International Preparatory Activities for the 1995 NGO Forum on Women*, Beijing: The Ford Foundation.

Woodman, S. (1999) 'Quelle liberté d'association en Chine?', *Perspectives chinoises*, January–February.

Wolf, M. (1985) *Revolution Postponed: Women in Contemporary China*, Stanford, CA: Stanford University Press.

Xie, L. (1999) 'How the Women's Federation is Facing the Challenge of Market Economy', abstract for workshop on 'Women Organizing in China', Oxford University, 12–16 July.

Zhang, Y. (1998) 'The Nature and Role of the Nongovernmental Sector in China', published paper from the symposium on A Changing Asia: Women in Emerging Civil Societies, Washington, DC: The Asia Foundation, 18 September.

CHAPTER THREE

Women's Higher Education in Ghana and South Africa

Education has long been considered an opportune site for development activity. Nonetheless, contemporary development institutions rarely take into account the realities of women's lives and of their educational needs. In this chapter, two scholar-activists report on their own field-work in African countries. In the case of Ghana, Vijitha Eyango argues that women reject higher education outright in favour of experience in the marketplace; rather than providing women with the skills they need as 'developing subjects', education hinders their access to viable and necessary money-making activities. Denise Newfield, writing in the wake of South Africa's political transformation, describes her involvement in building a new curriculum to drive South Africa's future as a nation. The majority of her students are women who traverse great distances to continue their education, especially when that education has been interrupted by the exigencies of economic survival. If education is to be a meaningful site for development, curricula must provide women with the professional training that will allow them to provide, in turn, for their families.

Although the two contributors to this chapter originally held opposing views on the efficacy of educational programmes for women in Africa, the unfolding of the post-apartheid period has brought them more into alignment. As this collection went to press, the situation in South Africa began increasingly to resemble that of Ghana. Both contributors reveal, ultimately, the inadequacy of formal schooling to meet the complex needs of African women today.

The Classroom or the Marketplace: Survival Strategies of Ghanaian Women

Vijitha Mahadevan Eyango

A mosaic of initiatives targeting girls has accompanied the appearance of gender on the educational map, as researchers, practitioners and policy-makers create new development paradigms aimed at addressing inequalities. The lack of female participation in formal education is typically attributed to factors such as pregnancy, early marriage, parental attitudes, and the traditional undervaluation of girls. This identification process begins a cyclical progression that continues with the theorization of reform strategies seeking to rectify imbalances, the initiation of action frameworks, and the hands-on implementation of solutions. Although much can be learned from global generalizations about gender equity in education, we have to be aware of their limitations when they are applied at the national level.

Analysis of the Ghanaian educational system reveals the impact of local socioeconomic factors on gender inequality. My contribution to the debate is that in explaining gender equities in Ghanaian education, we have to move beyond the issue of educational access, and address the quality and relevance of the educational programme itself. Fieldwork indicates that the lack of relevance of education for viable employment opportunities, coupled with the existence of a thriving informal sector, lures girls out of school and into trading.

At the moment of Ghana's independence from British rule, its economy showed many signs of positive growth. It had a well-developed infrastructure, large foreign exchange reserves, and one of the best civil services and educational systems in Africa. Yet the educational structure

Ghana inherited from the British, although considered impressive, was riddled with inequalities at all levels. Access to education was not evenly distributed across class, gender or race. One of the most visible in-equalities was the demographic spread of schools, a consequence of the economic and political strategies of colonialism, which resulted in the concentration of schools in southern industrial Ghana, leaving northern Ghana virtually untouched (Foster 1965: 118). There were also prob-lems with the curriculum in use, which was basically a British one with little local resonance.

Ghana's educational reform, brought into effect by President J.J. Rawlings and institutionalized in 1987, offered a fresh and promising approach to educational development. Its purpose was to target various shortcomings of Ghana's system of education, and rehabilitate it en-tirely. Objectives included reduction of the number of years spent in school, a broadening of the curriculum, and a more relevant system through 'Ghanaianizing' education to meet national needs. With the implementation of this reform, literacy levels and enrolment were expected to expand, and incorporate the large proportion of children who were not in school.

Despite impressive achievements in Ghanaian education since inde-pendence, and the country's massive educational reform efforts, the present state of education is one of crisis. Apart from intangibles such as declining teacher morale, there is a massive brain drain coupled with an overall deterioration of educational facilities. Given the relatively recent reform of Ghana's educational system, evaluation efforts are still in their initial stages; what has become apparent, however, is that markedly unequal representation of females in Ghanaian education continues at all levels of formal schooling, and across all age groups.

Gender Inequalities in Ghanaian Education

The participation of girls and women in Ghana's education sector has improved considerably since independence from colonial rule. For example, in a critical examination of the performance of West African countries from 1960 to 1990, Ghana was the country that recorded the lowest female illiteracy rates (Quist 1994: 133). Still, although major strides have been made to increase educational access for all, it is evident that there are glaring inequalities between male and female enrolments at all levels of formal schooling in Ghana. For example, primary gross enrolment ratios[1] for girls is 70 per cent, while for boys it is 83 per cent; secondary enrolment ratios are 29 per cent and 45 per cent, respectively, and tertiary enrolment ratios follow the same pattern of inequity – 0.6 per cent for women and 2.2 per cent for men. At some Junior Secondary Schools, not even one girl is registered (Scadding 1989). Even at the polytechnic level there are glaring disparities, with male enrolment accounting for 77 per cent of total enrolment and female for 23 per cent (UNESCO 1998: 3–25; Ghana Statistical Service 1992).

Enrolment inequalities in terms of discipline are also evident at higher levels of schooling, with women overrepresented in the arts and humanities, and men in the more scientific and technical fields of study. For example, during the University of Ghana's 1990–91 academic year, 655 of the 876 female students were enrolled in arts, social studies and law faculties (Ghana Statistical Service 1992: 100).

The lack of participation by women is not restricted to formal education, but is apparent in non-formal education as well. For example, the Institute of Adult Education at the University of Ghana organizes various literacy courses; nevertheless, only about one-third of the participants are women (Manuh 1984: 44). The People's Educational Association, a department of the institute, has an education for 'personal and national development', including activities such as organizing public lectures and literacy classes in workplaces in Accra; there were no females enrolled in those literacy classes, however (Manuh 1984: 45). The National Vocational Training Institute offers classes in auto mechanics, electrical work, metalwork, building, printing, dressmaking and catering. Most women attending the school are enrolled in dressmaking and catering, while the other, more 'technical', classes are dominated by men (Gage and Njogu 1994: 42).

Two major issues surface. First, fewer girls than boys are enrolled in school. Second, there is evidence that girls are routed towards the arts and boys towards the more 'scientific' subjects of mathematics and physics; moreover, schooling trains boys for jobs and encourages girls to work in domestic service positions (Scadding 1989). Although there are many critical questions surrounding the inequalities of education that are perpetuated at all levels of schooling and across all age groups, my concern is with the extent and nature of enrolment inequalities. The causes of inequality in enrolment are not clear. In this day and age, we can assume that girls are not innately lazy or mentally unable to perform at higher levels of schooling. Are girls prevented from enrolling and, if so, by what? Are parents or teachers responsible and, if so, why? Is the routeing of girls towards the arts responsible for the drop-out rates? What roles do household incomes play in the decision to

send a child to school? Do enrolment figures represent a case of outright sexual discrimination, or something more complex that traditional theories of education and Western feminism cannot account for?

Explaining Gender Inequalities

Feminist theoreticians in comparative education have attempted to
incorporate gender inequalities into their research and analysis, and
trace causes. Some explain the unequal access of girls to education as
something promoted by men in order to preserve a male-biased power
structure (Ferreiro and Teberosky 1990: 69). Kathleen Rockhill, who
focuses on women's access to literacy, gives one such analysis. Her
conclusion is that women yearn to become 'literate', but are prevented
from doing so by husbands who see the power of literacy, and pur-
posefully prevent their wives from acquiring it. As Rockhill views it,
'Men need to feel in control; not only does this mean having more
power than their wives, but controlling what they think and do.' She
describes the society she is working with as a 'gendered society where
the conception of rights is alien to women who have been told all their
lives that they must obey and care for others' (Rockhill 1987). Once
girls are married, they re-enter the educational system only with the
approval of their husbands, who are usually the ones to finance the
continuation of education.

Nelly Stromquist provides a broader framework of analysis in her
discussion of education, feminist theory, and the issue of gender differences in access to education (Stromquist 1990). Incorporating ideas
from liberal, radical and socialist feminist theory, she conducts a
systematic analysis in which the state emerges as the principal actor in
regulating access to education. Her synthesis of the various feminist
theories leads her to the conclusion that a fundamental restructuring of
education is not being carried out by the state, and that access cannot
be significantly improved unless such restructuring takes place through
women-run organizations beyond the formal educational arena.

Another prevalent theory is that gendered inequalities are caused by
parental influences. F.O. Akuffo's study on rural elementary schools
attributes female dropouts to parental preference for boys' education in
times of inadequate resources. She also states that girls, facing the
expectations of both domestic duties and education, are 'compelled' to
enter into trading and have relationships with boys; they finally end up
getting pregnant, and have to terminate their education (Akuffo 1978;
Bukh 1979). According to this explanation, parents encourage their

daughters to leave school because they do not view skills picked up during education as a good preparation for the children's adult lives. In this view, a woman's traditional role is to look after her children first and foremost, while the man is the breadwinner; therefore, parents place a greater emphasis on educating their sons rather than their daughters. Thus the emphasis placed on children and child-rearing has serious implications for education.

Others focus on cultural attitudes about power-sharing between men and women. They note the attitudes of parents and prospective husbands who express dissatisfaction with girls who have had 'too much' schooling (Blege 1972). Since the mean age of marriage for girls in Ghana is about eighteen-and-a-half, the prediction is that the decision to spend money on a girl's education is influenced by the conviction that she will not pursue her education past a certain age. With limited resources, why spend so much on a girl who will probably just get married and drop out of school?

Christine Oppong and Katherine Abu reviewed an earlier study of gender inequalities in Ghana. The study, carried out in the 1960s among the Northern Dagomba, examined parents' reluctance to send their female children to school. It was found that girls' labour was needed at home, as girls were expected to do more work in the house. There was also a perception that 'marriage prospects would be spoilt and loose ways learned' at school (Oppong 1973: 25).

Marriage, pregnancy and childbirth also emerged as factors influencing educational access (Etta 1994; Greenstreet 1986). Most girls marry early and produce children at an early age. Since many African societies have customs that prescribe a period of confinement before and after birth, during which a women is often expected to be secluded, the ability to attend school is severely constrained. In accounting for the high rates at which girls leave primary as well as secondary schools, Isabelle Deblé concluded that contributing factors range from early marriage patterns to the irrelevance of formal education (Deblé 1980). Similarly, Aysit Tansel pioneered an effort aimed at addressing the perceived direct and indirect costs of girls going to school. He analysed household decisions to send children to school in Ghana and the Ivory Coast, and concluded that the costs of education and the distance affect access to schooling. Using socioeconomic indicators of parents' education, household income, the costs of school, and rural–urban residence location, Tansel found that the indirect costs of schooling (in terms of forgoing children's inputs to household production and the labour market) were extremely high. As noted above, time spent at school was at the expense of time working on the farm or in the family business (Tansel 1993).

Claire Robertson, in her analysis of Ga women in Ussher Town, an urban district of Accra, discusses the mothers' costly burden of educating young Ga children, given the high rate of divorce and separation (Robertson 1976). She notes that demands for schooling are placed on mothers who are traders in the informal sector, and who thus face difficulties earning a cash income in Ghana's increasingly capitalist economy. These urban mothers see education as essential to upward mobility, but they do not find it easy to provide for their children, given their scant resources.

The analyses above cites the key factors affecting differential access to education, ranging from family values and attitudes, to pregnancy and early marriage. Reform strategies, proposed in response to these factors, have as their operating premiss that the lower participation of girls in education is indicative of their overall disadvantaged status, and that every effort needs to be made to remedy the situation. Accompanying this is the blanket focus on increasing enrolments for girls. Although these factors are essential to understanding educational access and retention, they do not adequately represent the realities of the Ghanaian socioeconomic context.

Curricular Relevance

The focus of the scholarship in feminist theory, comparative education theory, world systems theory, and sociological theory has been on educational outcomes and enrolments, with a view to the political agenda of how to distribute education more equitably, and how to ensure equal representation of boys and girls. Although this work is essential to understanding the general context of girls' access to education in Ghana, it is not entirely adequate as an explanation. It is therefore all the more important to uncover other significant factors that may have been ignored, buried or dismissed from consideration as a result of the general preoccupation with trying to 'fix' the situation.

My own fieldwork in Ghana began with numerous interviews with education officers, teachers, students and dropouts, and substantiated the general perception that the curriculum in use is not relevant and does not provide employable skills (Mahadevan 1995). Why were Ghanaian students learning about British history, not their own? Why Shakespeare, and not Ama Atta Aidoo? Why were they learning to knit sweaters for a climate that hardly ever went below 80 degrees Fahrenheit?

Given such a curriculum, becoming 'educated' ultimately led to serious constraints on the economic options available to Ghanaian girls. The majority of my interviewees said, in no uncertain terms, that the formal education system in Ghana prepares students for an imaginary job market. According to Headmistress Osei, of St Louis Secondary School,

> It does not matter if it's secondary school or university. Nor does it matter if it's boys or girls. There are hardly any jobs for those students who finish university. No jobs here in Ghana, that is. I would say that out of those who finish university maybe five per cent get jobs here in the civil service; the rest leave the country or take up employment totally unrelated to what they went to university for. In fact, the students graduating from those technical and vocational schools have a much higher likelihood of finding employment.

Opportunities for jobs in the civil service prevalent in the decades following independence no longer exist. The formal economy's job market has become saturated, and there are few options for employment for school graduates. Even for those who have managed to capture jobs in the public sector, most cannot exist without a second 'unofficial' job to supplement their income. Gifty Ampofol, for example, talked about the two other jobs she has in addition to her position as a teacher at Kumasi's University of Science and Technology Primary School:

> It is not possible to think about existing on the salary you get from your official job. Look at me, in my supposedly good teaching position. Who in the outside would believe that I have to sell eggs and *kelewele* [fried plantain] at night? I don't think in America teachers have to do that … but here you have to do that to survive … and don't think it's only us teachers that are in this position. It's all of us. Even my husband, who is a lecturer right here on campus … do you think he's doing research at night? No, he's struggling with his taxi business … with three children to clothe, feed and school, you don't have too many choices.

The overwhelming consensus was that inequalities in enrolment had to do with the reality of limited employment opportunities for girls. Once basic skills were acquired, the question then became whether or not it was a worthwhile investment in time as well as money to continue to go to school. Not only was there a paucity of job opportunities for females; they would be able to earn better money by going into business as hairdressers and tailors than as university graduates.

In a study that addressed the impact of formal education, Claire Robertson's overall conclusions were that formal education was not providing schoolgirls with skills for success in the marketplace. She takes the argument a step further to say that there were only two means for women to obtain financial support from men: as prostitutes and as wives. She concludes that formal education, rather than reducing female–male inequality, was reinforcing women's subordinate position (Robertson 1986: 658). Gracia Clark, in her study of the Kumasi Central Market, found that although formal school education provided some skills, traders found their education useful only in limited contexts (Clark 1994: 188). 'Graduates with qualifications that would have brought secure and respected positions a generation ago now compete for a restricted number of job openings, making family connections and business capital more essential' (Clark 1994: 308). The lack of relevance of formal education in providing viable employment opportunities cannot be complete without a discussion of Ghana's informal sector.

The Informal Sector

Ghana's informal sector encompasses economic activities not represented in formal statistics, including vendors of foodstuffs, fish, cloth, local medicines, pottery, soap, and other homemade crafts. In the informal sector, the majority of trade takes place in markets that serve as the primary channels for the distribution of local and imported produce and goods. Ghanaian women are well known for their high levels of economic activity. Since the fifteenth century, they have been integrally involved in the marketing system (Ardayfio 1984: 1). Women's market dominance has increasingly shifted to the informal sector (Gage and Njogu 1994: 45), and is now their most important means of earning an income (Ankomah 1996: 39). This sector has been the primary economic sphere in which women have been able to earn money specifically as traders – or 'market mammies', as they have been termed in recent decades. Thus, much of the work of Ghanaian women is invisible to the researcher and policy-maker.

Several characteristics of the informal sector serve to benefit women. First, this sector provides a steady and immediate source of income; second, it allows for flexible scheduling, enabling women to integrate their market hours with household responsibilities. It also accommodates childcare needs, as children can accompany their mothers to the market. It requires a low level of capital investment and does not have a schooling requirement. Many studies show that the majority of traders do not have any formal education. When the variation in traders' incomes was looked at more closely, it was clear that among educated traders 'higher incomes depend more directly on capital than education' (Clark 1994: 308).

Another interesting feature is that even though there are huge male–female enrolment disparities, this is not reflected in a larger proportion of unemployed females. Ghana's most recent population census (1984; Ghana Statistical Service 1987) and the Ghana Living Standards Survey (GLSS) of 1987–88 (Ghana Statistical Service 1989) show that in both rural and urban Ghana more girls that boys are employed in the economically active population. Ironically, given that women control the informal sector – culturally defined as a 'women's sphere' – boys and men do not consider the informal sector an option for employment.

The irrelevance of the curriculum for viable employment and the existence of a vibrant informal sector create conditions that deter girls from school attendance. Mrs Attah, a teacher from Ridge School, describes the situation of her brother and his wife:

> Don't joke with the market mammies here. My brother, a university professor at Kumasi's University of Science and Technology, with his big Ph.D. if you convert how much he earns to dollars, he gets around $75 a month.... His wife, she is a trader here at Makola market ... she makes more than $100 per month on simply selling *bronni wewo* [second-hand clothes] ... and that does not even include Christmas and Easter. In those times she gets plenty business and brings plenty more money to the house. Sometimes I even wonder why I am staying as a teacher when I could be earning such money.

Another reason why women select the trading profession, as Mr Frimpong, the National Statistician, pointed out, was that

> Most Ghanaian girls want to have their children at a relatively early age – if they think of the formal educational system, which consists of ten years of primary school, five years of secondary, three years of university and then national service, it scares off girls. Many girls will start trading before they even think of getting married. All in all, once you can earn your livelihood, you earn the respect of society: it does not matter what it is you are doing ... The informal sector is not represented in national statistics so it is very difficult to gauge the wealth of people who constitute the sector; however, Ghanaians have been able to gauge wealth by the obvious physical signs – car, trips abroad, recreation, and the rest. Lifestyles indicate wealth, and in the same token it is obvious that government employees do not earn anything compared to those earning in the informal sector.

Government officials make little attempt to examine the economic reality facing the Ghanaian student, the options open to her when she graduates, or the relevance of the educational system as a whole. The generally held belief of educators and policy-makers is that simply focusing on physical capital such as school buildings, expanding educational facilities and providing textbooks and supplies will gradually foster a better environment that will attract more girls into schools. This point was driven home in nearly all the interviews I conducted with organizational representatives in Ghana. Ghana's World Bank education representative gives a typical response:

> You're asking about gender inequalities. All I can say is that this year we are building 250 primary schools, and many more Junior Secondary and Senior Secondary schools ... build schools and thereby increase enrolments.... It is the physical infrastructure that needs building and support. We have already dealt with changing the curriculum to a relevant one. Back to gender inequalities: yes, of course we do know they exist, and this is our response: by building more schools, there will be more opportunities for girls to go to school, and those inequalities that you are talking about will disappear. We've been in this education business too long not to know that this solution works.

Conclusion

All too often, male and female inequalities are defined erroneously since researchers continue to use female subordination and male supraordination as their basis for interpretation. Implicit in much of the literature on gender inequalities is the monolithic view of women as victims labouring under disabling constraints within a patriarchal society. This inaccurate analysis of the situation tends to obscure the critical issues at stake. As we explore new development paradigms shaping women's lives, we need to create new intellectual tools to address imbalances in theory and practice. Although factors such as pregnancy and parental choice do play a role in the educational decision-making process, we still need to factor in the realities of the complex socioeconomic and cultural context in which Ghanaian girls and women function. We cannot simply view gender disparities in Ghanaian education in a vacuum but, rather, as the product of social, traditional and market forces, all of which have a tremendous impact on the goals and perceptions of young aspiring girls. The Ghanaian woman has had to choose the route that best serves her interest. Without rendering education more relevant to women's lives, and without contextualizing the complex survival strategies of Ghanaian women, the move to 'force' gender equity in education is destined to failure.

Denise Newfield's study, my companion piece in this chapter, is especially noteworthy in that she documents educational reform efforts in South Africa prior to ANC takeover, then provides continuity by following the programme beyond the 1994 change of government. One could, however, question how effectively a group of solely white South African women could design a transformative education programme without input from the black population they are striving to serve. No matter how well-intentioned this particular group of women may be, they are open to questioning on their *modus operandi* – not only because the author lays claim to being one of the group of women for change, but because of the sensitivity of race relations in pre- and post-apartheid South Africa. Still, as Newfield argues, the educational mission of the new curriculum must transcend race and ethnic affiliation if South Africa is to achieve its bid for a fully democratic society. Despite our differences, as African educators, Newfield and I both strive on a daily basis to understand the complexity of institutional policies that embody, create and reproduce knowledge.

Note

1. The gross enrolment ratio is the total enrolment of a given level of education, regardless of age, divided by the population of the age group which officially corresponds to that level of schooling.

References

Akuffo, F.O. (1978) 'High Wastage Rate in Women's Education: The Case of the Rural Elementary School Girls', *Proceedings of the Seminar of Ghanaian Women in Development: Volume II*, Accra: National Council of Women and Development.

Ankomah, A. (1996) 'Premarital Relationships and Livelihoods in Ghana', *Focus on Gender*, vol. 4, no. 3.

Ardayfio, E. (1984) *Marketing in Ghana: An Analysis of Operational and Environmental Conditions*, Addis Ababa: United Nations Economic Commission for Africa, African Training and Research Center for Women.

Blege, W. (1972) 'Alternatives in Education in a Developing Country: The Ghana Case', *Ghana Journal of Education*, vol. 3, no. 1, January.

Bukh, J. (1979) *The Village Woman in Ghana*, Uppsala: The Nordic Africa Institute.

Clark, G. (1994) *Onions are My Husband: Survival and Accumulation by West African Market Women*, Chicago: University of Chicago Press.

Clark, G. (1986) *The Position of Asante Women Traders in Kumasi Central Market, Ghana*, Ph.D. dissertation, University of Cambridge; Ann Arbor, MI: University Microfilms.

Clark, G. and T. Manuh (1991) 'Women Traders in Ghana and the Structural Adjustment Program', in C. Duncan, ed., *African Women Farmers and Structural Adjustment*, Gainesville: University of Florida Press.

Deblé, I. (1980) *The Education of Women*, Paris: UNESCO.

Etta, F.E. (1994) 'Gender Issues in Contemporary African Education', in *Afrique et Développement/Africa Development. Special Issues: Education and Development in sub-Saharan Africa*, vol. 19, no. 4.

Ferreiro, E. and A. Teberosky (1990) *Literacy Before Schooling*, trans. K.G. Castro, Oxford, Heinemann Educational.

Fogelberg, T. (1982) *Nanumba Women: Working Bees or Idle Bums? Sexual Division of Labour, Ideology of Work, and Power Relations between Women and Men in Gole, a Village in Nanumba District, Northern Region, Ghana*, Leiden: Institute of Cultural and Social Studies.

Foster, P. (1965) *Education and Social Change in Ghana*, Chicago: University of Chicago Press.

Gage, A.J. and W. Njogu (1994) *Gender Inequalities and Demographic Behaviour: Ghana/Kenya*, New York: The Population Council.

Ghana Ministry of Education (1994a) *Draft: Strengthening Educational Planning: Current Educational Trends with Specific Reference to the Participation of Girls*.

Ghana Ministry of Education (1994b) *Draft: Towards Learning for All: Basic Education in Ghana to the Year 2000*.

Ghana Statistical Service (1987) *1984 Population Census of Ghana: Demographic and Economic Characteristics: Total Country*.

Ghana Statistical Service (1989) *Ghana Living Standards Survey: First Year Report: September 1987–August 1988*.

Ghana Statistical Service (1992) *Quarterly Digest of Statistics*, vol. 10, no. 4.

Greenstreet, M. (1986) 'The Education of Females and Their Social Perceptions on Population', *National Conference on Population and National Reconstruction: Conference Proceedings, vol. II*, Accra: University of Ghana.

Mahadevan, V. (1995) *Education and the Reproduction of Gender Inequality: An Analysis of the Junior Secondary School Reform Movement in Ghana*, Ph.D. dissertation, University of California at Los Angeles,

Manuh, T. (1984) *Law and the Status of Women in Ghana*, Addis Ababa: UN Economic Commission for Africa.

Ninsin, K.A. (1991) *The Informal Sector in Ghana's Political Economy*, Accra: Freedom Publications.

Oppong, C. (1973) *Growing up in Dagbon*, Accra: Ghana Publishing Corporation.

Oppong, C. and K. Abu (1987) *Seven Roles of Women: Impact of Education, Migration and Employment on Ghanaian Mothers*, Geneva: International Labour Office.

Quist, H.O. (1994) 'Illiteracy, Education and National Development in Postcolonial West Africa: A Re-appraisal', *Afrique et Developpement/Africa Development. Special Issues: Education and Development in Sub-Saharan Africa*, vol. 19, no. 4.

Robertson, C. (1976) 'Ga Women and Socio-economic Change in Accra, Ghana', in N.J. Hafkin and E.G. Bay, eds, *Women in Africa: Studies in Social and Economic Change*, Palo Alto, CA: Stanford University Press.

Robertson, C. (1977) 'The Native and Effects of Differential Access to Education in Ga Society', *Africa*, vol. 47, no. 2.

Robertson, C. (1984) 'Formal or Nonformal Education? Entrepreneurial Women in Ghana', *Comparative Education Review*, November.

Robertson, C. (1986) 'Women's Education and Class Formation in Africa, 1950–1980', in C. Robertson and I. Berger, eds, *Women and Class in Africa*, New York: Africana Press.

Rockhill, K. (1987) 'Gender, Language and the Politics of Literacy', *British Journal of Sociology of Education*, vol. 8, no. 2.

Scadding, H. (1989) 'Junior Secondary Schools – An Educational Initiative in Ghana', *Compare*, vol. 19, no. 1.

Stromquist, N.P. (1997) 'Gender Sensitive Educational Strategies and their Implementation', *International Journal of Educational Development*, vol. 17, no. 2.

Stromquist, N.P. (1990) 'Gender Inequality in Education: Accounting for Women's Subordination', *British Journal of Sociology of Education*, vol. 11.

Tansel, A. (1993) *School Attainment, Parental Education and Gender in Côte d'Ivoire and Ghana*, Center Discussion Paper no. 692, New Haven, CT: Economic Growth Center, Yale University.

UNESCO (1994) *World Education Report: 1993*, Paris: UNESCO.

UNESCO (1998a) *Statistical Yearbook: 1998*, Paris: UNESCO.

UNESCO (1998b) *World Education Report: 1998*, Paris: UNESCO.

UNESCO, ECA and OAU (1991) *Development of Education in Africa: A Statistical Review*, Sixth Conference of Ministers of Education and those Responsible for Economic Planning in African Member States, Dakar, 8–11 July 1991.

Weis, L. (1979) 'Education and the Reproduction of Inequality: The Case of Ghana', *Comparative Education Review*, vol. 23, no. 1.

Weis, L. (1980) 'Women and Education in Ghana: Some Problems of Assessing Change', *International Journal of Women's Studies*, vol. 3, no. 5.

World Bank (1993) *Ghana 2000 and Beyond: Setting the Stage for Accelerated Growth and Poverty Reduction*, Africa Regional Office, Western Africa Department.

World Conference on Basic Education for All (1990a) *Appendix 1: World Declaration on Education for All: Meeting Basic Learning Needs*, endorsed by the conference on 9 March 1990 in Bangkok.

World Conference on Basic Education for All (1990b) *Appendix 2: Framework for Action*, endorsed by the conference on 9 March 1990 in Bangkok.

'Blessed with the Necessity of Transformation': Postgraduate Education in South Africa

Denise Newfield

The worst realities of our age are manufactured realities. It is therefore our task, as creative participants in the universe, to re-dream our world. The fact of possessing imagination means that everything can be re-dreamed. Each reality can have its alternative possibilities. Human beings are blessed with the necessity of transformation.

Ben Okri, *A Way of Being Free*

This essay attempts to capture an important moment in South Africa's educational history – a moment at which South Africa throws off its apartheid past and moves forward into a more equitable and productive future for all its citizens. More specifically, this is a practitioner's account of a particular project in South Africa – an educational intervention at the postgraduate level at the University of the Witwatersrand, one of the country's foremost tertiary institutions. It concerns the establishment of a Master's programme for educators within the field of English teaching and learning (the MA in English Education); the goal is to contribute to the national project of educational reconstruction by offering a programme for the development of leaders in the field. This intervention exemplifies an attempt to work in and for transformation. The project began in 1993, a year before South Africa's first democratic elections, with a decision to work for educational transformation within the constraints and opportunities provided by the particular professional/ institutional context. A group of lecturers in the field of teacher education, all white women,[1] knew that the education system had to be, and would be, changed when the African National Congress (ANC) government came to power; they sensed that few South African teachers would be able to cope with these changes, for historically determined reasons. Better-qualified teachers would be required at all levels, from kindergarten and primary school upwards through secondary school and tertiary levels. Working with postgraduates, our intention was to develop a body of teachers, lecturers, educational publishers and curriculum developers who would be informed and up-to-date in local and global knowledges, pedagogies and curricula, so providing leadership within their own institutions and contexts during the period of transformation.

Historical Context

A recently released South African feature film, *Fools* (1998), based on the short story by one of our most accomplished contemporary authors, Njabulo Ndebele, may be used to provide a portrait of schooling under apartheid. The film opens with a sequence depicting a black high school during the 1980s. Situated near a small town in the country, the school is shown in the grip of apartheid. The children, dressed in their school uniforms, are assembled in rows outside for the daily harangue by their headmaster. Under the watchful eye of a government official, the headmaster uses Afrikaans, the language of the oppressor, to oppress his own children. The stuttering sound of an unseen helicopter flying overhead – a signifier of surveillance – is heard on the sound track. The scene changes to the headmaster's office and the camera pans across the wall – ironically revealing framed photographs of the three past Afrikaner leaders, P.W. Botha, B.J. Vorster and Hendrik Verwoerd. A black teacher, the film's main character, who has raped a female student, has been summoned for an interview. The film's opening sequence evokes a sense of the political oppression that choked students, with a double oppression for black female students. The points are made with powerful economy and irony.

It is well known that until 1994 South Africa's political system was founded on the separatist philosophy of apartheid. Perhaps it is not so well known to what extent the educational infrastructure was built on that infamous ideology. Seventeen education departments existed for different racial and ethnic groups living in South Africa, excluding those in the Bantustans, euphemistically called 'homelands' or 'independent states'. Education was divided on racial grounds, and organized unequally in terms of resources, both human and material. White children received Christian National Education, with its local, Calvinist version of a Eurocentric curriculum; while black children received Bantu Education, a vastly inferior curriculum, designed by Hendrik Verwoerd, the architect of Grand Apartheid, to prepare black children for menial jobs. The disparity between these two systems was reflected in the matriculation results, where the pass rates for white candidates was close to 100 per cent, as against 25 to 30 per cent for black candidates, going down to as low as 17 per cent in some areas. The per-capita annual expenditure also varied according to race; in 1978, for example, the government spent an average of R640 per white child, R297 per Indian child, R197 for each 'coloured' child, and R68 for every black child (South African Institute of Race Relations 1997). These figures indicate the differential nature of school resources in relation to buildings, electrification, books and other materials. Whereas schools provided white learners with free textbooks, black learners were obliged to buy their own.

The film sequence from *Fools*, however, does not represent all schools prior to 1994. There were schools for black children whose principals were not government dupes, who instead challenged apartheid and worked actively with the children to develop their aspirations and their view of history. Only a handful of independent schools had experimented with racial integration and alternative curricula up until this point. But overall, much of mainstream schooling – for white as for black students and teachers during this time – was impoverished, even redundant, for it was preparing everyone for a future that would never materialize.

Genesis of a Master's in English Education at Wits

As in the primary and secondary school sectors, tertiary institutions had also been established for different population groups in apartheid South Africa. Universities and colleges of education existed for blacks, 'coloureds' and whites. Among the universities for white students, Afrikaans universities supported the official policy, whereas the liberal English universities were oppositional in terms of their ideological position, and to a certain extent in terms of their practices. The University of the Witwatersrand (Wits) was one of the four so-called 'open' universities in the country, which made some attempt to include black students, though on a small scale, defying legal regulations in certain instances, and challenging the ideology of apartheid. Its stand on academic freedom and its protests against apartheid led the Nationalist Party government to see Wits as a revolutionary hotbed, and the police force was not infrequently sent to the Wits campus to break up a demonstration. Since 1994, however, certain critics have claimed that Wits did not do enough during the apartheid years, particularly with respect to the recruitment of black faculty members and exploration of non-Eurocentric curricula.

It must not be forgotten, however, that many faculties took an oppositional stance to apartheid. This stance informed faculty members' curricula and their teaching activities. The departments of History, Political Science, Sociology, African Literature and Education were among those that sought to cultivate a critical independence of mind in their students, and to encourage opposition to apartheid. Others taught a Eurocentric curriculum that avoided confronting the realities of South Africa. The departments involved with teacher education were, by and large, strongly critical of apartheid education, as was evident in their courses on educational history and philosophy, and indeed in many of the subject methodology courses. The teacher education courses for English teachers,[2] for example, contrived, over a period of three decades, to alert its students and to contribute to the overthrow of apartheid. An excellent example is the English Methodology project that established South African literature as the major component in literature courses. Pre-service teachers were expected to research a work of South African literature, and to devise a handbook for teaching it in a South African school. Students were encouraged to select novels such as Sol Plaatje's *Mhudi*, Alan Paton's *Cry, the Beloved Country* or *Too Late the Phalorope*, Nadine Gordimer's *July's People*, J.M. Coetzee's *Waiting for the Barbarians*, or the poetry of Oswald Mtshali, Mangane Wally Serote and Mafika Gwala, which embodied the struggles and aspirations of black people in the 1970s and 1980s. It is important to note that this literature curriculum openly flouted the existing syllabuses in schools for both white and black children, where South African literature was actively discouraged, if not outlawed, owing to its overtly political nature. South African literature before 1994 is predominantly a literature of resistance against apartheid. Pre-service teachers also encountered South African writers not only on the page but in person, through an annual series of poetry readings at which writers read and discussed their work. Some of these writers, or some of their writings, were banned at the time under one or other of South Africa's infamous apartheid laws, such as the Suppression of Communism Act – an act frequently used to silence South African authors. White students during the 1970s and 1980s, and students of all races during the early 1990s, were given the opportunity during their English Methodology classes to experience the role that literature, especially poetry, was playing in the political struggle that was taking place, and to meet writers of all races who held views diametrically opposed to those of the state. A number of white students were amazed to encounter black people who were both brilliant thinkers and accomplished speakers of the English language.

These strategies encouraged the group of educators at Wits to engage in the project under discussion in this essay. Change was in the air; educational reform would be high on the ANC government's agenda, whenever that government formally took over the reins of power. Our group had become concerned with the fate of in-service teachers in the early 1990s, many of them in senior positions in schools and colleges of education, but with a training that was out of date and ill-suited to the transformation that was soon to come. My colleagues and I wished to move beyond critiquing the existing or past curriculum, a practice that was finely honed at Wits, towards reconstruction and innovation – the designing of new programmes that looked towards the future.[3] We formed a working group in order to develop a Master's programme for in-service English teachers and educators that would meet the needs and challenges of post-apartheid South Africa. Our curricular and pedagogic decisions were made on the basis of research on coursework Master's programmes in the global market – for there were no local models – and on the needs of the local context. We examined the broader, more inclusive ways in which the subject of 'English' was being constructed in the latter years of the twentieth century in answer to the challenges of technological development, multiculturalism, multilingualism and globalization. We took account of the phenomenon of English as a world literature, produced by colonized and postcolonial peoples all over the world. Most crucial, though, were local conditions – the content of teacher-training courses in the past, the needs of teachers, the needs of the country. The programme would be dynamic and fluid, open to new ideas and needs as they became apparent.

It is therefore accurate to say that this group invented the course programme in light of global theories and trends, as well as local conditions and needs. As the apartheid monolith was due to explode after South Africa's first democratic elections, the programme had to foreground issues of diversity – in terms of classrooms, culture and content – and promote an agenda of redress and equity. We hoped to bring in candidates who had the potential to transform education in their home sites; if these candidates did not meet the Wits entry requirements, we would recognize their prior learning and experience as fully adequate. The programme was designed to question the content of

'English' as a subject by offering a wide range of modules in literature (including African literature and world literatures in English), language, literacy, media, writing, and materials development, and it would teach and examine the modules in multiple ways. Assessment practices would include a range of cognitive and communicative methods in an attempt to provide a space for specifically South African ways of representing ourselves and our cultures – the oral as well as the written, the audio, visual, gestural, performative and multimodal, in addition to the linguistic. We would attempt to work with diversity in such a way as to see it as a resource rather than a problem. Our contribution would be towards the building of a new curriculum for English, to the production of greater agency and innovative disposition for teachers, and the development of a more equitable society.

Curriculum 2005

The Master's in English Education programme at Wits actually pre-empted South Africa's new national curriculum, so far as English was concerned. The Department of National Education of South Africa unveiled its new curriculum for schools in 1997. It became clear that there was much common ground between our Master's programme and the goals of this new curriculum for schools, dubbed *Curriculum 2005*, after the intended date of its full implementation. Determined to shed its prescriptive, discriminatory, content-based curriculum, which had encouraged rote-learning in schools for black children, the Department of National Education had opted to use an outcomes-based paradigm for its new school curriculum, geared towards multiculturalism, multilingualism, gender equity and democratic ideals. It was hoped that the new curriculum would help South Africa to achieve the following vision: 'A prosperous, truly united, democratic and internationally competitive country with literate, creative and critical citizens leading productive, self-fulfilled lives in a country free of violence, discrimination and prejudice' (Department of Education 1997a).

Although it was heavily criticized from its inception for a range of reasons, including the difficulty of its implementation, a number of commentators saw *Curriculum 2005* as a highly sophisticated, progressive, even radical curriculum of real merit. Since 1994 South Africa has produced a series of impressive human rights documents, such as the new Constitution of South Africa and the language policy documents. Seven critical outcomes cross all the learning areas of the new curriculum. They derive from principles enshrined in our new Constitution and are intended to ensure that learners gain the skills, knowledge and values that will enable them to achieve personal success, as well as contribute to the success of their families, their communities and the nation as a whole. In order to contribute to the full personal development of each learner, and to social and economic development at large, learning programmes should ensure that the students engage in the social, cultural, vocational and metacognitive activities outlined below. The concept of 'lifelong learning' is stressed in all major documents of the period. This provides a message to teachers that qualifications obtained at some point in the past are unlikely to suffice, and to underqualified teachers that they will have to enhance their qualifications to survive in the new system. The assumption is that learning is a dynamic, ongoing process.

Curricular Content

Courses were developed to serve the local and global demands of English educators in South Africa and beyond as we embark on the twenty-first century. Students are obliged to take the mandatory core module that is an introduction to the teaching and learning of English locally and worldwide, with an emphasis on our new national curriculum. The approach is critical, and concentrates on analysing past and present curricula. It is team-taught by mainly female staff in a rigorous but empathetic, varied, innovative way, using a range of multimodal assessment methods in keeping with the theme of diversity. The pedagogy may be said to be 'feminist' or 'feminine' in terms of its range of methods, its flexible, dynamic, dialogic approach, and its acknowledgement of the role of affect, culture and context in learning, as opposed to more rigid, norms-based 'masculine' pedagogies.

In addition to coursework, students are required to complete a research report within the field of English education. In the short life of the programme so far, students have produced a range of high-quality reports on topics that break new ground, are very localized, and demonstrate exceptional commitment to understanding local conditions and implementing transformed practice. Research has been done in the following areas: teacher attitudes and the processes of dissemination of *Curriculum 2005*; a multiliteracies[4] approach to *Curriculum 2005*; teaching literature in multicultural classrooms; 'othering' in the South African media; alternative assessment strategies for new English curricula in secondary schools; issues in assessment in adult basic literacy; collaborative approaches in the teaching and learning of poetry; visual literacy in language classrooms.

Outcomes

The initial response to the programme indicated that the course did in fact meet a need, and that educators in different regions of South Africa, and in different sites, and even in other parts of the African continent, were motivated to upgrade their qualifications and skills. Thirty educators (mostly women) were accepted into the programme in 1996, the first year. Our own admissions policy differed from the policy of our governing body, the Arts Faculty. We had to push strongly for the inclusion of applicants who did not meet the grade requirements of the Faculty, but who nonetheless had valuable professional experience and the potential to contribute to their communities. Initial interest in the course showed the commitment to educational change and empowerment that existed in the country at the time, and the rekindled enthusiasm of some English teachers due to their liberation from Christian National or Bantu Education. Both white teachers in privileged positions at top private schools or at historically white, now mixed state schools, and black teachers from state schools and colleges of education, wanted to unlearn some of what they had previously learned. They also wanted to upgrade their knowledge and skills in order to meet the demands of the new curriculum. Everyone wanted to interact with colleagues of other races, an opportunity they had previously been denied. Extracts from the letters of motivation for places on the course over the period of three years are revealing:

With the changes in education, the old methods and approaches are no longer useful in present classrooms. They pertain to the old system of education in black schools. Consequently, we as teachers are not able to meet the needs and interests of our learners. (Nancy, black teacher at a college of education for black teachers in a rural area)

With the changes taking place in education in South Africa, I believe that there is a need for courageous, adventurous teachers who are not deterred by differences across race, cultural practices, belief systems, language, class and other categories. There is a need to operate flexibly across community boundaries as never before.... I hope that through studying for this degree I will be able to take on these challenges and make a contribution to the education system of South Africa. (Lusanda, black lecturer at a college of education for black teachers)

I would like to be part of the larger debate going on in South African teaching.... I need to reflect on my personal experience, on the experiences of other teachers, and on the challenges facing us all. I want to do this not alone, but with other teachers and researchers. I know there is so much I don't know. (Alison, white teacher of disadvantaged first- and second-language speakers of English in a private, independent school)

Since I began teaching more than twenty years ago my students have changed radically with regard to their literacy backgrounds. I therefore urgently feel the need to study further so that I may be more qualified to encourage and develop literacy skills in these learners who come from so many different contexts. Presently, I hold the post of Head of Department of English in the school where I teach. In order to do justice to this post I strongly believe that there is a need to have a strong theoretical foundation. This will hopefully enable me to implement curriculum development in my school as well as policies which can cater to the challenges that *Curriculum 2005* presents. (Harriet, white Head English teacher at a private Catholic secondary school)

I wish to express my thoughts and feelings about English as a Second Language, especially in our black schools. My views on this are based on what I experienced as a learner of English, when it was very difficult for me to communicate with other people in English – I was only able to memorize what was taught. This problem is created by the traditional approach to English language teaching in black schools. I am interested in furthering my studies in English so that I can help black learners, because they are the victims of this situation.... Further studies in education are not for promotion, the economy, etc. ... rather, there are people around us who really need the knowledge we have. As educators, we need to build our country by sharing this knowledge, and our skills, and be willing to accept other people's ideas. (Lilly-Rose, black secondary-school teacher in a rural area)

Applicants for the programme have been mostly teachers and college lecturers, working in both formal and non-formal contexts with schoolchildren or adults learning basic literacy, and also educational publishers and examiners for school boards. Exceptional dedication has been shown on the part of the students, most of whom work full-time and attend the course part-time. A number of students commute five hours or more each way to get to the weekly seminar from their place of residence in a rural area far from the metropolitan centre of Johannesburg. Nancy and Lilly-Rose are cases in point. One a schoolteacher, the other a lecturer at a college of education in a remote rural area on the border of the Ciskei and Kwazulu-Natal, both full-time employees with families, they were prepared to make considerable financial and personal sacrifices for the sake of education in this country. Lilly-Rose and Nancy travelled seven hours by bus to their Monday afternoon seminar, then caught the night bus back at seven in the evening, returning home in the early hours of the morning to do a full day's work. A startlingly high level of commitment has also been shown by most teachers of the course, whose engagement with course content and pedagogies, and with their colleagues' experiences and ideas, has given rise so far to the attainment of a high standard of work, comparable to that in reputable international institutions.[5]

Challenges Facing the Programme

The Master's in English Education throws up many challenges for students and lecturers, since it involves issues of race, culture, ideology, identity and ultimately curricular transformation in a context where historically advantaged and disadvantaged students are brought together. It therefore requires critical self-reflection by all participants. Our staff meet every week to discuss issues and problems arising from the sessions. One such problem in 1998 involved an experiment with assessment. *Curriculum 2005* encourages a range of assessment practices, including self-assessment. Class members were asked to self-assess their final coursework assignment, in terms of a set of criteria. Our motives were twofold: affording a personal experience of self-assessment to teachers who might later implement the same technique in their own classrooms, in terms of the requirements of *Curriculum 2005*, and momentarily shifting the locus of power from the lecturers to the students in order to encourage the development of agency in them. The exercise caused an uproar. A number of students were most uncomfortable with this method – out of uncertainty with the techniques of self-assessment, modesty, or the inability to envisage evaluation as emanating from oneself. The experience highlighted the hegemony of the academy's assessment procedures – always a judgement from above, a norm-referenced assessment – and the way they had produced individuals unused to self-evaluation.

Race issues inevitably arose. Lusanda's story, presented below, emerged only in her final self-reflective assignment; a similar issue from a different vantage point was picked up in Joanna's reflections. Both students struggled with, and ultimately grew from, this experience of exclusion and inclusion.

> *Lusanda:* 'I believe that there has been a lot of development on my part since the beginning of the course. At the beginning I was seriously thinking of dropping out, as I could not find a grasp, but as soon as I found it, I held on for dear life. I had a nasty experience of being rejected by the group I was to present with, and it left a huge dent in my self-esteem. It came at a time when I thought I was beginning to enjoy the course and it set me off track and left me very bitter and raised questions of any real transformation in this country. Now that the course is over, I can sigh a sigh of relief, and

look at the whole experience as a giant step in my development as a teacher in South Africa, and I am confident it has empowered and enriched me.'

Joanna: 'I was affected by an aspect of the group dynamics in the sessions. Despite attempts by staff and students, it seemed that there was always a predominant sense of 'us' and 'them' between the cultural groups. Many of us tried to overcome this by deliberately mixing our groups for the oral presentations. This presented practical difficulties, as some of the black students had problems attending the preparatory meetings. I was conscious of the possibility that this might in itself contribute towards lowering the self-esteem of these students.... However, I was inordinately pleased when two of my fellow students, Rizwana (who is not silent anyway) and Lilly-Rose, separately phoned me at home to discuss assignments. I have to ask myself if my pleasure was connected in some way to a kind of patronizing tokenism on my part that somehow relieved my guilt. The 'guilt of the English' and the guilt of 'Whiteness': how much more guilt can I handle, and does it serve any useful purpose?'

Conclusion

Since 1994, education in South Africa has received enormous international attention. We have moved in the space of a few years from eighteen distinct educational departments and corresponding curricula to one national curriculum. Not only have we placed our hopes in education's important contribution to national productivity and to our future competitiveness in the global market; we have also assumed that education will assist in equalizing historically determined racial inequalities in skills and knowledge. Our new curriculum is explicitly non-discriminatory, an attempt to provide both the democratic principles of our country's post-apartheid national Constitution and the know-how, skills and attitudes required for the workplace.

Vijitha Eyango's analysis of the educational situation in Ghana in the first part of this chapter brings several questions immediately to mind. Is the South African effort all in vain? Is formal education of no long-term value in Africa? Is Eyango's argument confined to women, or does the underlying point about the gap between education and making a living cut across gender lines? Even with a reformed curriculum, will young women in South Africa find education irrelevant to their lives? These are frightening thoughts for us in South Africa. Will the history of education for South African women take the same path as it has in Ghana?

Perhaps we should be comforted by the fact that the differences between Ghana and South Africa may be too great to allow for correspondences between the two countries. Yet I am forced to concede that the optimism of the early moment of transformation that I have tried to capture in my essay has begun to give way to a less positive mood. The euphoric shift away from apartheid education in the mid-1990s did not give rise to utopia, nor to instant and ubiquitous improvement in the processes of teaching and learning. Rather, the issues that have come into focus are how wide the disparities had been in white and black schooling, how poorly resourced many schools were, how poorly qualified many teachers were, and how the culture of learning that had been destroyed in many contexts during the apartheid era would take a long time to restore.[6]

Women graduating from the Master's in English Education at Wits have, on the whole, been encouraged by their achievements both in the programme and in the workplace. The pass rate has been high, and even students who did not meet the grade requirements of the institution on admission ultimately achieved good results. Women entering the Master's Programme remain highly motivated, diligent, innovative and, most important, impassioned about the project of education in South Africa. They continue to see a key role for education in South Africa – in terms of the empowerment of individuals, groups and the nation as a whole. The work they produce reveals a strong grasp of the needs of particular educational contexts, and provides creative and effective ways of working with those needs. The women discover that they are able to participate and compete internationally within their academic field, and to play a positive role locally.

South Africa cannot afford to allow its women – or its men, for that matter – to give in to disillusionment about education as a key development process. I believe that we in South Africa have two choices. Either we capitulate to cynicism – as has J.M. Coetzee in his award-winning novel *Disgrace* – or we work actively, but with eyes wide open, under the trying conditions in which we find ourselves, regarding transformation as a fraught but blessed state that constitutes the present moment in our history.

Notes

1. Black representativeness was nil at the time, and remains so within the department under discussion. This is one of the legacies of apartheid in many departments at the University of the Witwatersrand. It is a problem the University is trying to rectify by a range of strategies, such as the 'Growing your own timber' scheme, which provides bursaries for promising young students of underrepresented groups with a view to training them as lecturers for future employment by the institution.

2. A key figure here was Jonathan Paton, son of Alan Paton, author of the well-known South African novel *Cry, the Beloved Country*.

3. Our approach was confirmed and elaborated in work done by Gunther Kress, whom we encountered just before our programme was launched – specifically, *Writing the Future: English and the Making of a Culture of Innovation* (Kress 1995); and, just after the MA in English Education programme was launched, by The New London Group's work, as outlined in their article 'A Pedagogy of Multiliteracies: Designing Social Futures', in the *Harvard Educational Review* in early 1996 (now republished in Cope and Kalantsis 2000).

4. 'Multiliteracies' has been a generative literacy concept as well as theoretical framework for the MA in English Education programme. Pertinent papers on the topic are The New London Group 1996 and Newfield and Stein 2000.

5. This view was expressed by the external examiner of the course in 1998, a professor of English and Education at the Institute of Education, University of London.

6. Specific issues of concern widely reported in the press during 1999 and 2000 include the total absence of textbooks in some schools, with which to implement the new curriculum; the lack of subject expertise among teachers; the poor management by principals and senior staff in some schools; the gap between high-achieving schools with good resources and those schools with few resources available, particularly those in rural areas and townships where black people live; the astonishingly poor matriculation results, with a number of schools throughout the country achieving a zero pass rate in the school-exit examinations at the end of 1999; the problems encountered by educational publishers, such as an inadequate budget for books in many schools; and logistical factors, such as the state's vacillating approach to the dates of implementation of the new curriculum for different levels of schooling; unsatisfactory conditions for teachers, including poor salaries, which remain below those of most other professions. In addition, many highly skilled teachers have lost their jobs during an initial period of rationalization. A number of teacher-training colleges have closed down, while others have merged. The end result is that many people in the teaching profession – teachers, publishers and lecturers – now feel demoralized.

References

Chapman, M., ed. (1981) *A Century of South African Poetry*, Johannesburg and London: A.D. Donker.

Cope, B. and M. Kalantsis, eds (2000) *Multiliteracies: Literacy Learning and the Design of Social Futures*, London and New York: Routledge.

Cornbleth, C. (1990) *Curriculum in Context*, Falmer: The Falmer Press.

Department of Education (1996) *Discussion Document: Lifelong Learning through a National Qualifications Framework*, Republic of South Africa: Report of the Ministerial Committee for Development Work on the NQF, February.

Department of Education (1997a) *Curriculum 2005: Lifelong Learning for the 21st Century*, Republic of South Africa, February.

Department of Education (1997b) *Outcomes Based Education in South Africa: Background Information for Educators*, Republic of South Africa, March.

Department of Education (1997c) *Senior Phase Policy Document*, Republic of South Africa, September.

Jansen, J. and P. Christie, eds (1999) *Changing Curriculum – Studies on Outcomes-based Education in South Africa*, Cape Town: Juta.

Kallaway, P., ed. (1984) *Apartheid Education: The Education of Black South Africans*, Johannesburg: Ravan.

Kane-Berman, J. (1978) *Soweto: Black Revolt White Reaction*, Johannesburg: Ravan.

Kane-Berman, J. (1991) *South Africa's Silent Revolution*, Johannesburg: SAIRR and Southern Books.

Kress, G. (1995) *Writing the Future: English and the Making of a Culture of Innovation*, Sheffield: Nate.

Lodge T. (1999) *South African Politics Since 1994*, Cape Town: David Philip.

Mattera, D. (1983) *Azanian Love Song*, Johannesburg: Skotaville.

Mbeki, T. (1998) *Africa – The Time Has Come*, Cape Town and Johannesburg: Tafelberg & Mafube.

Murray, B. (1982) *Wits: The Early Years*, Johannesburg: Witwatersrand University Press.

Murray, B. (1997) *Wits: The Open Years*, Johannesburg: Witwatersrand University Press.

New London Group (1996) 'A Pedagogy of Multiliteracies: Designing Social Futures', *Harvard Educational Review*, vol. 66, no. 1. Also published in B. Cope and M. Kalantsis, eds (2000) *Multiliteracies: Literacy Learning and the Design of Social Futures*, London and New York: Routledge.

Newfield, D. and P. Stein (2000) 'The International Multiliteracies Project: South African Teachers Respond', in B. Cope and M. Kalantsis, eds, *Multiliteracies: Literacy Learning and the Design of Social Futures*, London and New York: Routledge.

Paton, J. (1990) *The Land and People of South Africa*, New York: J.P. Lippincott.

Ramadan, S., dir. (1998) *Fools*, a feature film based on the short story 'Fools' by N. Ndebele, scripted by B. Peterson and S. Ramadan.

Shear, M. (1996) *Wits: A University in the Apartheid Era*, Johannesburg: Witwatersrand University Press.

South African Institute of Race Relations (SAIRR) (1953–2000) *Annual Surveys 1953–2000*, Johannesburg: SAIRR.

Taylor, N., ed. (1993) *Inventing Knowledge: Contests in Curriculum Construction*, Cape Town: Maskew Miller Longman.

Taylor, N. and P. Vinjevold, eds (1999) *Getting Learning Right – Report of the President's Education Initiative Research Project*, Johannesburg: Joint Education Trust.

Wolpe, A., O. Quinlan and L. Martinez (1997) *Gender Equality in Education. Report of the Gender Equity Task Team*, Pretoria: Department of Education, October.

CHAPTER FOUR

Making Peace
as Development Practice

Peace-making is the ultimate site for development in that it works towards building a stable environment in which to construct a better life for future generations. The contributors to this chapter – one Israeli, one Palestinian – live in the same country, and have been associates and partners in this struggle for ten years. Yet they still cannot go out to a restaurant together, or invite one another home for a cup of coffee. Only on a recent trip to Rwanda, where they served as peace mediators, were they finally able to live their friendship openly on neutral ground. These two women are co-founders of the Jerusalem Link for Women, a peace movement split in two, like their nation, between the Israeli Bat Shalom and the Palestinian Jerusalem Centre for Women. Through educational programmes, training seminars, non-violent demonstrations, mediation, e-mail exchanges and interviews such as they one they conducted with us to produce this chapter, they proffer strategies for developing trust, developing relationships, and negotiating difference in the most extreme of political circumstances.

Dialogue in the War Zone: Israeli and Palestinian Women for Peace

Sumaya Farhat-Naser and Gila Svirsky

Gila Svirsky: Sumaya always begins.

Sumaya Farhat-Naser: We have always had women and men who try to talk to each other, who crossed the barriers to speak to each other and do something for peace. But until 1992 it was forbidden to meet as politicians or to represent political positions. It was forbidden to talk to the other side – on both sides – because speaking with the enemy was treason, a form of recognizing the enemy, and so both the PLO and the Israeli government forbade it. But there were always groups of women, individuals who met. I remember in 1986 we met for the first time, six Israeli and six Palestinian women, to develop a programme on how to continue to work with each other. These meetings continued, hidden and informal for several years.

In 1989 a group of Palestinian and Israeli women were invited to Brussels by the Jewish Cultural Centre, which hosted a joint meeting. That meeting was a secret one during which the women worked together to form political principles and create a framework for our joint work. It was necessary to have political guidelines.

These guidelines guaranteed political protection for both sides, because these meetings were forbidden and we wanted to show our people that we were meeting for something that was good for both sides. We formulated principles such as the recognition of national and political rights, the recognition of the PLO, and our stand against violence.

In 1992 a second meeting was held, again in Brussels, because it was too difficult between 1989 and 1992 to continue meeting in

Jerusalem because of the Intifada. Our second meeting was entitled 'Give Peace a Chance', and we worked out amended principles. The event was extremely important, because four women who were elected to the Israeli legislature came to Brussels in their official capacity as parliamentarians. That made us realize that we had to include Palestinian women who were also elected officials, and so ten women from the Tunisian legislature came. Thus it was a meeting not only of women at the grassroots level, but also of responsible women in politics on both sides. This forced people on both sides to speak about the fact that it was illegal for politicians from either side to meet. We were happy to note that several months later this type of legislation was invalidated on both sides.

We presented our ideas in Brussels at a press conference. We emphasized that we had to work together as part of a joint venture for peace. We recognized that our main enemy in the current situation was false or inadequate knowledge about one another. There was so much fear and mistrust rooted in misinformation, and the fact that we were kept apart by political barriers and exclusive ideologies that conditioned our peoples to remain separated. The Occupation policy and policies fostering animosity caused these fears, and the belief that we could only be enemies.

What we were trying to do was to encourage both sides to view one another as partners, having parity in everything – equal rights; the right of both peoples to live in peace, dignity, and security; and accepting the notion that we both belong to this piece of land. It belongs to us both as two states for two peoples.

We believe that Jerusalem belongs to both, as an open city that can serve as two capitals for two states.

We reject all kinds of violence.

We have not only the right but the obligation to involve ourselves in politics, to shape our political future constructively, and to influence the formation of a civic, democratic society in both nations. We want to see ourselves as one front working for peace for the benefit of both sides.

Those are the main principles that we have been working for ever since.

Now, practically speaking, we received support from the European Union to establish two centres in Jerusalem – Bat Shalom for Israeli women and the Jerusalem Centre for Palestinian Women. Together both centres comprise the Jerusalem Link. It was meant that these two centres should be in this same city. It would have been a serious error to have only one centre, because we have an asymmetrical situation.

On one side is an established, fifty-year-old state with a well-organized, highly developed structure, all the attributes and infrastructure of a state. This includes a high level of educational, technical and economic development. And on the other side, we have a society that has been plagued by the thirty-year revolution and Occupation, and is totally destroyed, yet is on its way to beginning its dream of becoming a state. This asymmetrical situation means that the women of the Jerusalem Centre must deal with much more difficult and very different problems than those faced by Bat Shalom. The Israeli women also face an unbelievably complex situation and difficulties that they have to deal with differently. And so we need these two separate centres.

This also demonstrates that both sides want to achieve independence and freedom, and do not want to distort themselves to accommodate the other. We wish to retain our political and cultural identity. Therefore it is important that we should be able to stand in front of each other and look into the other's eyes knowing that we are different, and simply respect that each side is different.

Bat Shalom is located in West Jerusalem for the Israeli women and the Jerusalem Centre is in East Jerusalem for the Palestinian women. Each centre has its independent programmes that comply with the immediate needs of its own society. We also have joint programmes that address the political situation, and empower women for political activity. We discuss political principles, and are aligned with the negotiations and the Peace Process. We are committed to the Peace Process and the international covenants, laws and references for this Peace Process. Together, we address the problem of human rights, especially in Jerusalem. We make joint statements concerning what is happening; for example, if a terrorist attack takes place, irrespective of who did what against whom, we issue a joint statement condemning the event, which points out responsibility for this action and takes a stand on the event. This is very important in terms of public education for peace. As a women's organization, we are also members of the Palestinian Women's Association, and we are very involved in educating women about democracy and human rights.

So we are forced to work and struggle on different levels. We work internally for the development of a civic, democratic society, and in doing this we are very much in confrontation with the whole political and legal system, because we are trying to promote a Palestinian legal system. As women we also have to fight for our women's rights together with other women. We have Palestinian–Palestinian dialogue on the Old City of Jerusalem, where Palestinian women – Christian and

Muslim, as well as Christians from different churches – come together to talk about their problems and present their own visions for society. We have civic education for the women of the Old City. The Old City was neglected for such a long time. Palestinians were not allowed to present any sort of developmental plans there, nor was the Old City part of any Israeli development plan. Consequently, there is a lot to do.

We also have a dialogue between Palestinian women from the West Bank and Palestinian women with Israeli passports from Galilee. The main theme is the idea of national identity. Both groups are Palestinian, on the one hand, in their culture, religion and emotions; but on the other hand, one group has Israeli passports and has gone much further in terms of exposure to Israeli society and their way of life. Therefore we have to recognize our connection to these women from Galilee, and analyse our triangular relationship. How do we make peace work, have a vision for coexistence with dignity for all parties?

The core of our work is our third dialogue programme called 'Women Making Peace', which provides training for dialogue between Israeli and Palestinian women. This is the most difficult programme, because many people on both sides want to meet, and are eager to do so. But it is not enough to have good intentions and a desire to meet. A suitable infrastructure must be in place. When we have lived fifty years knowing each other only as enemies, with pain and bitter experience very much alive on the Palestinian side, it is very difficult to say 'Let's sit together and hug.' We can't hug. Without proper training, women on both sides think, 'Now we can come together, and I will show them what I have experienced.' Yet everyone has, in the back of her mind, the idea either of defending herself or of attacking the other. After just two sentences, the whole discussion explodes: 'You see, they are so bad. I don't want to see them again. I knew that it was no use meeting with them. I knew that they were terrible.'

To prevent this from happening, we conduct dialogue training. We train both groups, independently, about how to meet, how to learn to respect one another's vision, how to know that there are at least two versions, not one, to every story. Although meeting together is painful, we must learn to bear this pain, to defend ourselves from feeling this pain, and learn how to cross this painful stage. We must address our fears, speak our hopes and visions aloud. But to do this, we must also lay the groundwork by training women in political analysis, teaching them to analyse the information around us. What is going on behind the scenes; what does it mean to speak about refugees, borders, Jerusalem? How do these issues affect one side or the other?

When both sides feel that they are prepared to look into the eyes of the other with respect, to heal, to listen, to understand how to contribute to a logical discussion, to be sensitive in wording, in attitude, then the groups can meet and begin working together. The aim is not to learn to drink coffee together. Anyone can drink coffee together. The aim is to discuss political issues, very difficult political issues, and to come out of these discussions with a consensus that is good for both sides. This is the aim for this dialogue programme that caters to young women, old women and target groups such as students and police-women.

Gila: I'm really going to miss hearing these speeches. I'm always inspired by them.

At the same time, I'm always struck by how the approaches of each side are different. The work of Bat Shalom is also different from the other peace movements in Israel.

First, perhaps I can capture the difference between us by saying that the Israeli women come to dialogue with Palestinian women so that they can sleep better at night. They can assuage their guilty feelings about being in the camp of the oppressors. On the other hand, Palestinian women come to the dialogue group to prevent the Israeli women from sleeping well at night. I think that pretty much captures the different stances that each side takes. We have had dialogue work for about three years now. We have had some very difficult times in the groups, and also some superficial times in the groups. The dialogue work is always marked by the determination of the Palestinian side to get to the political issues, to talk about what Israel is doing wrong, and to have the Israeli women understand that they must pressure their government to change things. Whereas the Israeli women come because they want to be friends with the Palestinian women. They want to drink coffee, they want to talk about their children and about good books they've read. They acknowledge the faults of the Israeli government but, at the same time, they want to get past it. But the Palestinians are not past it.

The Oslo Declaration of Principles – and the famous handshake on the White House lawn – happened in September 1993, but there is no peace. There has not been an end to the Occupation. In some ways, in fact, the Occupation has got worse. Although Israelis in general – especially the Left – recognize that we are a long way away from the final peace agreement, many people think that peace is in the bag. All we have to do now is work out the details.

But peace is not yet in the bag. On both sides, it's our task to clarify to our respective societies that not only are some things worse, but some very, very painful decisions will have to be taken – on both sides – for peace really to be in our pockets. Our job in Bat Shalom is to prepare Israeli society for some of those painful concessions. Bat Shalom serves a different function in Israeli society from the other Israeli peace organizations. It's not only because we're women, but I think being women has a lot to do with it. The principles that we signed jointly with the Jerusalem Centre for Women (JCW) were much more progressive – in fact, radical – principles than had been signed previously by any joint gathering of Palestinian and Israeli peace advocates. They were way ahead of their time. Some of the statements made in those principles are matters of consensus in Israel today, but some of those statements remain on the radical fringe, and it will take a few years before we move towards them.

Let me give you a couple of examples. Sumaya mentioned them in the Palestinian context. Let me present them in the Israeli context.

The first statement is that there must be a Palestinian state side by side with an Israeli state. This principle was considered anathema to the Israeli public when we first began to talk about it. It was beyond the pale. We spoke of it without going into detail. We are now ten years past our initial dialogue groups, and we can look with gratification at public opinion in Israel and say that it has moved a long way on this subject. Today, 60 per cent of Jewish Israelis believe that Palestinians have a right to a state of their own, side by side with the state of Israel. Sixty per cent! Ten years ago, it was less than 20 per cent. An additional 10 per cent of Jewish Israelis believe that while the Palestinians may not have a right to a state, this state is inevitable. Which means that 70 per cent of the Israeli Jewish public believes that there is a state around the corner and the great majority feel that it is justified. This is an enormous stride forward.

A second joint principle, which is not yet acceptable to the Israeli public, is that the city of Jerusalem must be a shared capital. If you ask Israelis today what they think about Jerusalem as a shared capital, 80 per cent will tell you that Jerusalem must be the exclusive capital of Israel. An additional 15 per cent have creative ideas about how to go about solving the problem of joint claims to the capital. Only 5 per cent accept the solution which the Jerusalem Link supports: the concept that Jerusalem must be a shared capital, in united and shared sovereignty – part of the city will be the capital of Israel and part of it will be the capital of Palestine. That is still a principle on which we are way out on a limb compared to the rest of Israeli society.

I'd also like to point out something that Sumaya mentioned in passing and for which the Jerusalem Centre for Women deserves enormous credit: their courageous position on the rejection of violence as a political strategy. For the Palestinians that meant condemning all forms of Palestinian violence, even at a time when the Palestinians had very few other tools to make their claims or focus world attention on the injustice done to them. Nevertheless, the Palestinian women's centre said 'No' to violence. For us Israelis, condemning Israeli violence means condemning the Israeli army for its acts of state terrorism. This includes using live ammunition to control demonstrations, grabbing land by force, destroying homes, and even denying Palestinians their fair share of drinking water. These are all forms of state terrorism used against a weak civilian population, and we condemn them, even though they happen under the auspices of a legally elected government. We regard this as a form of terrorism; condemning it was our own courageous contribution to the principle of non-violence.

I'd like to talk about the ways in which the women's peace work at Bat Shalom is different from the type of peace work that takes place in the rest of the Israeli peace movement. First of all, the mainstream peace movement in Israel, the mixed-gender movement, is very conservative. It looks at the issues and asks itself: will the security of Israel be strengthened? Security is the ultimate criterion for them. It looks at any of the proposed solutions or political accommodations and asks: what are the security safeguards? What's in it for Israel?

We believe that this turns the question on its head. It's our belief that a peace agreement holds the best – indeed, the only – hope of security. A peace that is acceptable to both sides is the only way to achieve security for Israelis, as well as Palestinians.

Our methods are different, our goals are different, and our vision of peace is different. The mixed-gender peace movement in Israel seeks a peace of mutual deterrence. This would include closing the border, locking the door, and throwing away the key. No more Palestinians mixing with Israelis. They want limits set on the extent to which the Palestinian side can arm itself – no tanks, no warplanes, no artillery. I'd like to set those same limits on Israeli society. I'm not arguing for tanks on the Palestinian side, but for banishing tanks from the Israeli side as well.

The difference is that while the mixed-gender Israeli peace camp argues for mutual deterrence, the Bat Shalom women argue for a culture of peace and mutual co-operation. We argue for a future in which our destinies are intertwined, in which we have economic, cultural and recreational co-operation – in sport, in fashion, in business, whatever. Our economies should have some integration, while at the same time maintaining the independence of both states.

I argue forcefully for the economic integration of both communities because of the terrible disparity between the two economies. The per capita GDP in Palestine is approximately $1,600 per year. The parallel figure in Israel is $16,500. That's ten times more. Israel's per capita GDP is roughly the same as that of Italy and Spain, modern European countries. Palestine's economy is Third World. This enormous disparity between Palestine and Israel fosters instability between our two societies. And we have learned from history that you cannot have two neighbouring societies with such a huge economic gap between them and expect political stability. There will always be volatility unless there is some parity. So we in the women's peace movement argue for a shared future.

There are also important differences in our activities. In the women's peace movement, we do different sorts of things. The mixed movement embraces the 'big bang' theory of organizing. It has a big rally where a hundred thousand people show up, hug each other, and then all go home again until the next rally six months later.

The women's peace movement has consistently advocated ongoing peace activities – ongoing in every way possible, using every strategy imaginable to build bridges between our societies and to educate Israelis about the importance of peace. For example, in addition to the dialogue groups that have already been mentioned, the Israeli women make condolence calls to some Palestinian families when a family member has been killed by the Israeli authorities. Conversely, the Palestinians do the same thing on our side by visiting – where they would be welcome – families of Israelis who have been killed by terrorism.

We have public education activities. We run seminars and open-panel discussions. We have our own newspaper, and we pay for advertisements in national media to air our views. We had a meeting just last week to begin our analysis of a very difficult issue: the refugee problem. How can we resolve the problem of almost a million Palestinian refugees created by the 1948 war, who have now grown into a population of several million? We have begun this series of meetings to come up with a solution that makes sense.

Finally, Bat Shalom women have been physically courageous in their activities, in a way that the mixed peace movement has not yet begun to dream of. Bat Shalom is willing to engage in civil disobedience. We're willing to break the law if we believe it to be an unjust law. We act in the spirit of Mahatma Gandhi, who said that non-cooperation with evil is a sacred duty. We believe that very strongly. A case in point is the demolition of homes that has taken place over the last few years. Over 5,000 Palestinian homes have been destroyed by the Israeli authorities under the pretext that they were illegally constructed, but in reality this is an effort to move Palestinians out of areas that Israel wishes to claim as its own.

The Israeli women of Bat Shalom have joined Palestinian protests, thrown themselves in front of the bulldozers together with our Palestinian sisters and brothers, defied laws, pushed past soldiers, put ourselves on the line because we know that non-cooperation with evil is a sacred duty. The consensus-driven peace movement in Israel would never participate in this way, and has shunned these activities of ours. We act in conjunction with a few men who have the same take on the politics of the region as we do, and we appreciate their presence. The women's peace group in Israel has taken leadership within Israel in terms of its courage, its progressive political beliefs, and its feminist vision of peace – not just an end to the belligerence, but peace with dignity and co-operation on both sides.

Sumaya: We Palestinian women in the Jerusalem Centre have many difficulties convincing our people that this joint work is fruitful, and that we must go on with it. We have these difficulties because we work openly with Israeli women, and are stamped as a joint venture. For example, the Palestinian network association for NGOs in Palestine has refused us membership because we work with Israelis. However, because we are already stigmatized, in a sense this gives us the freedom to dare to do things that others cannot do. This is a strength in itself. We have taken small steps towards success in showing people that it is possible to reach consensus with the other side. First we have to persuade the Israeli side that we have rights, and then we must convince our own people that some Israelis are willing to recognize our rights. We try to see these small steps as something big in order to encourage ourselves, to defy the despair and disappointment we sometimes feel.

We always have the feeling that we are in a state of alarm. We have to be careful not to make political mistakes, so that we can show our people that we are keen to protect our rights and do not want to give anything up, that we never compromise. This is very tiring, and a great pressure. We have a concept in Palestine called 'normalization'. Normalization means the establishment of normal relations with the Israelis. This is strongly rejected – people say: how dare you try to make something normal in a situation where nothing is normal? We are still under occupation; they are still the occupiers. They are still taking land away, they are still restricting our movements, destroying our houses, detaining our people, depriving us of our rights, and so forth.

We have to be very careful to avoid being pushed into that corner of normalization. Normalization can be something great, the fulfilment of living together in peace. But we are not there yet. We always have to persuade or to ask our Israeli partners to understand that we cannot do many things we wish to do because we are afraid of being accused of normalizing relations. For example, meeting in a restaurant and eating together, or visiting each other at home. We cannot do it. We are afraid of it. We become vulnerable, unprotected, if we do it. On the other hand, we know very well that if we do do these things, we will become much closer to each other. The process of understanding and making a relationship will be greatly enhanced. So it's always one step forward, two back, then perhaps try another step forward. That is what we must do in this very sensitive situation. So working for peace in Palestine is very, very difficult. We must always defend why we do it. We must always consult people. We must always fear for our safety. We must be very cautious, and involve both people on the ground and people in decision-making positions so that they can give their seal of approval. We are so pleased to see that officials are now using the same phrases, the same words, we used three or four years ago. We say things today, knowing that in a few years officials will say them. This is our contribution.

Gila: On the Israeli side, the media have completely ignored us until recently, and I think this is part of the general syndrome of marginalizing women's activities. When we stood in the Women in Black vigil for many, many years, we were covered by every major international news network. We were on CNN, the BBC, all the major networks, and had a segment on 'Sixty Minutes' in the US, but in Israel we never made it into the newspapers until the fifth year of our vigil. By and large, the Israeli media ignore women's work.

Sumaya: The majority of our people don't yet see the importance of the work we are doing. We see that our work together is preparing the ground for the people who will build peace together when the peace settlements are achieved. But our people still have difficulty believing that the Israeli government wants peace with us. They are reluctant to believe that our work is necessary. I myself hesitate to go to the media to say I am doing wonderful things in Israel. It can provoke a backlash, backfire on us and hurt our work. Our strategy to let people know about us is to work with groups of women, girls, boys, who participate in our courses. Every year we have five or six hundred participants in our courses. We are afraid of being attacked if the media turn their lens on us. Abroad, in Europe or the States, the media are interested in knowing about us, and academics in particular are interested. They do research on us. Journalists, on the other hand, want action, and they love to show violence, bloodshed. But our work, moderate work, is measured in small steps. There are no immediate results. We make dialogue groups; it takes time. How can this be covered by a journalist? When there is a violent act, the whole world knows about it in ten seconds. We must learn how to use the media better; we must become better skilled at presenting our words, our ideas, our message. How to make coalitions. To seek assistance. We need to work on this.

We also need to work on fostering economic development, but unfortunately that kind of development is inevitably linked with the official political system. In Palestine, any co-operation with Israelis, especially economic, must be via the official political establishment. There is an undefined relationship between NGOs and the Palestinian authority, officials, administration. We are working on that. But again, I have received several letters from Israeli businesswomen and organizers who are seeking connections with Palestinian businesswomen. They met several times just for discussion, but nothing came out of it because Palestinian women feared normalizing relations with Israelis. 'I don't need to do this', says the Palestinian woman to herself; 'my business is doing well. I must wait until this co-operation is fully accepted, not just ten per cent.' Except those who are in the Palestinian Authority. They have good relations; they work together. Especially the businessmen, who have the power. The women feel that it is forbidden as soon as they begin, because of the patriarchal structure, the authority of men. Men maintain the difference between business and politics. We don't think this is correct.

Gila: Yes, this is terrible. People who were once involved in the worst forms of oppression against the Palestinians are today businessmen making money from the connections they had as perpetrators of torture or demolishers of homes or agents in the secret service organizations. Some of these Israelis are making money today through partnerships with some corrupt politicians in the Palestinian Authority, as well.

Editors: How does the Jerusalem Link work out its differences? What sorts of skills have you developed over the years for mediating conflict? Do you have anything formal in place? [Sighs from both Sumaya and Gila.]

Gila: That's a hard question. Well, sometimes we ignore the differences. [Laughter on all sides.] If there's a difference of opinion, such as we had for a long while about what we mean when we speak of sharing Jerusalem – what kind of model we have for the city – I think we agree not to talk about it. Wouldn't you say so, Sumaya?

Sumaya: Yes. But I have to tell you: I have been the spokesperson for the Centre for more than two years now. Before that, I was on the Board of Trustees; I was a co-founder. In these years, we always had disputes. And always there is some sense of suspicion. Do they really mean what they say? There have always been issues we have not dared to speak of. But even as a responsible person, I tended until now to ignore these things, and sweep the disputes under the table. But now I am at a new stage. I have a new project with the former director of Bat Shalom in which we are trying something I suggested. We try to talk about our differences, and to address them now. You need a certain degree of maturity in order to face these disputes. So I decided to write an article about our differences in which I say why I had quarrels with Bat Shalom on this issue or that. I wrote about fifty pages, addressing twelve disputes in this single document. These were the things we couldn't talk about. Whenever we started, we quarrelled again. So I thought it would be more effective to write about them, to write about things we can't say face to face. Now that we have started, I give the article to my colleague, and she answers in writing from her point of view. Afterwards we might meet together to say: 'Isn't it too bad we quarrelled; how crazy we were.' Or we can say: 'I had not realized what you meant.' We also saw, through this process, that it is possible to solve problems once and for all. We are working on it right now; we already have sixty shared pages. For example, she was very upset with me because I write exactly as I speak, enumerating my political points: one, two, three, four. I ignored the fact that we had worked together for so long. I called her 'the Israeli' or 'the co-ordinator.' I never used her name, Daphne, or 'my friend'. And I responded: 'How can you expect me, after just two years, to say that you are my friend? You are not yet my friend. It is not that easy, especially if I am representing an official political stance in my work with you. I am afraid of being accused of normalization. You are asking me to behave as if I am living and enjoying a state of law in Israel, with all the reassurances that go with that.'

Through this writing we are trying to promote understanding. Through this writing I introduce my culture, my thinking, my behaviour, in the context of the culture and the education I had at home in the street. It is a very important process that can be followed in conflict management.

I also have many things to write to Gila – about our disputes, and problems, and difficulties with her. These are completely different from the difficulties I had with Daphne. It is so interesting. I hope this process continues.

Editors: Could you talk about the difficulties you face today?

Gila: Allow me to begin. The Jerusalem Link recently voted to change its founding principles. To be more honest, actually the Palestinians came to the Israeli side and said they had to have the principles changed. I liked the old principles because they were a broad, general vision of what peace should be. The Palestinians wanted the principles to be more specific. When we went over them point by point, the recommended changes turned out to be ones with which I found it hard to agree. Ultimately I resigned from the directorship of Bat Shalom over this. I don't want to go into great detail here over these principles, but the general dynamic was that the Palestinians would ask for a particular change and the Israelis would immediately concede. I would raise my hand and say: this is not acceptable to me; it's too extreme. Then the Israelis would say: it's OK, the Palestinians need it for their purposes; it's no big deal for us. And I would say: but it's a big deal for me. But I was in the minority at that meeting. Eventually the principles approved at that meeting were taken to the wider membership of Bat Shalom, and it became evident that there were many women in Bat Shalom who felt that they could not live with the new principles. There were a number of resignations as a result.

This is a really fine example of a poorly handled dynamic. The situation was not set up to allow for discussion, or even for the existence of a safe space for those who disagree to express their point of view. I said earlier that often we handle conflict by not talking about things. This was different. This was a situation in which the Palestinians said: 'We need this', so the Israelis, after so many years of being the oppressor, felt that they could not disagree with what the Palestinians were asking for. I think that in America in debates over race relations this is called 'white guilt'. We felt unable to make legitimate counter-proposals. In separate meetings, the Israelis spoke of bringing to the Palestinians some suggestions for compromise wording, and we did. But as soon as each suggestion was raised, there was initial resistance on the part of some Palestinian women – the younger, more extremist ones – so the Israelis immediately backed down without a full discussion. I blame the Israelis for not being more honest, more open. Instead, we were constantly backing down against real or even imagined Palestinian objections. There was no real engagement on those issues. To this day, the matter of the principles has not been resolved.

Maybe an example will help. Both sides knew that we had to make a statement about how to resolve the problem of several million Palestinian refugees created by the war of 1948 – Palestinians who once lived in areas that are now Israel. The Palestinian side proposed a wording that included the sentence: 'This solution must honour the right of return of the Palestinian refugees in accordance with UN Resolution 194.' In my opinion, this resolution – passed fifty-two years ago, in 1948 – is outdated today. It would give Palestinian refugees the right to return to their former homes in Israel, thereby evicting Israeli families and compounding one injustice with another. Even my very mild suggestion that we say 'in the spirit of UN Resolution 194' rather than 'in accordance' with it was rejected. And the Israeli side did not stand up for this revision, even though many Bat Shalom members cannot live with the wording as it now stands.

I hope that following this turbulent period there will be engagement on the issues and frank discussions about what the problems are, what solutions would be agreeable to both sides. Final-status peace talks are being launched, and I want the Israeli women's peace movement to come to the Israeli politicians not with an untenable fifty-two-year-old position, but with viable, rational proposals for resolving the issues in contention.

Sumaya: For us, the Palestinians, it was very necessary that we re-evaluate and amend our principles to include certain details of the Final-Status Negotiations. We have received more and more pressure from our society to the effect that working with the Israelis is useless. But we are very clear. We want to work with you. And we push for our joint work. First, we want to show our people that we are working on very sensitive issues, and working together with the Israelis, preparing the ground for those who are the negotiators and for those who are on the street to understand what is going on in the negotiations. Second, we feel that we have been misled by the Israeli government so many times

over the past years of the peace process. The agreements that were
signed went back on those written before, and each time fewer rights
were given to us than in the previous agreement. The feeling was that
the Israelis are cheating us. You can't trust agreements with them. We
have nothing to revert to.

We need a very clear reference for our work together. We feel that
our legitimacy comes from the Oslo and UN resolutions, for example.
We feel that we need to be much more specific, so that we can count
on some rights. It is important to us that the basis for the two states
be the borders as they were on 4 June 1967, before the war broke out.
Why should we now make concessions before we begin to negotiate?
In any negotiation, both sides must make compromises. Why should we
in the Jerusalem Link begin with a compromise that benefits the Israeli
side? This is how our side viewed it. The re-evaluation of our declaration
was a kind of self-protection, self-defence in our society, but also to
initiate the discussions that we hope will begin. We wanted to include
specifics – the refugees, the settlements, Jerusalem. We also thought the
weakness of the Oslo agreements were that they did not address the
problems of the Palestinians, yet they claimed that they had brought
peace discussions to the final stages. We felt that we did not get even
a small part of the rights to which we were entitled in the previous
agreements. Thus we cannot go to the final negotiations with only 8 per
cent of the land – if earlier agreements had been honoured, we would
enter the Final-Status Negotiations with 30 per cent of the land.

This is to show you the immediate and critical necessity for re-
evaluating and amending our principles, from our point of view. I
must say frankly that it was a shock to see that this produced such
turbulence in Bat Shalom, and that its director – Gila – quit. We were
very surprised by this. Nobody could believe it. We worked together;
we expected her to understand. How could she work with us and not
share our vision of our rights? How can any individual be against the
UN resolutions? She can afford to say it because everything is settled
in her state, and its legitimacy is based on UN resolutions. But we are
now struggling so that those same resolutions should be applied to us,
and nobody can tell us they shouldn't. It was a very important discussion. The problem is that there was no room for discussion. What Gila
says is right. We wanted to amend things. But they gave up immediately,
so as not to have a dispute and to show they can work with us. Let's
show that we get along together. So we hid our disputes and real
messages again.

Letter

Gila to Sumaya

Dear Sumaya

This dialogue with you, like the many we have had in the past, has been marked by openness, honesty, and an empathetic listening, even where we disagree. I have had the feeling at all times of speaking as equals, without holding back difficult words, without making 'discounts' for the differences between us.

And yet I have also been painfully aware of the need you have to maintain distance – what the Palestinians refer to as preventing 'normalization'. Even though this has continued to sadden me, as I have longed for a 'normal' and close friendship with you, someone with whom I share so much and feel so warm towards, I know and understand that you cannot allow this to happen under the rules that you have agreed to live by. Distance is a political statement of your own, as well as protection for you against those who attack your efforts at reconciliation. I know that you need to protect yourself and your family from those voices and acts of criticism, but I ache to think how politics can come between people.

Another ache I have is the thought that you and your colleagues on the Palestinian side have not been able to understand or appreciate my decision to resign as director of Bat Shalom, based on my objection to the new principles that the Jerusalem Link adopted. You were 'shocked', you note in the interview. I do feel the need to try again to explain. Not just as someone who might have been your friend in a world that was more just, but as one who continues to be a political ally in our common cause.

Let me say at the outset that I was in complete agreement with the previous Jerusalem Link declaration. That document reflected the principles common to us all – the shared yearning of Israeli and Palestinian women for a just and enduring peace in the Middle East.

The new document, however, although it may be a suitable statement for the Palestinian side of the Jerusalem Link, does not take into consideration Israeli needs. Some of the new principles adopted are not fair to the Israeli side, in my opinion, and will alienate Bat Shalom from even the progressive elements of Israeli society that we have worked so hard to nurture and expand, including many of its own members. These new principles will weaken Bat Shalom's ability to influence political opinion, and hence political decision-making, inside Israel.

Some of the new principles return us to old conflicts, rather than lead us to new and creative solutions, to a healing of the old pain. In my opinion, the following three principles advocate positions from an earlier era which are no longer tenable:

- Principle 1 calls for 'establishment of a Palestinian state alongside Israel on the June 4, 1967 boundaries'. Calling for these borders without acknowledging the inevitability of 'adjustments agreed upon by both sides' is unrealistic. I had proposed that at the very least we insert the words 'based on' the June 4, 1967 boundaries, suggesting that amendments can be made, but this formulation was rejected.
- Principle 6 calls for solving the Palestinian refugee problem 'in accordance with UN Resolution 194'. This resolution – passed more than fifty years ago, in 1948 – is outdated and irrelevant today. For example, it would give Palestinian refugees the right to return to their former homes in Israel, thereby evicting Israeli families and compounding one injustice with another. I do believe that a just solution for the Palestinian refugee problem must include the Palestinian right of return to the area that is now Israel – for those who so choose – but I cannot agree that Israelis who currently live in these homes must now be turned into refugees.
- Finally, principle 4 notes that the permanent settlement negotiations must resume without delay (with which I certainly agree), but then adds: 'the terms of reference being all relevant UN resolutions....' I think it is absurd to invoke the 2,000 pages of UN resolutions that have been enacted since 1948 as the 'terms of reference' without a thorough reading and review of their applicability to contemporary times. Indeed, many of these resolutions foment anger and divisiveness, rather than offer constructive solutions. The previous Jerusalem

Link declaration correctly referred only to Resolutions 242 and 338, which are still the key and relevant resolutions, and did not resurrect old hurts.

These were my three main objections, and they were key matters of principle for me. You yourself saw that at the meeting where the Palestinians raised these proposals the Israelis were fearful of expressing their uneasiness with them. You saw the dynamic that was created – of going along with whatever the Palestinians said. I was the only one who consistently found the voice to speak honestly, and that is because I spoke as an equal with you, having had years of frank and fruitful dialogue. It seemed to me that the other Israelis spoke out of 'white guilt' – shame over the years of oppression by Israelis of Palestinians. The Israeli discomfort with the principles became evident only when we met separately as Bat Shalom.

Sumaya, my disappointment was with the Bat Shalom board, which consented to these principles without making any effort at all to create a statement that would be fair and relevant to our side as well as yours. Those few on the Israeli side who pushed for the new principles acted in utter disregard of the negative implications for Bat Shalom. Although their primary motivation was to provide the Palestinian side with a document that they felt was necessary for Palestinian needs, in my opinion the damage rendered to Bat Shalom will ultimately harm the Jerusalem Link.

It seems that the honesty that you and I have had as directors of the Jerusalem Link has not filtered down to our respective organizations. Perhaps because they have not had the ongoing contact with each other, as you and I have had.

This matter of the new principles and my resignation as a result often evokes in my mind the words of the Lebanese writer Kahlil Gibran: 'When your friend speaks his mind you fear not the "nay" in your own mind, nor do you withhold the "ay".'

Dear and trusted colleague, thank you for your ongoing cooperation throughout our work together. I hope that the day will come when concerns over 'normalization' and ideology will no longer prevent us from actually becoming friends.

Sincerely,

Gila Svirsky
29 January 2000

Letter

Sumaya to Gila

Dear Gila

Thank you very much for your kind words and sincere feelings in describing the relations between us, which have developed through our sensitive and hard work, the joint management of conflicts, and the growing process of our personal maturity – perceiving, learning, and ultimately acknowledging each other's positions. We have become very close, and while we share almost the same feelings, attitudes and perceptions about many points, we also have our differences – which is normal and correct – derived from our respect for the identity and uniqueness of each. Opening up and expressing our common concerns and aspirations has helped us both to understand the importance of circumstances and context when searching for solutions. The willingness to put oneself in the place of the other has made it possible sometimes to reach consensus on difficult issues. When we fail to reach consensus, it has sometimes been because of insufficient time and also an unwillingness to have intensive and comprehensive discussions. Even though we know the importance of having a frank and thorough discussion, we often avoid it because we fear confrontation. We would rather conform than confront.

Thank you, Gila, for understanding the complex issue of 'normalizing relations', which will exist as long as our peoples consider each other the enemy. Political reconciliation must precede social reconciliation. When it does, then it will be easier to meet, work jointly, and plan for a common future. But as long as one side is politically, economically and ideologically taking advantage of the other, peace work is perceived by the majority to be not just nonsense, but also dangerous. Based on their daily experience, my people believe that Israel is fulfilling Zionist ideology by acquiring as much Palestinian land as possible by force and illegal means, and aims to control our people for ever. They see Israel as engaged in a process of dictating, rather than negotiating. In peace, both sides must win; in war, both lose, although the loss of one side is greater than that of the other.

Why do I write all this to you? I know your thoughts, attitudes, humanity and desire for justice. I also know your political stand and, based on personal discussions, I understood your motives for resigning. But this does not make up for the sad feeling I have in losing you as a trusted colleague and partner. I highly respect and value your thought and character. What shocked me was your quick resignation, your setting of priorities while dealing with the matter. We are both aware of the difficulties in each centre. It had always been a relief to relate, compare and share these problems. I have the feeling that both our boards did not discuss the principles thoroughly, bringing dissatisfaction and new conflicts. Addressing disputes is the basis of our efforts to reach reconciliation. And yet we are still at the starting point, and must develop this as a valued culture to guide our behaviour.

I understand your concerns about borders, refugees and UN resolutions. This is not only a matter of principle, but also a matter of trying to convince each other. The UN resolutions are the only legal documents that Palestinians have to protect our rights. We cannot drop these resolutions before even beginning to negotiate, or receiving a sign from your side that you are prepared to acknowledge responsibility and admit guilt. I know you are far from thinking about these issues, but I feel that it is my responsibility to address the linkage between responsibility and guilt, and thus open the door to compromise. This is the basis for the first step in reconciliation. I understand your concern about not wanting to evict Israelis from the homes they now live in, the Palestinian homes from which the owners were forced to evacuate and become refugees. First admit the injustice that was committed and recognize the rights of the Palestinian refugees, so we can then find options for solving the problem. Your fear of seeing your people become refugees is respected and understood only if you prevent the creation of refugees on the Palestinian side. We two peoples have the same values! What an appreciative reaction and feeling of relief spread among my people when they read about the Israeli researcher who published an acknowledgement of the massacre of Tantura, a village near Haifa, where 200 Palestinian people were killed in 1948, and the village was destroyed. Such forms of acknowledgement open the heart and mind to rethink, reconsider, and search for solutions.

I have interest and desire to continue this dialogue with you on political issues and on a social and personal level. I feel enriched by it. The obstacle is only the accumulation of work in the office and at home. I am sure we will do it, and I am very happy to know that you will always be there to share our concern and participate in our joint mission.

Dear and trusted colleague, I also thank you for your ongoing co-operation and because I have learned a lot from you. I hope that the barriers preventing us from becoming close friends will diminish. There are not only physical walls set by law, but the psychological barriers are also still thick and diverse. On your side, you can work for peace and be proud; you will be admired and encouraged by most, even though some will reject you. On our side, my work for peace is perceived by most people with doubt, question marks, accusations, and sometimes a sense of shame. Sometimes we have to hide from or avoid public meetings and events. My work is not only difficult and sensitive, but could turn unappreciated and even dangerous.

Most painful to me is that I consider my work very important, necessary and vital for our joint survival. I believe in that, and this is what keeps me strong and gives me the strength to continue and start again and again. The main source for my strength and courage is knowing that there are hundreds of wonderful women and men on both sides who share my vision and work sincerely and with commitment. I hope that these people on both sides will become one front that grows and grows into thousands and millions. I not only hope, but I do believe that we will make it.

Sincerely,

Sumaya Farhat-Naser
3 February 2000

CHAPTER FIVE

What's in a Name? (Re)contextualizing Female Genital Mutilation

This chapter revolves around an issue that has received enormous attention from feminists throughout the world, and that remains a highly visible site for development work in Africa, the Middle East, and many countries in Europe. The three contributors to this chapter bring unique perspectives to the debate: each defends an ideological position that she links inextricably to discourse, the very choice of a word. For Molly Melching, an American-born activist in Senegal for twenty-five years, female genital cutting (FGC) is a practice that is gradually being abandoned by villages via holistic education programmes, community theatre, and a groundswell of local opposition to its continuation. For Obi Nnaemeka, a scholar–activist currently teaching in the USA, feminist activism in the area of female circumcision cannot be separated from the language – verbal, visual – in which the issue is framed, and the wider context of Western imperialism. Finally, for French lawyer Linda Weil-Curiel, female genital mutilation (FGM) is a crime of child abuse, requiring sanction and punishment by law in her home country. All three agree in theory that female genital cutting should come to an end; but each develops different practices for the achievement of such a shared goal.

Abandoning Female
Genital Cutting in Africa

Molly Melching

A well-known children's story describes the competition one day between the sun and the wind when they saw a man walking along the
road. 'I am sure that I can make that man take off his coat sooner than
you', said the wind. 'Fine! Go ahead and try, and we'll see who wins!'
replied the sun. The wind blew and blew with all his might, but the man
merely pulled his coat tighter and tighter around him. The wind blew
stronger and stronger, but the man only wrapped the coat around him
more to keep it from blowing off. 'Let me try now', said the smiling
sun. With much gentleness, the sun beamed warm rays of sunlight down
on the man walking along the road. The man loosened his grip on the
coat and soon, basking in the warm sunlight, he took off his coat.

In the West African country of Senegal, 174 villages have made the
unprecedented decision to end the harmful practice of female genital
cutting (FGC) in their communities for ever. The women, men, religious
personalities and traditional leaders of these communities organized
public declarations to share this historic decision with the Senegalese
nation and the rest of the world. No pressure came from the outside
and no force was exerted to achieve these results. Rather, the women
of the communities participated in a non-directive, holistic and rights-
based educational process implemented by the non-governmental
organization TOSTAN.

The educational programme developed by TOSTAN – which means,
literally in Wolof, breaking out of the egg – includes six basic modules
and four continued-education modules. It was developed with the
philosophy that literacy skills alone are not sufficient to prepare learners

for active participation in the social, political, economic and cultural decisions related to the development of their community, and ultimately their country. TOSTAN therefore promotes an integrated approach to learning which offers a comprehensive curriculum in national languages not only for reading, writing and maths, but also for improving the life skills and socioeconomic conditions of participants. The use of innovative pedagogical techniques inspired by African traditions and local knowledge has contributed to making the sessions relevant, lively and participatory. Themes of problem-solving, hygiene and health, leadership, management skills and democracy, help the women to analyse their situation, set goals for the future, develop critical thinking skills, find solutions to problems, and rehearse strategies for social transformation throughout the learning process – in short, it helps them achieve the breakthroughs implied by the TOSTAN name. Participants immediately link learning to action, and thus to meaningful results that compensate for hours spent in the classroom.

TOSTAN classes are also fun to attend. Reinforcing and giving value to traditional elements of African culture such as singing, dancing, theatre, music and poetry attract the women and give them confidence in their ability to participate and give voice to their concerns. Encouraging positive African skills of dialogue, mediation, and finding consensus around issues, all the while maintaining respect for the individual and the group, are effective means of inducing change from the people's own perspective. The class is thus seen as the catalyst for frank, open and, above all, peaceful dialogue between men and women, children and adults, inside and outside the classroom – dialogue previously hindered by traditional taboos and beliefs related to age and gender. In this context, women discuss strategies for positive social transformation, and find ways to bring about change within the context of their daily lives.

Problem-solving

The women and men most involved in the process of ending female genital cutting pointed out specific information they learned in the TOSTAN modules that was useful in making their decision to end the practice.

In the process of working on collective problem-solving in Module 1, the participants learned to work together to achieve a common goal. They often referred to this process as helpful in organizing their ideas and activities. In the first village that declared an end to FGC, Malicounda

Bambara, the women had already used it to carry out village hygiene activities, to solve problems with their village facilitator, and to create a soap-making project for the class. As they were planning social mobilization activities on FGC in their village, the women tried to envision possible problems (Step 3 – Planning the Solution – Obstacles). Foreseeing these obstacles helped them to avoid certain problems, and prepared them to respond with confidence when difficulties arose. The rehearsal through role-play or theatre used in class sessions helped participants to reflect on the best ways to present new ideas or decisions. They were also prepared to respond to arguments or opposition to their ideas.

The first step of the problem-solving process, problem analysis, helped women to gain insight into the importance of cause and effect. With regard to female genital cutting, they had always believed that 'bad spirits' were the cause of any health problems observed in their girls. Learning, for example, that infection after circumcision was related to other causes was a surprise to the women, but one they were capable of understanding because of their knowledge of the transmission of germs, acquired in Module 2.

The Transmission of Germs: An Essential Notion

In one Module 2 activity, a bowl of water to which perfume is added by the facilitator is passed around the class, and each woman is asked to rinse her hands in it. Although the participants admit that they can't see anything, they nonetheless know there is something else in the bowl, because they then smell the perfume on their hands. This something is like germs – invisible. Women often made the analogy to this class experiment when they were discussing how one razor blade used on several girls can transmit germs to all the other girls who are cut with the same blade.

In one Bambara village, the religious leader was opposed to the women ending the practice of FGC, and made a statement about how FGC could not be the cause of certain infections and illnesses such as AIDS, as had been insinuated by health workers. One woman who had been through the TOSTAN programme commented: 'If he had studied TOSTAN Module 2 he would understand that "the tradition" doesn't lead to the infection; it's the transmission of germs from a non-sterile razor blade from one girl to another which can lead to infection!' Germ transmission and the need for hygiene were also emphasized throughout Module 3, in the context of diarrhoea and vaccinations.

Leadership Skills and Decision-making

The leadership sessions in Module 5 helped to reinforce leadership skills among the women, and provided the opportunity to discuss the decision-making process and characteristics of good leaders within the nurturing space of the classroom. When the women stood up to defend their decision to end FGC, their confidence, determination and leadership skills were evident to all present.

The module containing the information which best helped the women in making their decision to end FGC was Module 7. Learning about their bodies, particularly the reproductive organs and the importance and interdependence of all the body systems and functions, was important in helping the women to understand better the dangers linked to genital cutting. Many of them did not realize that other women in the world are not circumcised, and even if they were aware of this, they did not know exactly what it meant. Many had no idea what normal female organs looked like, and were seeing pictures and diagrams for the first time in their lives.

The session on sexuality played a role in the women's decision to end FGC. This session turned out to be one of the most popular of the module in all villages, whether they practised FGC or not. The content helped women to understand, through discussion, that women indeed have the right to a healthy sexual life. Once again, role-play was used to help the participants practise discussing this sensitive issue with their husbands. In evaluation after evaluation, the women noted that because of Session 7 of the Module, they found ways to approach their husbands about their sexual needs for the first time. The session never mentions circumcised women specifically. However, the women who had undergone this operation realized that their sexual satisfaction might be less than that of other women.

Strategies for bringing about social transformation through organizing women's support groups and working with traditional, religious and local administrative leaders is also emphasized in many of the Module 7 sessions. Peace is a key concept in Senegalese society; therefore, it was extremely important to encourage peaceful methods of change in the village. The women felt comfortable using these strategies, because it allowed them to involve the important opinion-leaders of the community in their activities in a respectful way. Many found that the men and religious leaders were more supportive and progressive than they had imagined. In fact, the men were extremely pleased to be included in these discussions, and felt that the women were taking their viewpoints into consideration. Thus they became more open to change. This process led to new dialogue and consensus around other important issues of the community, not only FGC.

For the Module 7 sessions, TOSTAN asked the women to adopt a sister or friend (*ndey-dikke* in Wolof) with whom they would share the information learned during the module each day. This system proved highly effective, for several reasons:

- The women were motivated to write down summaries of what they learned in class, thus reinforcing their reading and writing skills as well as their own understanding of the topics.
- The experience was an empowering one for the women – in evaluations they stated that their *ndey-dikke* showed them great respect because of their new knowledge.
- Many women chose to share their information with more than just one woman, organizing small groups in the neighbourhood. In the St Louis region, the women also said that they adopted their husbands and the village religious leaders as well as a friend.
- The practice the women received in teaching the new information gave them confidence in sharing the information on a larger scale. Many participants developed themes from Module 7 at their larger women's group meetings, or held public sessions for the entire village.

Another new element of Module 7 was the effort of the TOSTAN team to include an action objective for each theme, and sometimes each session. Thus this module became more action-oriented, and the results were immediately observable in the many participating villages.

The Human Rights Education begun in Module 7 was also a powerful contributing factor in the decision to end FGC in the villages. TOSTAN began human rights education after the extensive participatory research with hundreds of women in developing Module 7 in 1994. The results of that research indicated that the women's problems related to the family, health, education, the environment, law and the economy were often due to a lack of knowledge of their rights and responsibilities, as well as of those of the community. This lack of knowledge also compromised their participation in public life. TOSTAN then decided not only to inform the village women of their rights and responsibilities but also to help them appropriate these rights. We did this by using their own stories and experiences, then providing a nurturing space where they could find solutions and help achieve desired change based on the social, cultural and economic environment in which they live.

TOSTAN believes that experience with this active human rights education has led to rapid and positive social transformation, not only in the area of ending female genital cutting but also in other areas. For example, after studying Module 8 on Early Childhood Development, which uses universal children's rights as a reference in all sessions, the women of Touba Toul recognized that they were violating their children's rights by sending their 10–12-year-old girls to work as maids in neighbouring towns: their rights to live with their parents, to education, to love and affection, to be spared from unsuitable work or not to be exploited by others, and finally the right to play. The class decided to use strategies discussed in the module to change the situation. The president of the Women's Group called for meetings in the different neighbourhoods of the village. There the women presented a play and poems on children's rights, and the negative consequences of sending children off as maids at such an early age. These were used to provoke comments, and encourage debate with other villagers. They then discussed the human rights abuses involved in this practice, making reference to specific articles violated to make more of an impact. In March 1998 they organized a special day of consciousness-raising on sending children to work as maids, inviting village leaders and local government authorities to attend and speak out on the practice. That day a communal decision was made to stop sending young girls off as maids, and a committee was elected to discourage abuses.

It is important to mention this other experience to show that the Malicounda Pledge and the Diabougou and Medina Cherif Declarations were part of a broader movement for social justice.[1] This example demonstrates the impact an entire village can make when the members of the community fully participate in the decisions which affect their lives and those of their children; when they have the skills, confidence and courage to envision and develop strategies for positive social transformation in respect of human rights norms, taking into account their own sociocultural environment.

Perhaps the most important contributions of the TOSTAN basic education to ending FGC in Senegalese villages were the methods developed by the programme which allowed the women to discuss this normally taboo issue in a non-threatening environment. In Senegal, it would seem that dialogue should be a natural aspect of an educational situation, since it is a country known for dialogue and conversational exchange. According to a well-known Wolof proverb: *Xuloo amul, ñaq waxtaan moo am* ('Fighting doesn't exist; only a lack of discussion exists'). Unfortunately, the dialogue and exchange of ideas that occur naturally in Senegalese society in the marketplace, in the home, or under the village baobab, almost never exist within the formal classroom situation.

The French educational system and Islamic religious education have both so influenced Senegalese society that the idea of education and learning is now associated with a 'master' who teaches and inculcates knowledge to learners who have the passive role of memorizing, often without the opportunity to question information received from the teacher. Over the many years during which the TOSTAN programme was developed, the most difficult pedagogical notion for trainees to comprehend and use was the right of the student, whom we called 'participant', indeed to 'participate', to speak up, to have a different viewpoint from the teacher, whom we called the 'facilitator'. Most facilitators who had received a formal education felt that they were not good teachers if they did not provide lengthy lectures. Not only were they worried about what the students' perception of them would be if they did not behave like most other teachers in the country; they were also worried about being judged negatively by outsiders coming to visit the class.

TOSTAN worked with trainers, facilitators and participants to help them discover that the participatory form of education is in fact African in origin. Sitting in a circle (as one does in a traditional African village square); allowing each person to express his or her idea (as happens in a village meeting); listening carefully and patiently to others' ideas (as is taught in traditional African education); coming to consensus through negotiation and mediation (well-known African skills) making use of the oral tradition; learning by observing and doing oneself (as is the method for traditional learning of jobs such as blacksmith, shoe-maker, or hair-braiding) are all methods that were reinforced and used in the TOSTAN training.

The TOSTAN team also strove to write sessions in such a way as to provoke discussion among participants, and to train facilitators capable of allowing class participants to work out issues among themselves in small groups or in the larger group. The practice gained in the classroom transferred to real-life situations, and the women began to participate more and more in village meetings, often speaking their minds publicly for the first time. Exchanging experiences also led to opening up to one another and gaining confidence in the other women in the class. This was essential to the process of ending FGC in participating villages.

On many occasions the women of the villages were asked how they would replace the initiation rites. 'The TOSTAN class will replace our initiation rites' was often their – significant – answer. 'The members of the class are now like the women with whom we went through initiation. We have shared ideas, experiences and secrets as we learn in the classroom, and we now have a common bond based on mutual trust. We have also seen how our lives improve when we work together for the same goal.'

Although the TOSTAN basic education programme has been essential in helping women to understand why they want to abandon FGC, TOSTAN now understands that it is not, in fact, sufficient actually to end the practice. We now believe that, in order for this to happen, a public declaration is necessary to ensure that everyone does indeed stop. Two researchers helped us to understand the importance of the public declaration – two researchers living thousands of miles apart, unfamiliar with each other's analysis of the reasons for the difficulties in ending FGC in African countries.

The first researcher was Demba Diawara, a 66-year-old religious leader and former participant in the TOSTAN Basic Education Programme from the village of Ker Simbara, whom I always introduce as having a doctorate in Wisdom and Social Transformation. Although Demba once supported the practice of FGC for the women of his village, he changed his mind after going through the TOSTAN basic education programme and attending the first declaration in Malicounda Bambara to end female genital cutting, which took place on 31 July 1997. Demba Diawara reflected on the situation of his own village, and explained that they could never do the same as Malicounda Bambara. 'Ker Simbara is small, but Ker Simbara is big. Beyond our small village are many other villages where our relatives are living. If they do not agree with our decision to end FGC, we will have insurmountable problems. Our children will not be able to marry their children. My own wife comes from those villages!' So Demba put on his shoes and walked from village to village, explaining to others why it was important to end female genital cutting. During those sessions, women stood up for the first time to reveal the sufferings they and their daughters had endured throughout their lifetime because of the 'tradition', as they themselves call it. Demba was more and more convinced of the importance of his mission. He came to see me in January 1998, and explained that his educational work was having positive results, but it was not enough: 'We must meet together now and make a communal commitment to end the practice. This must be a family decision and all must be able to voice their opinions, then stand up together and agree.' That meeting was held on 14 and 15 February 1998, and led to the first written pledge for ending FGC, called the Diabougou Declaration. Thirteen villages publicly announced

the end of FGC in their communities, with measures for enforcing the
decision decided upon by the members of these communities. The
Committees elected for that purpose have reported no cases of female
circumcision since.

It was at that time that the second researcher I mentioned contacted
me after reading an article in the *International Herald Tribune* about the
Malicounda Bambara and Diabougou Declarations. Gerry Mackie, a
researcher at Oxford University, had written an important article two
years earlier about the similarities between footbinding in China and
female genital cutting in Africa. According to Mackie, these are both
conventions:

> A peculiar characteristic of a convention such as FGC is that even if each
> individual in the relevant group comes to think that it would be better to
> abandon the practice, no one individual acting on her own can succeed.
> Every family could come to think that FGC is wrong, but that is not enough;
> FGC would continue because any family abandoning it on its own would
> ruin the futures of its daughters. Enough families must abandon it at once
> so that their daughters' futures are secured. One way to do this is to declare
> a public pledge that marks a convention shift. (Mackie 2000)

Mackie predicted in his article that FGC could be ended by using the
same strategies as the footbinding reformers in China: widespread
education followed by public pledges. This theory corroborated the
experiences of Demba Diawara and TOSTAN in the field, and helped
partners in the programme, notably UNICEF and the government of
Senegal, to grasp the importance of supporting such events.

Thus, when the TOSTAN participants in eighteen villages of Kolda
who had studied the TOSTAN Basic Education Programme requested a
meeting with surrounding villages to discuss the issue, they were given
immediate support by everyone. Representatives from these villages
announced their written pledge to end FGC on 1 and 2 July 1998 in
the presence of the media, the government, and many development
partners. All the women in those villages formerly underwent FGC,
which is practised by 88 per cent of the population on the depart-
mental level. There also, the villagers themselves formed follow-up committees to ensure that no one deviates from the communal decision. As
of September 1999, no cases of FGC have occurred in the eighteen
villages. However, the president of the Women's Group, Lala Balde, told
me about a neighboring village that had initially refused to participate
in their declaration. Unfortunately, when that village held its circumcision rites this year, one of the girls died from haemorrhaging. The

villagers then regretted not having listened to their relatives, and quickly decided to adhere to the declaration.

In our opinion, the Public Declaration has become a central and crucial aspect of ending FGC. Drawing from our own experience in Senegal, TOSTAN now believes that there are three possibilities which can lead to effective, meaningful Public Declarations to end FGC:

- The Public Declaration, which follows a non-directive basic education programme lasting two years, such as TOSTAN's, offering ten modules of learning including reading, writing and maths.

- A programme such as the Women's Empowerment Programme now being implemented in Senegal, Mali and the Sudan: after months of studying the elements of the basic education programme which, we believe, led to the ending of female genital cutting in participating villages, TOSTAN selected the subjects crucial to ending female genital cutting. This new adapted programme offers human rights training, problem-solving skills, basic hygiene and women's health over a shorter period. After seven months of village-based training for 1,848 participants in thirty villages in the region of Kolda, 92 per cent of whom were women, the results were the most positive TOSTAN has experienced in any educational or literacy programme we are aware of in Senegal. The attendance rate, with the women meeting four times a week for two to three hours a session, was 92 per cent, and in many villages 96 to 100 per cent. The dropout rate – which for most literacy programmes in West Africa averages 50 per cent – was only 6 per cent.

- The third method for achieving Public Declarations exemplified by the work of Demba Diawara involves social mobilization activities by participants in the programme and members of the same ethnic group who seek to stop the practice at the same time as their relatives. This is the case for the Diabougou Declaration and two similar declarations made in the village of Baliga on 19 and 20 June 2000, and on the island of Niodior on 7 April 2000. The Baliga Declaration was particularly significant, because it involved the leading Bambara religious leader in the village of Njassane, where Bambaras from Senegal, the Gambia and Mali come in pilgrimage every year. The family of this religious leader sent a large delegation to Baliga publicly to present Islam's position in favour of girls' and women's health. They also asked their numerous talibés or followers to stop. Thirteen villages representing approximately 11,000 people were represented at that public deliberation.

These methods for ending female genital cutting show respect and
understanding for the people involved. Trying to force change through
coercive action and condemnation has alienated people in the past, and
can be dangerous, because it causes people to cling with even greater
determination to their traditional beliefs. Many examples exist to prove
the ineffectiveness of such an approach. A law against FGC is helpful
only after people have gone through a process of non-directive education, and truly understand the risks involved in the practice. It is our
conviction that with the implementation of empowering educational
programmes for millions of villagers in African countries where FGC is
practised, followed by Public Declarations, there is an unprecedented
reason to have great hopes for a rapid and universal end to FGC in the
coming years.

Update

Over a hundred villages declare an end to FGC in Kolda,
27–28 November 1999

Thousands of villagers from 105 communities in Kolda, the southern
region of Senegal, gathered to participate in the biggest Public Declarations to end female genital cutting to date in Africa. Men, women
and children arrived on 27 November 1999 in the village of Bagadadji,
piled in the back of huge trucks or packed into local transport vans.
Many walked for miles to witness this historic celebration, marking the
end of an ancient, traditional practice which has harmed and killed
countless girls and women throughout the centuries. Lively traditional
Fulani musicians, singers and dancers performed throughout the night
as women ran one by one into the middle of an enormous circle,
pounding their feet, flinging their arms and chanting to the rhythm of
the drums. A mood of community and purpose permeated the atmos-
phere as people anticipated the forthcoming morning ceremony.

Thirty of these 105 villages recently participated in TOSTAN's Village
Empowerment Programme which includes themes on Human Rights,
Problem-solving, Basic Hygiene and Women's Health, over an eight-
month period from February to October 1999. This programme was
implemented by TOSTAN in collaboration with the local NGO, OFAD/
NAFOORE, and financed by CEDPA through the PROWID/USAID Washington project.

The crucial decision to end female genital cutting emerged from the
villagers' own initative. During the training period, the women shared
the information they learned with their families and other members of

the community, but also went to neighbouring villages to discuss issues of health and human rights. By the end of the programme, sixty villages had made important changes to improve the health and well-being of all members of their community, such as ending violence against women and children, vaccinating children and pregnant women, using local health facilities more frequently, and practising family planning. Perhaps the villagers' most important decision was to end female genital cutting, practised at a rate of 97 per cent before the programme began. OFAD/NAFOORE requested assistance from TOSTAN, CEDPA and UNICEF in organizing a public communal declaration to announce the decision of the sixty villages. When other members of their organization learned of the forthcoming declaration, they called village meetings, and forty-five additional communities joined this grassroots movement for the promotion of girls' and women's health.

Twenty-seven journalists from Dakar and regional radio stations around the country arrived in Kolda on Saturday 27 November and visited Ngoki, a participating village, to talk with the women's class. The participants explained how knowing about their right to be protected from all forms of violence and their right to health helped them to make their important decision. They also spoke of the health problems associated with FGC, and their firm commitment never to allow cutting to take place again within their community. One woman talked about how her young granddaughter had died from the operation two years ago, and how she had known then that it was simply wrong to continue: 'The programme has saved me', she explained, 'because now everyone agrees and is stopping as a community.' The women sang a song about human rights, and the responsibility they now have in protecting the health of their daughters: 'We women have endured needless suffering; we women now must take a stand. We will be firm and never go back to this practice of pain.' One of the journalists asked the women what they thought of one religious leader's decision to oppose the end of FGC, particularly in the northern region of Senegal. The president of the class responded: 'Well, I don't know of this religious leader you are speaking of, but I would say that he doesn't know of the suffering we women undergo related to the practice of female circumcision. I would suggest he talk to women about this matter and then I am sure he would change his mind.'

The local religious leader of the area, Dr Oumar Balde (holder of a doctorate in Islamic Civilization from the Sorbonne in Paris), met the journalists on the Saturday afternoon to explain his support for the forthcoming declaration. 'FGC has nothing whatsoever to do with Islam', he explained to the attentive group. 'I have ended the practice in my family, and feel that it is a tradition which should be abandoned by everyone throughout Senegal.'

On the Sunday morning, a delegation including the Governor of the Region of Kolda, the President of the Regional Council, the Prefect of Kolda, five Deputies from the National Assembly, including the Vice-President of the National Assembly and the Head of the Population and Development Network, the Representative of the Ministry of the Family, Social Action and National Solidarity, representatives from the Ministries of Health, Community Development and Education, TOSTAN, UNICEF, the Director of the International Child Development Centre for Children in Florence, Italy, representatives from CEDPA Washington, USAID Washington, USAID Senegal, the Population Council and the Belgian Embassy, as well as traditional and religious leaders from the area, National Television, Peace Corps Volunteers, representatives from former declarations in Diabougou, Baaliga and Medina Cherif, and journalists, arrived to a joyous welcome by the local Fulani traditional instrumental and dance groups. Approximately 2,500 people were present to represent the 80,000 villagers in 105 villages affected by this decision.

Several key figures active in the decision to end FGC from the Region of Kolda addressed the assembly. The President of OFAD gave the welcoming speech for OFAD and TOSTAN and explained the process that led to this important day. A TOSTAN programme participant spoke of the extraordinary impact the education class had made in her village. As a former cutter, she described with emotion why she decided to give up her lifelong means of income, and end the practice of FGC in order to preserve the health of girls and women. The Head Doctor for the Region of Kolda powerfully communicated the dangerous health consequences of FGC, and gave the example of a young girl recently brought into the regional hospital bleeding profusely following the traditional cutting ceremony. The girl died. Dr Oumar Balde addressed the assembly, and was unequivocal in his opposition to a practice which has such negative health dangers for young girls and women. The guests at the ceremony also awarded 907 diplomas to the president of each of the thirty classes.

The declaration to end FGC, written and approved in consensus by the 105 villages, was read by a woman village participant in Fulani, then in French:

Today, the 28th of November 1999, we 105 villages [the entire list of villages followed in the original statement] for ever renounce the practice of female genital cutting as of this same day in the presence of our religious and traditional leaders. The negative consequences this practice has on the health of girls and women, as well as the opinion and advice of religious leaders and human rights militants, encouraged us in making this decision. We have furthermore taken all measures necessary to ensure a total and sustainable respect of this decision.

We thus announce our firm commitment to disseminate this decision not only in our own communities, but throughout the country and even throughout the world. We also pay homage to the pioneer communities who began this movement.

We would like to thank the media for the important role they have continued to play in informing the populations on the problems linked to the practice of female circumcision. We thank the trainers in the programme for their personal commitment and all the work they have carried out to promote women's health.

We thank the Government of Senegal and particularly the Ministry of the Family, of Social Action, and National Solidarity, the Ministries of Health and Education, OFAD/NAFOORE, TOSTAN–UNICEF, CEDPA, USAID, and all our other development partners.

We ask to benefit rapidly from:

- The opening of other basic education centres to deepen our knowledge on human rights, and the promotion of women and children's health.
- Appropriate technology to alleviate women's work and help them attend classes.
- Health huts to better respect our right to health.

Lastly, we pray God that our decision will be an inspiration to other communities across the world. Yesterday there was one village, then there were ten, today there are more than 100, tomorrow there will be millions of us in Senegal and across Africa who seek to preserve and assure the well-being of all people.

The Bagadadji Public Declaration was given wide media coverage, particularly on regional radio stations in areas where FGC is practised. Full-page coverage of the event appeared in four daily newspapers. On 30 November, a television report on the 8 p.m. and 10 p.m. national news led to widespread discussion of the event, and both TOSTAN and OFAD received numerous calls from around the country expressing astonishment at the number of people who had decided publicly to renounce this ancient practice and celebrate their courageous decision with the rest of the world. TOSTAN and OFAD have already received more than two hundred requests from other neighbouring villages to benefit from the education programme.[2]

Notes

1. Public Declarations of 282 Villages for the Abandonment of Female Genital Cutting in Senegal:

31 July 1997   The women of MALICOUNDA BAMBARA (Region of Thies) announce their decision to end FGC following the TOSTAN–UNICEF non-formal education programme.

6 November 1997   The community of NGUERIGNE BAMBARA (Region of Thies) makes the decision to abandon the practice of FGC following the TOSTAN–UNICEF non-formal education program.

15 February, 1998   Eleven villages from the Bambara ethnic group decide to end the practice of FGC at the DIABOUGOU declaration (Regions of Thies and Fatick) following social mobilization activities and the TOSTAN programme.

1–2 June 1998   Representatives from eighteen Pulaar and Mandinka villages publicly declare an end to FGC at MEDINA CHERIF (Region of Kolda) following the TOSTAN–UNICEF non-formal education programme.

20 June 1999   Public declaration of twelve Bambara villages to abandon FGC at Baliga (Region of Thies) following social mobilization activities and the TOSTAN–UNICEF programme.

28 November 1999 Public declaration of 105 Pulaar and Mandinka villages at BAGADADJI (Region of Kolda) to abandon FGC following the TOSTAN programme (CEDPA funding) and social mobilization activities.

7 April 2000   Public pledge in NIODIOR of representatives of twenty-six islands of the Sine-Saloum River (Serrere Niominka ethnic group) to end FGC following social mobilization activities and the TOSTAN programme.

25 March 2001   Public pledge of 108 Pulaar and Mandinka villages of the Rural Community of MAMPATIM (Region of Kolda) to abandon FGC, end early marriage and promote family planning following the TOSTAN–UNICEF programme and social mobilization activities.

2. The Niodor Declaration to Abandon Female Genital Cutting – involving men and women from twenty-six islands in the Sine-Saloum River in Senegal – followed on 7 April 2000. Experimental programmes based on the TOSTAN model are currently being launched in Mali and the Sudan, funded by the Wallace Global Fund.

References

All reported quotations, with the exception of the reference to Gerald Mackie, are from conversations recorded by the Director of TOSTAN.

Mackie, G. (2000) 'Female Genital Cutting: The Beginning of the End', in B. Shell-Duncan and Y. Hernlund, eds, *Female Circumcision in Africa: Culture, Controversy, and Change*, Boulder, CO, and London: Lynne Rienner.

If Female Circumcision Did Not Exist, Western Feminism Would Invent It [1]

Obioma Nnaemeka

Development and Its Discontents:
Human Rights without Human Dignity

Iji nma, jide ji./You have the knife and the yam.

(Igbo proverb)

Ngwelenine makpu amakpu na amaro nke afo nalu/Because all lizards lie on their stomach, it's difficult to know which one has a bellyache.

(Igbo proverb)

Despite the billions of dollars purportedly spent in the past four decades to develop Africa and her peoples, many parts of Africa are worse off than before. The failure lies not so much in the fact that Africans are not 'developable' but, rather, in the mythology of development itself – mythology in the Barthesian sense of the word: a lie, a cover-up. Indeed, the irony of the development enterprise is that an intervention intended to herald and maintain progress has, to a large extent, become a clog in the wheel of progress. To move forward, an archaeology of the mythology of development is pertinent, imperative and urgent. Vincent Tucker ably engages with such an archaeology in his essay 'The Myth of Development: A Critique of Eurocentric Discourse' that unmasks the 'cover-up' called development:

> Development is the process whereby other peoples are dominated and their destinies are shaped according to an essentially Western way of conceiving and perceiving the world. The development discourse is part of an imperial process whereby other peoples are appropriated and turned into objects. It is an essential part of the process whereby the 'developed' countries manage,

control and even create the Third World economically, politically, sociologically and culturally. It is a process whereby the lives of some peoples, their plans, their hopes, their imaginations, are shaped by others who frequently share neither their lifestyles, nor their hopes, nor their values. The real nature of this process is disguised by a discourse that portrays development as a necessary and desirable process, as human destiny itself. (Tucker 1999: 1–2)

The language of development is the language of necessity and desirability (the so-called Third World needs and must have 'development') and, by implication, the language of the indispensability and relevance of those who believe it is their prerogative to make development happen. It is the language of those who 'have the knife and the yam' (as my people say). But the illusion of indispensability carries in its articulation the seed of resistance – the resistance of those for whom development is manufactured as a panacea. It is in this respect that the issue of female circumcision has become one of the contested terrains in development discourse and engagement. The disagreement is not about the urgent need to put an end to a harmful practice – most people (both Africans and non-Africans) agree that the practice must end. The resistance from Africans is not necessarily against the termination of the practice; rather, it is against the strategies and methods (particularly their imperialistic underpinnings) used to bring about this desirable goal. The resistance is against 'an imperial process whereby other peoples are appropriated and turned into objects' (Tucker 1999: 1) – exhibited, viewed and silenced.

The danger of globalization lies in its unidirection and hegemony, which dam the multiplicity of voices (particularly voices of disadvantage and resistance) and create wider divides at all levels – class, gender, racial, economic, digital, and so on. Globalization and the internationalization of African women's issues have produced a recontextualization and rearticulation of such issues. For example, about two decades or so ago, female circumcision was addressed primarily as a health issue, and the question of widowhood practices in Africa was addressed largely as an economic issue (specifically because of their economic impact on widows). The past decade has increasingly witnessed the tendency to herd all categories of suffering into one battlefield: human rights. 'Human rights' has become the mantra for all the *causes célèbres* generated in recent times; it has become a cure-all for all African women's problems. Not surprisingly, international human rights documents – conventions, protocols, and so forth – proliferate reports, essays and books on African women produced inside and outside Africa.

To mobilize Africa against female circumcision, many have called on African governments and organizations (the OAU, for example) to live up to the spirit and letter of the international human rights documents – the Convention on the Elimination of All Forms of Discrimination against Women (CEDAW), for example – to which they are signatories, or to adhere to the spirit and letter of their respective constitutions. One critic is quick to remind Nigerians that

> Chapter IV of the Constitution of Nigeria delineates the 'fundamental rights' of Nigerian citizens. It states that '[e]very individual is entitled to respect for the dignity of his person, and accordingly – no person shall be subjected to torture or inhuman or degrading treatment.' In light of the explicit language in these provisions, Nigerians need look no further than their own constitution for injunction against female circumcision as violation of women's and children's constitutional rights.[2]

Well said. But the question of 'respect for the dignity of his person' and that of 'degrading treatment' must be addressed fully. Indeed, the word 'dignity' is at the core of all the basic human rights documents that have emerged from the United Nations since its formation over fifty years ago. The very first sentence of the Universal Declaration of Human Rights (1948) contains the word 'dignity': '[w]hereas recognition of the inherent dignity and of the equal inalienable rights of all members of the human family is the foundation of freedom, justice and peace in the world.' The very first sentence of the oft-cited 1981 Convention on the Elimination of All Forms of Discrimination against Women (CEDAW) includes the word 'dignity': 'Noting that the Charter of the United Nations reaffirms faith in fundamental human rights, in the dignity and worth of the human person and in the equal rights of men and women' (Center for the Study of Human Rights 1996: 1).

Female circumcision has been condemned as a 'torture' or 'degrading treatment' that shows lack of 'respect for the dignity' of women and girls. And it should be. Unfortunately, some of the most egregious manifestations of 'degrading treatment' and lack of 'respect for dignity' lie in the *modus operandi* of many Westerners (feminists and others) who have intervened in this matter. The resistance of African women is not against the campaign to end the practice, but against their dehumanization, and the lack of respect and dignity shown to them in the process. For the Western interventionists and insurgents to lay claim to any credibility and legitimacy, they must first of all put respect and dignity back where they belong. In my view, the ultimate violence done to African women is the exhibition of their body parts – in this instance, the vagina – in various stages of 'unbecoming'. This acute voyeuristic inclination would have fizzled out if the victim had been Western.[3] What is good for the goose is also good for the gander! It is not necessary to violate African women in order to address the violence that was done to them. In effect, African women are doubly victimized: first from within (their culture) and second from without (their 'saviours').

The images (as photographs) of African and Muslim women in books, magazines and films about circumcision are disturbing at best, and downright insulting at worst. A couple of examples will suffice – the first is explicit; the second is more subtle. Not too long ago, I received an e-mail offering me a book on circumcision that had just been published. I acquiesced, and a couple of weeks later the book, titled *The Day Kadi Lost Part of Her Life* (Rioja and Manresa 1998), was in my postbox. After reading the book and looking at the pictures, I retitled it: 'The Day Westerners Lost All of Their Mind'! A promotional insert in the book reads as follows:

> We 'meet' Kadi on the morning she is to be circumcised when she is still blissfully ignorant of what is about to happen to her. We see her at home, going about her daily chores, eating her breakfast and then accompany her on the journey to the village where the operation is to take place. Photos depict the sacrifice of a chicken as precursor to her own circumcision and then witness as Kadi is taken by the 'buankisa' (circumciser), made to undress, held down and then cut. While the photographs are very confronting, they are portrayed with sensitivity and delicacy, yet evoke sadness and anger, which we hope will serve to rally readers against this practice. (Rioja and Manresa 1998: no folio)

This book – which, incidentally, was short-listed for the Australian Awards for Excellence in Educational Publishing – gives a bad name to 'sensitivity and delicacy'. The book is replete with photos of Kadi (this poor girl from a nameless African country) in different states of undress – the most disconcerting being the pictures where she is held down (legs spread out) by the emaciated legs of an old woman, and screaming her head off as her clitoris and a razor are held in full view for the reader. The photos come with captions such as:

> With the first incision, Kadi's screams cut the heavy air of the sky, threatening a storm. The *buankisa's* hands are covered with blood, again…. The pain is unbearable and Kadi fears the incision will never end….

> The strength of the old woman is insufficient against the instinctive reactions of Kadi's pain, and the cuts of the razor, used on each girl until the point of bluntness, are repeated despite her movement. (Rioja and Manresa 1998: no folio)

In fact, in the picture that carries this last caption, the child that is being cut does not look like Kadi (although the name is ascribed to her) – she's much younger and has more baby fat than Kadi – and the hands circumcising her are different from the ones circumcising Kadi. This observation may seem minor or insignificant, but it certainly plays a role in revealing the making of 'Kadi', on behalf of whom money will be raised (like other Kadis who have been used to swell bank accounts). The reader is reminded in the promotional insert that '*part* of the proceeds of profits' (my emphasis) will go to FORWARD – the Foundation for Women's Health, Research and Development. (Like other 'development' promotional materials before it, this insert is silent on where the bulk of the proceeds go.)

This choreographed text (like most such texts) is presented to us as a chance meeting of two journalists from Spain who stumbled into Africa with cameras and films to '"meet" Kadi on the morning she is to be circumcised'. This may not be as fortuitous as one is led to believe. The text was written by Isabel Ramos Rioja, editor of *La Vanguardia* newspaper, and the photographs are by Kim Manresa, who has won many photojournalism awards, some of which were probably given to him for taking photographs of little girls' clitorises in Africa. 'Kadi's' predicament is cause for concern, but so should be that of the emaciated, hungry-looking old woman who is holding her down. Fortunately, Manresa's camera documents a wider and more complex landscape: Kadi and the context (human and material) of her existence. Unfortunately, the book, in its articulation, ignores the complexity of the context and focuses instead on Kadi's clitoris and the razor that eliminates it. So goes the mythology of circumcision as it is thrust on to the international stage. So are the decontextualization and banalization of African women's lives as they take centre stage in the narratives of feminist insurgence against female circumcision.

It is no secret that Westerners and Western media organizations have offered money, and used all sorts of coercion, to have girls circumcised so that Westerners could shoot pictures for their magazines, newspapers, books and documentaries. Pratibha Parma's account of the encounter with Bilaela in Gambia is instructive:

> Our first meeting with Bilaela went badly. I felt cheated and upset that she had not been straightforward. We'd made a monetary agreement by phone from London, which I'd confirmed in writing by fax.... Bilaela now says she has spent all the money we had allocated.... I am afraid Bilaela thinks we are like the crew members from a major US television network who were here three weeks ago. According to Bilaela, they had plenty of money,

stayed in five-star hotels, and had many rest days by the pool and on the beach. Bilaela was the American crew's local liaison, and apparently had problems getting the money they owed her and thinks we are probably not going to pay her either. Bilaela said…that if we were willing to pay for some girls to be excised, she could arrange for us to film it. She said she'd done that for the New York crew. (Walker and Parma 1993: 161–2)

And these voyeurs want me to believe that they are fighting for the human rights and dignity of African females! The role that money, the politics of poverty, and the politics of the belly play in these campaigns and interventions demands extensive research. In the so-called Third World, poverty makes people more vulnerable and exploitable.[4] Such vulnerabilities cast a shadow on the authenticity of claims about 'Third World' 'collaborators'.

In March 1999, Germany was hit by a barrage of billboard announcements developed by the advertising agency Young & Rubicam for the German-based organization (I)NTACT, whose main focus is the campaign against female circumcision. (I)NTACT used what Young & Rubicam produced to: '(1) Inform the public about FGM; (2) to make known the organization (I)NTACT; and (3) to stimulate giving' (Levin in Nnaemeka and Ezeilo). There are four announcements, each of which has a picture of an object: an old, rusty, crooked, bloodstained knife; a long threaded needle; a rusty, bloodstained pair of scissors; and a rusty, bloodstained razor. Tobe Levin, a dedicaed feminist advocate for the end of female circumcision, translates the German inscriptions on the announcements as follows:

Above the scissor, for example, subway passengers can read: 'Whoever thinks about cutting hair has never seen the eyes of a child who, without anesthesia, is having its clitoris cut out.' Above the needle, bus riders can read: 'Whoever thinks about darning socks has never held the trembling hands of a baby whose vagina was sewn up.' Above the knife, pedestrians can read: 'Whoever thinks about peeling potatoes has never experienced the torment of a bride whose vagina is cut open on her wedding night.' Above the razor blade, motorists can read: 'Whoever thinks about shaving has never heard the screams of a four-year-old whose labia are being cut off.' Under all four objects is written: 'Each year worldwide two million girls and women are mutilated, physically and spiritually, as a result of circumcision. (I)NTACT helps.' With thousands of posters attracting attention throughout the nation, the action has inspired hundreds of newspaper articles, a swollen treasury, and not a little criticism from African women. (Levin in Nnaemeka and Ezeilo)

(I)NTACT's effort is supposedly intended as a counterpoint to the prevailing exposure of African and Muslim women's genitalia. However, even this 'kinder, gentler' and subtle version is devastating in its com-modification (African females are pushed as one would push detergent, toothpaste or shaving cream in a television commercial). Obviously, the language, the disturbing parallels and troubling juxtapositions are in-tended to attract attention and shock readers/viewers into opening their wallets to (I)NTACT. It worked: (I)NTACT laughed all the way to the bank.

Renaming to Misname:
Strategies against Voice and Resistance

> If you want to see the way that the world has treated the Igbo man, look at the names his children bear. (Chinua Achebe)
>
> It is not what you call me, it is what I answer to. (Igbo proverb)
>
> Until the lion has a voice, the tales of the hunt will be only those of the hunter. (Eritrean proverb)

Censorship, as an imposition of silence on others, works in different ways. In the debate about female circumcision, the tactic of renaming to misname and silence has been deployed to marginalize voices which are making legitimate arguments against the pitfalls and wrongheaded-ness of Western-driven campaigns against female circumcision. African women who have objected to the *modus operandi* of the Western insurgents have been labelled, indicted and dismissed as defenders of female cir-cumcision. The Western-inspired name game that obfuscates the real issues in this matter is the type of diversion that the campaign to bring an end to female circumcision does not need. Many years ago, a con-ference on women responding to racism was held in Connecticut, USA. One of the participants, Audre Lorde, exposed the renaming-to-misname tactic used by the local print media:

> Women responding to racism is a topic so dangerous that when the local media attempt to discredit this conference they choose to focus upon the provision of lesbian housing as diversionary device – as if the *Hartford Courant* dare not mention the topic chosen for discussion here, racism, lest it become apparent that women are in fact attempting to examine and to alter all the repressive conditions of our lives. (Lorde 1984: 128)

Renaming to misname (changing the subject) has been used by anti-abortion advocates in the USA to put pro-choice activists on the defensive – a tactic that is tantamount to censorship and resistance to self-affirmation and self-determination. The abortion debate in the USA has intensified with the shifts in the language to articulate it, primarily owing to the entrenched ideological positions and profound ethical questions that have been injected into it as polarizing factors. The naming and renaming of the combatants in this bitterly contested terrain – from pro-abortion/anti-abortion to pro-choice/pro-life – is instructive. Claiming to be sole custodians of life, pro-lifers cast voices of opposition as anti-life ('baby-killers'), thus putting the pro-choice advocates in the difficult position of spending time and energy to defend themselves against a name they did not call themselves and, at the same time, assert that pro-choice and pro-life are not mutually exclusive.

Female circumcision has also been thrust into the name game – from gruesome sexual castration and female genital mutilation to the 'kinder and gentler' female genital surgeries, and now female genital cutting. But in this instance, one must not underestimate the impact of the renaming for people (Africans) whose cultures attach an importance to naming so profound that ceremonies are performed to mark it. From people, like Alice Walker, who have labelled African cultures 'mutilating cultures' (Walker and Parma 1993: 73), to the German Bundestag, which declared in a 1998 multi-party motion that 'the term 'circumcision' shall no longer be used by the government', Westerners are quick to appropriate the power to name, while remaining totally oblivious of and/or insensitive to the implications and consequences of the naming. In this name game, although the discussion is about African women, the subtext of the barbarism of African and Muslim cultures, and the relevance (even indispensability) of the West in purging the barbaric flaw, mark another era where colonialism and missionary zeal determined what 'civilization' was, and figured out how and when to force it on people who did not ask for it. Only imperialist arrogance can imagine what Africans want, determine what they need, and devise ways to deliver the goods.

The relevance or indispensability of the West in African affairs thrives on the availability of problems and crises. If the problems are not there, they are kept alive in our collective consciousness through imaginings, speculations, manufacture and reinvention. Western fascination with African women's *body parts* and sexuality has a long history. In 1810, Sara Baartman – a 20-year-old Khoi San woman – was taken from her home in South Africa to London to be exhibited as a freak of nature, because of her larger-than-'normal' (by European standard) buttocks. In 1814, when the British had had an eyeful, they shipped poor Sara to France, where the French used her for 'scientific research' until her death in 1815. The 'scientific research' continued after her death, with her body parts – sexual organs and brain – displayed in the Musée de l'Homme in Paris for one hundred and seventy years. In the nineteenth century, the problem was the African woman's buttocks. The current debate is about another body part – the vagina. Indeed, Alice Walker dedicated her novel *Possessing the Secret of Joy* to the offended body part: 'This Book Is Dedicated With Tenderness and Respect To the Blameless Vulva.' Who knows what the next body part for discussion will be! Ultimately, the circumcision debate is about the construction of the African woman as the 'Other'. The title of this essay seeks to capture the inventions and reinventions.

But naming, renaming and misnaming have their impetus, goals and consequences. During the apartheid regime, for example, naming and renaming of people based on shades of skin colour was linked to the right to vote or disenfranchisement. Not much is accomplished by substituting what the people who engage in the practice under discussion call it – female circumcision – with 'female genital mutilation' except to (1) exhibit the arrogant claim to the power to name;[5] (2) justify the indictment and opprobrium heaped on Africa and the Muslim world; and (3) create the urgency necessary for effective fund-raising. Indeed, the third reason relates also to the number of circumcised African women that is floated around: over a hundred million. What we have not been told is whether the hundred million were circumcised in one year, ten years, or since Africa and Africans came into existence. As far as I know, when the statistics of people murdered in the USA or women raped in Germany are given, the time period is specified – usually a six-month or one-year period. More importantly, we are often reminded that in Africa female circumcision is such a taboo subject that people are hesitant to talk about it. If people are silent on the issue, who provided the figures for circumcised African women that are floated around? In my view, it makes no difference if two, three, or a trillion African females are circumcised. If one is circumcised, it is one too many. The point I am raising here is that of trust between the helper and the 'helped'. Trust among collaborators, and between giver and recipient, is the most important ingredient in fashioning meaningful change with regard to female circumcision and similar campaigns. During their 1993 two-week whirlwind tour crisscrossing the Senegambia region for their documentary *Warrior Marks*, Alice Walker and Pratibha Parma came to grips on a few occasions with the issue of trust/mistrust and its consequences. Pratibha Parma notes with disappointment and frustration her unsuccessful interview with Madame Fall:

> After all the waiting, the interview turned out to be a great disappointment. In our previous conversations, Madame Fall had spoken of the joys of sex,

how important it was to her, how circumcision took this pleasure from women. She had laughed, had been informative, entertaining, persuasive. None of this occurred in our filmed interview, and none of our promptings produced what we were looking for. Instead, she talked about her 'leader' and the political party she belonged to. Fortunately, the interviews with the two sisters were inspiring. One of the sisters said, 'you cannot ever come to terms with pain.' (Parma and Walker 1993: 207)

Obviously, Madame Fall did not trust Pratibha Parma and her group enough to give them 'what [they] were looking for'. More important, Parma and company are not interested in what Madame Fall wanted to talk about – politics. This encounter reveals some of the salient issues at the core of the debate about and campaign against female circumcision – the unequal power relations between the West and the so-called Third World; the reduction of the myriad issues facing African women to female circumcision; the reduction of the complexity and totality of the African woman to the clitoris; the objectification and silencing of African women; the obsessions, prejudices and deafness of the West.[6] Parma and her group came to Africa in search of Africa. Their documentary was already made before they set foot on African soil. Any African whose interests, concerns and priorities ran contrary to the group's already-made documentary (in their heads) was irrelevant, and what he/she had to say was worthless. African women see and live their lives in ways that are much more complex than the obsessive one-dimensional and one-issue-oriented depictions that appear in books and films about female circumcision.

People name themselves and things in their environment for specific reasons and particular purposes. Africans do. TOSTAN, a Senegal-based non-governmental organization (NGO) that has accomplished huge successes in its campaign against female circumcision (see Molly Melching's essay in this chapter), calls ending the practice 'abandonment', not the popularly used 'eradication'. The former term has specific meaning for the people on behalf of whom TOSTAN has launched its campaign. To insist that TOSTAN use the 'accepted' latter term instead of the term that works for the communities it serves will certainly undermine the work of the NGO. 'Abandonment' makes sense if one examines closely the context in which female circumcision occurs. In Ivory Coast,[7] female circumcision is performed in a hut during initiation ceremonies. But what goes on in the hut is much more than female circumcision. Young girls are taught hygiene, sex education, and other lessons of life they need. Outsiders who demand that the 'circumcision hut' be destroyed meet with resistance from the community. The com-

munity is not resisting because they can no longer circumcise their
girls due to the demolition of the hut; they are resisting because the
destruction of the hut will mean the erasure of all the educational
activities that occur in it. What the local NGOs did, with government
support, was to argue for the retention of the hut minus one activity
(female circumcision) that takes place in it. This seems to me to mark
the difference between 'abandonment' and 'eradication'. One can 'abandon' one aspect (female circumcision) of the context without 'eradicating' the entire context (the hut). Also, by renaming female circumcision
'female genital mutilation' in which knives, razors and other instruments are used, Westerners have inadvertently narrowed the field of
struggle. Little do they know that female circumcision is not always
about knives and razors. There are communities that use hot water to
numb the clitoris. I am – in collaboration with an Africa-based NGO
– in the midst of a campaign against this practice. The communities
will remain nameless for fear of the spectacle of Westerners rushing off
with cameras to these communities in search of women with buckets
of hot water to photograph and/or dispossess.[7]

In Search of Solutions: A Question of Method

Those who fight against circumcision have always blamed it on 'tradition'
and 'culture' and, consequently, have proceeded to exorcize Africa's and
Islam's past. Tradition is not about a reified past; it is about a dynamic
present – a present into which the past is trajected, and to which other
traditions (with their past and present) are linked. It is to the present,
and to how we as members of local and global communities are implicated in creating and maintaining traditions, that we must respond.
Pratibha Parma worries about the 'return' to a reified tradition in
nationalist movements, and its nefarious consequences for women:

> the worrying and dangerous tendency in cultural nationalist movements,
> which in their bid to return to traditional values deny women their free
> agency. It is women who bear the brunt of these patriarchal traditions. For
> instance, women in Iran have been forced to put back the veil in the Islamic
> drive for a return to traditional values. While a sense of cultural nationalism
> is often crucial to the fight for self-determination, this should not be at the
> expense of half the nation's population! (Parma and Walker 1993: 213)

But two decades ago, in her preface to The Hidden Face of Eve, Nawal El
Saadawi wrote a more probing analysis of the rise of Islamic fundamentalism and its manifestations (for example, the upsurge in the use of
the veil) in the Arab world in general, and Iran in particular (El Saadawi

1980). In her analysis, Saadawi linked the rise of fundamentalism to foreign – particularly American – intervention in the region. This intervention, the ousting of the Shah, the return of Ayatolla Khomeini, and the rise of Islamic fundamentalism are linked. In this instance, as in others, 'traditional values' and 'these patriarchal traditions' (according to Parma) are invoked by internal forces purportedly to protect the inside from the outside. Foreign intervention, therefore, becomes an alibi for enforcing and justifying repression within. In the final analysis, women become pawns in the struggle between repressive, authoritarian internal forces and external imperialistic forces. What is at issue here is our collective responsibility for the so-called traditional practices. Unfortunately, those who have invented globalization are quick to grab the benefits, but renege on the responsibilities.

The problem with this circumcision *business* is that many Westerners who plunge into it do so thoughtlessly. It is not sufficient to read about female circumcision, then quit your job, set up shop, and raise tons of money 'to save young girls from being mutilated'. Of course there are many who are thoughtful and genuinely committed. But as my people say, 'Because all lizards lie on their stomach, it's difficult to know which one has a bellyache.' At any rate, a noble, thoughtless cause is a dangerous oxymoron. To combat female circumcision, we must first diagnose the problem; and to do that effectively we must ask questions (lots of questions); we must have a sense of history; we must have the humility to learn (not to teach); we must have the capacity to listen (not to preach). In 'dialogues' between Africa and the West, one party is listening and not speaking; the other party is garrulous and deaf. Not only do such 'dialogues' not promote social change; they undermine attempts to bring genuine social transformation. One of the most memorable graffiti I read at the University of Minnesota as a graduate student was the following exchange between two students – First student: 'Jesus is the answer.' Second student: 'What was the question?' Many Western insurgents against female circumcision have all the answers, but ask no questions. But we *must* ask questions: why *was* circumcision done and, more importantly, why is it still done? Why is it no longer done in certain places where it used to be done? Who brought it to an end? Why is it done in certain African countries and not in others? Why is it done in one community and not in another within the same country? Where else, other than in Africa and the Islamic world, has it been done, why and when?

The global sweep of female circumcision is not in dispute (although many would claim to be ignorant of it). Female circumcision is not just an African or an Islamic problem; it is a global problem. It was not imported into the West by 'Third World' immigrants, as some would suggest. It happened in the West before the immigrants arrived.[9] Nawal El Saadawi pointed to this fact during the heated argument about circumcision that erupted at the 1980 mid-Decade For Women conference in Copenhagen:

> In Copenhagen, we had a lot of disagreement, we women from Africa and the Third World, with her [Fran Hoskens, publisher of WIN News]. In our workshops, we argued that clitoridectomy has nothing to do with Africa or with any religion, Islam or Christianity. It is known in history that it was performed in Europe and America, Asia, and Africa. It has to do with patriarchy and monogamy. When patriarchy was established, monogamy was forced on women so that fatherhood could be known. Women's sexuality was attenuated so as to fit within the monogamous system. But she doesn't want to hear any of this. (El Saadawi, quoted in Patterson and Gillam 1983: 90–91)

In my view, the important question should not be about 'tradition', geography (Africa or the Middle East) or religion (Islam). The crucial question should be: Why is the female body subjected to all sorts of abuse and indignity in different cultures and different places (including the West)? Western feminist insurgents need to link their fight against female circumcision to an equally vigorous fight against the abuse of the female body in their immediate environment. Charity, they say, begins at home. Their first task should be to straighten out their own men by inviting other women ('Third World', Muslim, and so on) to join them in their endeavour (a task 'Third World' women will perform creditably!). Such collaboration will earn Western women a place in 'Third World' women's struggles. It is unwise for Western women to think that they are fully capable of solving their own problems, whereas 'Third World' women need their help because they are totally incapable of doing so. Such thinking breeds resistance. The problem of women living under patriarchy is a global one that requires global action.

The issue I raise here is that of agency. African women do not lack agency, whether others wish to attribute it to them or not. My earlier questions – Why is it no longer done in certain places where it used to be done? Who brought it to an end? – are pertinent here. Female circumcision is no longer practised in some African communities not because Fran Hoskens publishes WIN News (which most women in Africa do not read) or because Alice Walker produced the film Warrior Marks (which most African women have not seen and will probably never see). Walker's 'dream' for Warrior Marks makes the point: 'While planning the film, I dreamed of taking it from village to village, but now I've visited many African villages, and there are absolutely no audio-visual facilities. Barely, sometimes, drinking water. None that we foreigners could drink' (Walker and Parma 1993: 82). It does not occur to Walker that there may be a relationship between female circumcision and this 'absolute' lack she documents throughout in her book *Warrior Marks*. Who is Fran Hoskens writing for? Who is Alice Walker filming for? Certainly not for the African women who are there on the ground working tirelessly against female circumcision. There is a huge difference between writing and filming *about* African women, on the one hand, and writing and filming with/for African women, on the other. That difference plays a role in determining the success or failure of the fight against female circumcision.

Indeed, foreigners and foreign organizations have contributed money and material resources to women and organizations in Africa campaigning against female circumcision, and these individuals and organizations should be applauded. However, the thinking that things are changing in Africa because of Beijing (or any such UN gatherings) is grossly erroneous. The fight against female circumcision in Africa predates 1975 (the beginning of the first UN Decade for Women). Post-UN decade involvement by outsiders has accelerated progress in some respect and impeded progress in other areas. But much of the credit must go to African women (men too!) and Africa-based non-governmental organizations (NGOs) that actually do the work. African women do *not* lack agency. What may be lacking are the material and structural conditions necessary for the accomplishment of their goals.

Culture, the Humanities and Development

The rest of this essay will be devoted to the work of two Africa-based NGOs that have been successful in their campaigns against female circumcision: Women's Issues Communication and Services Agency (WICSA) in Nigeria and TOSTAN in Senegal. To understand and appreciate these NGOs' success, it is necessary to examine how they do their work. But before getting into the specifics of their strategies, I would like to address briefly the limitation of the notion and articulation of development. In an earlier essay I argue that the inordinate focus on politics and the economy in development study and work needs to be relaxed to create room for what I call cultural forces – culture as a positive force in development (Nnaemeka 1997). Often, culture ('cultural practices', 'cultural values', 'cultural impositions', and so on) is evoked as a negative element that impedes development. I argue that culture and its manifestations in different media have a positive role to play as well, and should be put in the service of development. Africa-based NGOs are cognizant of this fact, and have designed and executed their work accordingly.

Also, there are the issues of context, complexity and interrelationships. Each 'cultural practice' is a link in a chain whose demise may depend not on a surgical removal of the link but, rather, on adjusting the other links to which it is attached. It has been shown that many people in the 'Third World' would have fewer children, with an improvement in the context of their lives – education, material conditions, and so forth. It is not sufficient to preach to the woman who sends her child to hawk goods in a Lagos market about child labour and child abuse when the child's very existence depends on the hawking/labour; when the economy has so broken down that the mother had to withdraw her child from school because she could not afford the fees; when forces beyond her control – internal fiscal irresponsibility coupled with the unfair and strident monetary policies of international institutions such as the International Monetary Fund (IMF) – have paralysed her economically.[10] The child is not abused by his or her mother (who is devising ways to ensure the child's survival); the child is abused by the internal and external forces mentioned above. For the child to be saved from hawking, the context of his or her existence must change – a change that can be brought about by the meaningful collaboration and genuine commitment of the internal and external forces that abuse the child. Therein lie the complexity and interrelationships.

The Africa-based NGOs which I have observed, and with which I have been fortunate to work, are mindful of context, complexity and interrelationship as they engage in their campaigns against female circumcision. Unlike some of the organizations that are mushrooming in Europe and America, with only one item on their agenda – female circumcision – Africa-based NGOs campaign against female circumcision as part of an overall campaign *for* and *against* other myriad issues (Africans have things to campaign for, too!). Furthermore, they place culture and cultural expressions (visual and performing arts, for example) at the centre of their work as a positive force. The importance of the humanities (particularly the visual and performing arts) in development can be neither underestimated nor ignored, particularly in view of the fact that the majority of the people for whom the campaigns are launched are illiterate. The Nigerian NGO Women's Issues Communications Services Agency (WICSA) has developed a 'travelling museum' of paintings and sculptures for its campaign against female circumcision. WICSA gathered both male and female artists for its project. This point is important, and will be addressed below. The works of art are contextualized, and the accompanying literature (brochures and so on) is in European languages and, more importantly, in local languages as well. WICSA brings the 'museum' to the people in their immediate environment (both urban and rural) – a strategy that encourages the participation of a wider audience, which would not have been possible if the 'museum' were housed in one location to be viewed by communities for whom transportation is either inadequate or non-existent. WICSA has also succeeded in bringing its work to the attention of international audiences. In 1998, it was invited to participate in the second Women in Africa and the African Diaspora (WAAD) conference on 'Health and Human Rights' held in Indianapolis, USA. Tobe Levin was so impressed by the workshop organized by WICSA that she collaborated with the NGO to organize a six-month exhibition tour of Germany.

TOSTAN (literal meaning: 'breaking out of the egg'), a Senegal-based NGO directed by Molly Melching, one of the contributors to this chapter, has truly engineered a breakthrough by bringing cultural understanding to bear on development, and achieving outstanding results. TOSTAN, supported by funding from UNESCO and UNICEF, played a pivotal role in the banning of female circumcision in Senegal in 1998. Through its eighteen-month modular basic educational programme (developed by a group of Senegalese villagers and African and American non-formal education experts) that links basic education to life skills, TOSTAN has been able to teach rural women reading and writing skills in their local languages, encourage them to start and maintain income-generating projects, train them in health-related issues, give them self-confidence, and mobilize them to initiate and participate in social change (for example, the successful campaign to ban female circumcision). The groundswell of opposition to female circumcision in Senegal has its roots in the relationship between TOSTAN and the women of Malicounda who participated in the TOSTAN basic education programme. Armed with knowledge about health, leadership and human rights, the literate, confident graduates of the TOSTAN programme decided to tackle the issue of female circumcision. The women did their homework, and argued their case in the presence of the village council, which subsequently banned female circumcision in their community in 1997. Word spread to other communities, which also decided to endorse 'the oath of Malicounda'. In the community of Ker Simbara, the campaign was spearheaded by two men who had participated in the TOSTAN programme. The February 1998 'Diabougou Declaration', which got thousands of villagers to commit to the cessation of female circumcision, was drawn up by the village authority and the women.

A common thread runs through these two success stories – sensitivity to context and complexity, cultural understanding and its integration in project design, participatory processes, use of local languages, collaboration between women and men, participation of local religious and 'traditional' authorities, and genuine, meaningful collaboration between local communities and foreign entities. TOSTAN provided a context of empowerment for the women of Malicounda, allowed them to determine what their priorities were, and encouraged them to pursue and accomplish their goals. The women invited the participation of men because they are culturally attuned to such thinking, coming from an environment in which women's issues are village/community issues requiring the participation of villagers regardless of sex. The women are politically astute in ensuring the participation of all branches of local authority, regardless of which gender holds the authority. They also believe, as many African women do, that if the men are part of the problem, they should also be part of the solution. The problem with Western feminist insurgents against female circumcision is that they go to Africa to interview women, while alienating and putting down the men. The one man whom Alice Walker and Pratibha Parma discuss interminably in *Warrior Marks* is their Gambian driver, Malign. The one time Walker made an attempt to talk to the men who hold authority in the village was when she visited the chief's compound:

> The men around here are blandly gracious, like slave-masters, I suppose. We paid our respects to three graying patriarchs representing the *marabout* or *alacar* (not sure of the word they were using for chief; something Arabic) of the village, who was away on business. The men sat on chairs, the women on the ground. As a guest, I got a chair but could barely stay in it. The women had to recite in detail, and several times, everything we'd done since arriving in the village. They seemed bored, weary of their own subservience. I hadn't realized no one can leave the village, even guests, without this ritual of being 'released' by the chiefs, who are, of course, always men. This answers the question of why women don't run away. And, too, where would they go? (Walker and Parma 1993: 43)

To decode and analyse Walker's statement would require another essay. Suffice it to say that the arrogance and disrespect that turn a courtesy call into a treatise on bondage account for the failure of many Western-driven interventions. One does not have to look too far to see why

WICSA, TOSTAN, and similar NGOs succeed where self-serving projects like Alice Walker's have failed to make any positive and lasting impact on the lives of African women.

Notes

1. The title of this essay is a rephrasing of Jean-Paul Sartre's famous statement on anti-Semitism – 'If the Jew did not exist, anti-semitism would invent him' – in *Anti-Semite and Jew* (1960).

2. 'What's Culture Got to Do with It? Excising the Harmful Tradition of Female Circumcision', *Harvard Law Review* 106, June 1993, p. 1954.

3. In February 2000, within one week two tragic accidents occurred in two parts of the globe. A Kenyan Airline, with almost 170 crew and passengers (mostly Nigerians) on board, plunged into the Atlantic ocean off the Ivory Coast. There were only ten survivors. A few days later, an Alaskan Airline plane crashed into the Pacific off the California coast, killing all 88 people on board. During the recovery period, the Western media updated viewers with the number of victims recovered off the California coast (viewers heard about the numbers, but did not see the victims). But the same Western media exhibited on television grisly images of bloated and decomposing bodies/body parts recovered off the coast of Ivory Coast. Such disrespect is shown to the African dead or alive.

4. Betsy Hartmann (1995) has documented cases in India where population-control experts and organizations can get women to 'accept' sterilization in exchange for a couple of saris and a bag of rice.

5. When the Europeans came to Igboland, they met people who called themselves *ndi Igbo* (Igbo people). Claiming that they could not pronounce 'gb', and did not have the time or inclination to learn how it is said, the Europeans renamed *ndi Igbo* 'Ibo people', and eternalized the renaming and misnaming in their books. The same Europeans told the Igbo people that they could not pronounce *anya* (eye), but Igbo people have recently discovered that Europeans can pronounce 'Netanyahu' correctly and with ease!

6. I am aware that the two major figures in the making of the documentary – Alice Walker and Pratibha Parma – are women of colour. By referring to them as Westerners, I wish to state that what is at issue here is not skin colour but the mindset (mentality) that emanates from a particular location. It is instructive that Parma conferred Nigerian citizenship on the well-known Kenyan writer Ngugi wa Thiong'o – 'film being directed by the Nigerian writer Ngugi' (Walker and Parma 1993: 214) – despite her claims of affinity to Kenya: 'I was born in Kenya, East Africa and schooled in England, yet I was brought up to think of India as home.... Kenya gained independence in 1963, and my family moved to England a few years later' (Walker and Parma 1993: 89).

7. The Ivory Coast case was narrated by the Ivoirian Minister for Health during the second international conference on 'Women in Africa and the African Diaspora: Health and Human Rights' held in Indianapolis, USA (October 1998).

8. During a recent visit to Germany, I listened to a presentation by the wife

of a top German politician who is leading a campaign in Germany against female circumcision. She proudly exhibited the knives and razors she confiscated from circumcisers during one visit to Benin, I believe. How naive to think that the circumcisers have been put out of business because a couple of their knives are now in Germany!

9. Some would argue that female circumcision as 'female genital mutilation' was not performed in the West. But this is the case in many African communities where the practice goes on. Many of these communities have never heard of or practised the radical versions that can conceivably be called mutilation. The problem with the Western-driven campaign is that it chooses the worst-case scenario and makes it a generic term for the practice. The issue of 'urgency' I raised above applies here as well.

10. See Chinyere Okafor's short story 'Beyond Child Abuse', the epilogue to this volume.

References

Center for the Study of Human Rights, Columbia University (1996) *Women and Human Rights: The Basic Documents*, New York: Columbia University.

El Saadawi, N. (1980) *The Hidden Face of Eve: Women in the Arab World*, trans. and ed. Sherif Hetata, London: Zed Books.

Hartman, B. (1995) *Reproductive Rights and Wrongs: The Global Politics of Population Control*, Boston, MA: South End Press.

Harvard Law Review (1993) 'What's Culture Got to Do with It? Excising the Harmful Tradition of Female Circumcision', vol. 106, June.

Lorde, A. (1984) *Sister Outsider*, Trumansburg, NY: The Crossing Press.

Nnaemeka, O. (1997) 'Development, Cultural Forces, and Women's Achievements in Africa', *Law & Policy*, vol. XVIII, nos. 3 and 4.

Nnaemeka, O. and J. Ezeilo, eds (under consideration) *Engendering Human Rights: Social and Cultural Realities in Africa and the African Diaspora*.

Patterson, T. and A. Gillam (1983) 'Out of Egypt: A Talk with Nawal El Saadawi', *Freedomways*, vol. XXIII.

Rioja, I. and K. Manresa (1998) *The Day Kadi Lost Part of Her Life*, Melbourne: Spinifex Press.

Sartre, J.-P. (1960) *Anti-Semite and Jew*, trans George J. Becker, New York: Grove Press.

Tucker, V. (1999) 'The Myth of Development: A Critique of Eurocentric Discourse', in R. Munck and D. O'Hearn, eds, *Critical Development Theory: Contributions to a New Paradigm*, London: Zed Books.

Walker, A. (1992) *Possessing the Secret of Joy*, New York: Harcourt Brace Jovanovich.

Walker, A. and P. Parma (1993) *Warrior Marks: Female Genital Mutilation and the Sexual Blinding of Women*, New York: Harcourt Brace.

Female Genital Mutilation in France: A Crime Punishable by Law

Linda Weil-Curiel

> Violence resulting in mutilation or permanent injury is punishable by up to ten years' imprisonment and a 1,000,000 franc fine.
>
> Art. 222–9, *Code Pénal* (French Penal Code)

> The above infraction is punishable by up to fifteen years imprisonment if it is perpetrated on a minor fifteen years of age or younger.
>
> Art. 222–10, *Code Pénal* (French Penal Code)

On 16 February 1999, a French criminal court sentenced an exciser to eight years in prison for cutting the genitals of forty-eight girls. The trial was hailed as a milestone, because this was the first time the victims appeared in court to accuse their mutilators publicly. How did this come about? And how did I, a member of the Paris Bar with no personal link to Africa, come to defend the cause of children born on or brought to French soil in order to protect their right to bodily integrity? The account that follows is both personal and polemical. I am adamant that excising the genitals of young girls – albeit in the name of tradition – is a mutilation, and as such should be punishable as child abuse. The existing legislation, quoted in the epigraph above, was sufficient at some twenty-five trials before this landmark trial to convict the perpetrators.

Over the years, France has become home to a large number of West African immigrants who continue to practise female genital mutilation (FGM). In the French context, two opposing attitudes prevail. First, there are those who consider that this is a cultural tradition with acknowledged disastrous consequences, but feel that it is better to proceed tactfully and cautiously in order not to offend the feelings of those who practise it, assiduously avoiding any 'imperialistic' attitude. Then there are those, like myself, who believe that such traditions constitute a violation of basic human rights; bodily harm of this order on daughter-citizens must be ended by recourse to law when persuasion has not proved successful. Alongside the educational programmes designed to provide information to the families and disseminate the illegality of the practice, then, I believe that strong preventative measures should be taken. The practice of female genital mutilation, like those of slavery and apartheid, will not simply disappear on their own by the exercise of good sense.

For me, it all began with a story that made headlines in July 1982. The press reported that a three-month-old baby born on French soil, Bobo Traore, had died of severe haemorrhage following her clitoridectomy. Her parents, fully aware that the procedure was illegal, hesitated so long before bringing her to the hospital that when she arrived not a drop of blood remained in her already dead little body. From that moment, France opened its eyes to this practice, and public opinion began to take shape. Paediatricians who examined little girls during childhood checkups began calling for guidelines in an effort to stop the practice. Finally, the head paediatrician of a Paris hospital asked the Ministry of Justice to determine whether such practices were regulated by French law. The Ministry's response was unequivocal: anyone perpetrating physical harm on a child's body shall be punished under the terms of the French Penal Code, Article 312 (until February 1994, when the new Penal Code, Articles 222–9 and 222–10, quoted in the epigraph above, came into effect). Since that time, doctors have been required to report any evidence of mutilation to the authorities, just as they would report any other form of abuse, and they are absolved of the code of professional secrecy to do so. Interpreters have been provided to assist immigrant families in hospitals. Many associations that work to abolish the practice have received funding from the French government. Yvette Roudy, then Minister for the Rights of Women, set up a working group that included African women to study the issue; a first set of meetings was to determine how to persuade Africans living in France, via educational programmes, to desist from practising FGM; the second set was to determine whether new legislation to outlaw excision would be necessary. I was a participant in the study group; I took the position that special legislation was not needed and, moreover, would only point an accusing finger at the African population in France.

Shortly after Bobo's death and the prosecution of her parents, and that of other families whose children had been excised, a heated debate took place in the French press. Some journalists played the cultural card, arguing that it might be harsh to convict parents who felt that they were doing right by their child. Excising a daughter, for these parents, was rendering her eligible for marriage. For us to permit such practices to African families – because 'after all, it's their tradition' – strikes me as frankly discriminatory, even contemptuous. Would we permit such mutilation of the bodies of white children? Tradition or not, good intentions or not, I could not stand by and watch parents absolved of responsibility for violating the basic rights of their children. This is why I decided to take part in the legal proceedings as a civil party on behalf of several associations, among them the League for the International Rights of Women, founded by Simone de Beauvoir, and the CAMS, the Commission for the Abolition of Female Genital Mutilation, founded by Awa Thiam, a Senegalese professor and author. Our objective was to defend the right to bodily integrity of all children, regardless of their origin and of their parents' culture, and to show that France owed each child the same protection under the law. It is clear, however – and I accept that responsibility fully in the name of my beliefs – that the ineluctable consequence of this campaign was the penal sanction of African parents.

Some thirty such cases have been tried in the past twenty years. At the time of Bobo Traore's death, and until 1994 – when the new Penal Code came into force – Article 312, which punished acts of violence on minors, was applicable. In the existing legislation, it is stipulated that if the act causes invalidity for more than a week, the punishment is a prison term of two to five years. Such a case is judged by a court composed of three professional magistrates. But if the result is mutilation or death, then it is judged as a crime meriting punishment by a prison term of ten to twenty years. In this case the trial must come before the *Cour d'Assises*, the highest criminal court in France. Before the trial, an examining magistrate and the police conduct investigations. At the end of the trial, the court, which is composed of nine citizens and three judges, must answer the following questions: 'Are the defendants guilty?' 'Are there extenuating circumstances in their favour?' If, after deliberation, the defenders are found guilty, the court pronounces the penalties.

Back in the years 1982 to 1983, what were called *excision cases* were brought before the lower court by the prosecutor, until I interfered. I could do so because the code of legal proceedings allows organizations to join in those proceedings under certain circumstances, acting as a joint party to the prosecution in favour of the victim (*partie civile*). I immediately raised the point that lower courts had no legal competence to try people accused of performing or having given orders to perform excision because the practice leads to mutilation, which is legally a crime. In fact, I argued that, first, the law applies to anyone living in France, whether a French national or a foreigner; and, second, that other traditions and cultures cannot absolve parents of any breach of French law. On 20 August 1983, the French Supreme Court (*Cour de Cassation*) ruled that 'the clitoris and labia minora are the female erectile organs; their absence as a result of violence constitutes a mutilation', as defined then by Article 312–3 of the Penal Code. Interestingly, the case leading to the historic judgement of 20 August 1983 involved a woman who was French born and bred (and had no ties with Africa), but she had nonetheless cut her daughter's genitalia. The question then arose as to whether this jurisprudence could be applied to Africans claiming that excision was a traditional practice, and that they had no intention of causing harm. I successfully argued in court that the cultural weight of the practice does not affect the criminal indictment, because mutilation is the result of a deliberate act; the stoning of a woman, though permitted under the *sharia*, would be equally against the law in France.

In February 1999, one of the excision trials caused a considerable stir, because for the first time a case was triggered by a young woman, Mariatou Koita, who not only denounced her exciser but also filed a complaint against her own parents. Hawa Gréou, the woman who performed Mariatou's excision, had been arrested on 9 May 1994 and imprisoned until her trial because the investigating judge, who had ordered Gréou's telephone to be tapped, had proof that she was continuing to excise other girls secretly. The seizure of Hawa Gréou's address book led to the arrest – and ultimately the indictment – of many parents who had used her services.

Mariatou Koita was born the eldest of five daughters to a Malian immigrant family. A social worker placed three elder daughters and a boy in the home of a foster family, where they spent several happy years. When the girls were returned to their biological family in 1983, they were quickly taken by their mother to be 'vaccinated'. To the girls' horror, they were taken to an exciser's house, forced down on to a rubber cloth by three women, and excised sequentially. When Mariatou struggled and cried, she was told she was a disgrace to the family. After their mutilation, the girls were made to walk home. When the social worker came to the house a few days later, the girls were forbidden to speak of what had happened.

It was not until Mariatou attended a class on sex education in high school that she finally understood what had been done to her. (Other girls discovered that they were 'not normal' the first time they attempted to have sexual relations with a boy.) Her family refused to talk about the practice to her when she raised the issue at home. When another little sister was born in 1990, she tried desperately to prevent the baby's excision. But Hawa Gréou, a friend of the family and exciser of all the other Koita girls, brought her razors to their home, and Mariam was mutilated too. On the day of her eighteenth birthday, Mariatou left home never to return, and went straight to the Juvenile Judge – who subsequently opened the investigation that culminated in the trial. Three of the daughters testified against their parents, the most moving testimony coming from Maimouna, who described her experience to me as 'a rape that caused moral and physical suffering that would last for a lifetime'. She named it 'barbaric' and, with her sisters, asked the court for justice. The unrepentant mother called Mariatou and her sisters 'liars' who had brought shame to their people. The community rallied around her. During the trial, an association called Afrique Debout Unie en Marche wrote to the judges supporting the practice of excision on health grounds – claiming that it was a gynaecological procedure that assured hygiene and facilitated the birth process – and on religious grounds – declaring that 'over a hundred years ago, the prophet Ibrahim instituted the practice' (Sanogo and Magassy 1999). I pass over these inaccuracies without comment. But the judges and the jury found in favour of the girls, setting them free psychologically to rebuild their lives. Mariatou is now in law school. When she was asked, after the successful trial, if she, too, wanted to become a lawyer, she shook her head and pointed to the podium where the judges of the Cour d'Assises sat. 'No', she told me. 'I want to be up there with them.'

This case set a significant number of judicial precedents in the French battle against female genital mutilation. First, this was the first time victims, no longer minors, had appeared in court to accuse their mutilators publicly. Second, the court awarded damages: 80,000FF were awarded to each of the forty-eight victims. The exciser received an eight-year prison sentence, and Madame Koita was condemned to two years' imprisonment without possibility of parole. The other twenty-four parents received sentences ranging from three to five years, but they were not required to serve the time in jail so long as they did not commit the same crime in the five years following the trial. The parallel with the case of the French woman who had mutilated her daughter without having the excuse of tradition was invoked to show that a child's skin colour makes absolutely no difference in France, as the law protecting a child's bodily integrity is applied universally.

The success of such trials has been a strong deterrent to further excision of girls on French soil. The message has clearly got across to those who practise FGM in France. In March of 1999, I talked to one of the mothers after her trial. She told me that although she and the other mothers resented being convicted as *criminals*, they now understood the harm they had done to their daughters. She vowed to return to Senegal in order to convince the women of her village to stop the practice.

To return, however, to the concern with naming that prompted this chapter: I wish to clarify my own choice of the word *mutilation*. The other contributors have been more comfortable with words like *cutting* and *circumcision*. I applaud the excellent results obtained by the means Molly Melching describes in her essay on TOSTAN, and recognize the need for empowering communities in Africa to abandon those practices by evolutive means. I do want to say in passing, however, that a report from the Population Council I received recently on the reconversion of excisers and the education of communities by health-providers in Mali and Burkina Faso is less encouraging. Even those excisers who had agreed to 'put down their knives' continued to excise little girls on a case-by-case basis when asked to do so by the families, and the local healthcare providers admitted to feeling uncomfortable discussing the cutting with their patients ('FGC Excisors Persist Despite Entreaties' 2000: n.p.).

As a French citizen and lawyer, I cannot permit a second, tacit set of laws for the African population living in France, one that condones practices that are illegal for the rest of us. Moreover, young African women born in France wish to live like other young women of their generation. To consider them as somehow under a 'community authority' would be to negate the idea of a nation, and would also subject them to discrimination which would constitute a form of exclusion. I will never be convinced that groups of people living within the boundaries of the state should determine alternative laws by which they will abide. Excision is an issue that concerns an entire society, and not simply immigrant families. The transmission of the positive aspects of a culture is, of course, beneficial, but the rigid insistence on maintaining cultural identity by means of the practices of excision and forced, early marriages should be discouraged; the law must be leaned on to guarantee the protection of the weak – that is, our children. I believe that

the cultural or national origin of any child should be of secondary
concern when it is a question of protecting them from bodily or psychological harm; and that recourse to the law should be made when
parents remain deaf to the information provided.

In any case, the term *female circumcision* will never be acceptable to me.
How do you expect African parents to measure the harm done to their
girls if the same term is used for both practices, when in fact the
procedures and the consequences are dramatically different? The use of
any term other than *mutilation* is not only misleading, but also medically
incorrect. It seems senseless to me to try to end the genital mutilation
of little girls while shrinking from using the proper word, as we can
defeat only that which is clearly named. Africans who excise their
daughters are far from ignorant. They know very well what a difference
there is between cutting a hood of skin and cutting off an organ, since
the removal of the clitoris *for a specific reason* is precisely what is required
by their traditions: the control of female sexuality by the excision of
the organ of pleasure. This is far from the goal of male circumcision,
making the use of the same term for both acts very suspect. Given that
these women have been deprived of their clitoris, they often have no
knowledge of what is lacking, no sense of clitoral functioning, and
little sense of their own bodies. This last consequence of FGM strikes
me as one of the gravest inflicted by the practice, as I consider it
profoundly prejudicial to women's interests and, finally, capable of
rendering women insensitive to their own interests. This is why, in
France, we use the word *mutilation*, because the term corresponds to the
sad reality. It seems we have as much a battle of words as of laws on
our hands.

In conclusion, I would like to turn to Obioma Nnaemeka's essay in
this chapter, in which, I contend, it is feminism and the West that are
on trial, not female genital mutilation – the ending of which, we both
agree, should be our shared goal. Reflection on the brutality of such
practices is singularly absent from her argument, which makes of FGM
some sort of a construction in the imaginations of Western feminists
avid for sensationalism. The messenger bearing the bad news is accused, but not the perpetrator. African women should legitimately resist voyeuristic 'saviours' who insult them by exhibiting their body
parts in books and films. But what are we talking about: the cutting off
of an ear, of a toe, or of the clitoris? In addition, Nnaemeka fails to
mention anti-FGM activism among African men and women. She does
not mention, for example, that the film she criticizes, *La Dûperie* – in
which we see a little girl undergoing excision – is the instrument used

by the Inter-African Committee to encourage its constituencies to abandon this practice. Nor does she note that in this film voice is given to African speakers, who use a wooden carving to show villagers what incalculable and irreparable damage to a woman's sexual parts is done by excision and infibulation. Here we are a very long way from the exorcism of Islam, and of African culture and traditions, that Nnaemeka sees in the abolitionist campaigns.

All human societies have known behaviours that were disrespectful of human dignity, but neither slavery nor apartheid, as I have noted above, disappeared without coercion. Wherever we come from, we must critically examine any behaviours which undermine human bodily integrity and human dignity. It is precisely because the cause of women's rights knows no geographical boundaries that the fight against female genital mutilation remains a universal one, and all available means should be used to bring it to an end.

References

All citations from the trials are from an unofficial transcript of the court register and reported quotations are from informal conversations conducted by the author at the trials.

'FGC Excisors Persist Despite Entreaties: Mali, Gender and Empowerment', *Resumés of the Population Council* (2000), Dakar, Senegal.

Sanogo, A. and J.H. Magassy (1999) Letter from Afrique Debout Unie en Marche to Madame, Monsieur le Juge, Tribunal de Grande Instance de Paris, in defence of Hawa Gréou, 8 February.

CHAPTER SIX

Reading the Local and the Global: Literature as Development Practice

The novels and autobiographies discussed in this chapter call into question – as indeed has much outcome research on gender and development – the advisability of continuing to polarize the local and the global, the South and the North, theory and practice. In addition, each essay suggests that literature, as a crucial record of subject formation, should take its place in an interdisciplinary, international development debate. In the first essay, Deirdre Gilfedder analyses autobiographies written by members of the 'Stolen Generation' in Australia, commissioned by the Human Rights Commission in its effort to restore subjectivity, agency and dignity to victims of assimilation practices. Françoise Lionnet focuses on a novel written in English (and Creole) by Mauritian novelist Lindsay Collen in order to show how subjects experiencing the development process bear witness to its energies, its deprivations and its ambivalences. Finally, Celeste Schenck writes about two novels written in English for differently construed international audiences, and suggests that a new genre of literature is emerging as a result of globalized publishing practices. All three contributors are concerned with the dialogues, the doubled voices, the linguistic mixtures, the racial and generic *métissage*, and the ingenious and various forms of resistance that characterize and intertextually link the fictions of women writing in different local situations across the globe. These 'new writings in [e]nglish', as the contributions to this chapter attest, share certain new practices and politics – most notably the analysis of social, cultural and economic difference, and its continuing impact on the bodies, the identities and the choices of 'developing subjects'.

Testimonial and the Stories from the 'Stolen Generation' in Australia

Deirdre Gilfedder

I now understand why I find it so very hard to leave my home, to find a job, to be a part of what is out there. I have panic attacks when I have to go anywhere I don't know well and feel safe. Fear consumes me at times and I have to plan my life carefully so that I can lead as 'normal' an existence as possible. I blame welfare for this. What I needed to do was to be with my family and my mother, but that opportunity was denied me.

Woman from South Australia, fostered at 18 months in the 1960s,
Confidential Submission 483 in *Bringing Them Home* (1997)

What effect can the life story of an ordinary person have on the political life of a nation? Can literature create an impulse towards the development and the rights of Indigenous peoples? These questions arise from the impact of the increasing number of autobiographies by women of Aboriginal descent in Australia. Although these are by no means the first to appear, this phenomenon of the last decade invites us to consider why so many have been written at this moment in time. The stories that emerge coincide with political issues that have created turmoil in Australia at the turning of the millennium – above all with the issue of the 'Stolen Generation', those now-adults of Indigenous descent who suffered removal from their families at the hands of the Australian state.

The telling of *true stories* by Aboriginal authors, and the growth of Indigenous people's literature in general in Australia, has indeed forged a new place for Aboriginal subjectivity. At last, Aboriginal voices are speaking of their own experience at the epicentre of the Australian public sphere, doing so not only through traditional and alternative politics but also through literature and non-fiction publications. However, how are these texts being read? Is this literature exclusively about producing an effect of development upon the authors and their communities, or does it also develop the consciousness of those non-Indigenous Australian readers confronted with certain truths?

To answer these questions, I sought the aid of the Aboriginal writer, activist and expert on Indigenous literature Mary Graham.[1] In an interview with me, she spoke, in particular, of the Aboriginal approach to stories. From her perspective, the stories emerging at the current moment should be told in a way similar to traditional Indigenous stories: 'Stories are told continually which have been handed down over the generations, recounting the events of the last two hundred years as the people themselves have experienced those events and also the land has experienced it.' These autobiographies are interesting, therefore, 'not as one individual's story but, rather, as one story among many in the tradition of oral history'. The compulsion to tell these stories nonetheless stems from a desire for social justice: 'These stories and the recording of them are being used as evidence to help Indigenous people regain some measure of equality.' In this sense, telling life stories is transformative. As Graham would have it, a primary role of Indigenous literature is to advance the Aboriginal cause: 'land rights, the relief of social disadvantage and simply the cathartic relief of publicly sharing grief at the unhappy memories'.

Others have discussed the benefits to Indigenous people of finally having their voices heard, of breaking what W.E.H. Stanner called the 'Great Australian Silence' (Stanner 1968): those official histories that in the past ignored the accounts of Aboriginal Australians. Some recent autobiographies have been praised as 'releasing the tongues' (Cooper 1995: 140) of Indigenous Australians in the spirit of what could be characterized as a 'return of the repressed' (Sommer in Brodzki and Schenck 1988: 111). This new literature in English shares with postcolonial texts the subject and function of resistance, a resistance that can clearly have a therapeutic effect for the storytellers who are dealing with past trauma. In this essay, however, I wish to focus less on the question of developing subjectivities than on the role autobiographies might play in an overall perspective of Reconciliation in Australia. I propose that development be seen as a process of truth-learning in a complex and communal rewriting of Australian official history.

I wish to discuss autobiography both as a published literary genre and as it might figure in non-literary contexts. My project is to focus on one particular area, the stories of the so-called 'Stolen Generation'.

Thus I will look at the question of the 'testimonies' given to the Human
Rights Commission for their Report on the removal of children from
their Aboriginal families; such removals occurred over much of the last
century. These accounts are not to be classed technically as autobiography,
but they cross over at some points with published autobiography and
fiction that also draw upon this chapter in Australia's history. It is the
intersection between testimony, autobiography and fiction that I wish
to address in order to focus on a political role for life stories in Australia
today.

The publication of these accounts, interestingly enough, coincides
with a rich, fast-growing literature by authors of Indigenous Australian
background, so that many voices are being raised today to put questions
of Australian literature and historical memory into perspective. For
example, Donna Meehan's award-winning short story 'Joy Ride',
published in 1997, is an autobiographical account of her forced separation from her mother as a small child. Placed by state authorities on
a train with her brothers, she tells of her shock at seeing her mother
remain on the station platform as the train pulled away: 'Then Mum
waved a white hanky and I pressed my face against the window pane
as hard as I could, watching her. Watching until her blue dress faded
into a tiny blue daub of colour. I looked back at the station as far as
I could until it was out of sight' (in Bird 1998: 100). No information
having been offered by the authorities who had taken her, she was then
separated from her brothers and placed in an adoptive family in
Newcastle, New South Wales. This happened in 1960, yet it is with
cinematic memory that Meehan recounts the scene, and the confusion
and emotion she experienced. Her individual experience could be said
to speak for or to the many adults of mixed descent who suffered forced
separation from their Aboriginal parents as children. The experience has
also been sung about by singer-songwriters Archie Roach and Bob
Randall, and has recently been fictionalized in such riveting novels as
Doris Pilkington's Follow the Rabbit-Proof Fence, Alexis Wright's Plains of Promise, Romayne Weare's Malanbarra, and Kim Scott's Benang. Speaking of these
fictional works, Graham reminded me of the role of a

> chorus, as in Greek drama. The chorus/voices are not just some colourful
> backdrop to the main action, they are an intricate part of the fabric or
> praxis of our existence. They reflect the overall feeling, emotions, thoughts
> and beliefs of the time/moment while the current action is taking place on
> centre stage.... They also give an indication as to how the current action got
> to be centre stage.

These stories appeared in the decade which was to see the publication of the results of a National Enquiry into the forced separation by the Australian State of Aboriginal and Torres Strait Island people from their families in the twentieth century. The Report of the Human Rights Commission, called *Bringing Them Home* (1997),[2] traces the history of Assimilation and 'foster-care' programmes instigated by the Australian government between 1911 and the mid-1960s. In 1911, the Chief Protector, head of the Aboriginal Protection Board of each State of Australia, was given extensive power to control indigenous people; in some states he was made the legal guardian of all Aboriginal children, in a move that displaced the rights of parents. In the 1920s and 1930s, 'Absorption' – or, later, 'Assimilation' – meant that children of mixed descent were taken away, mostly forcibly, from their Aboriginal parents and communities in order to be merged with the 'white' community.

Among the confidential evidence included in the Report is the story recounted by 'Rose' of her own life. Her parents had hidden her from the Welfare officers in the 1950s for fear of her removal. One day in 1958, while her parents were working, she went into town to seek their aid for the younger children. There she learned that her brothers and sisters had been taken away by authorities. This is how she remembers it:

> The next day I knew that the Welfare had taken my brothers and sisters. This lady who I stayed with overnight: her brother came that morning and told her the Welfare had taken the kids to the homes. She called me aside and said, babe it's no good you going out to the camp today because the Welfare has taken your brothers and sisters away to the homes. I started crying and said to her, no I have to go back to the camp to see for myself. She got her brother and sister to take me out there and I just couldn't stop crying. All I could see was our little camp. My baby brother's bottle was laying on the ground. And I could see where my brother and sisters were making mud pies in a Sunshine milk tin that we used for our tea or soup. I didn't know where my parents were. (HRC 1997: Submission 316)

The Human Rights Commission estimates that in the twentieth century between 50,000 and 100,000 Aboriginal and Torres Strait Islander children were removed; that is to say – given the present population of around 280,000 Indigenous Australians – few have been untouched by the history of removal. In the 1920s and even after, the reasoning was often unashamed Social Darwinism: an attempt to engineer the extinction of the Aboriginal race, to breed out blackness from Australia. The fear of mixing inspired eugenic theories, such as that of Chief Protector of Western Australia A.O. Neville in the 1930s, whereby 'half-castes' were to blend entirely into the white race after two or three generations.

Later in the postwar period, official government discourse stressed, rather, the need to provide all children with what were seen as living conditions of a good standard – the principles of 'sound education' and 'suitable housing.' Courts nevertheless continued frequently to rule Aboriginal parents as negligent, and children were taken away as late as the 1970s. Assimilation was officially stopped in the 1960s under the government of Harold Holt, and then replaced by a general policy of 'self-determination' in Aboriginal affairs under the Whitlam government in 1972. Nowadays, Aboriginal affairs are managed by the Indigenous-governed body Aboriginal and Torres Strait Islander Commission (ATSIC), as well as by local Indigenous councils whose goals are to make self-determination a reality.

The Human Rights Report also details the failure of 'Assimilation', highlighting not only the effects of removal but, sadly, also the racial discrimination in employment and education that so often hindered the integration of those who had been separated. In the early years, the stolen children were often conceived of as a potential servant class, and accounts of unpaid labour abound in the Report. The following Confidential Submission is an example:

> They sent me when I was 16 from Parramatta Girls' Home out to M, a property 137 miles from Nyngan. We never had a holiday. We weren't allowed to go into town with them. If you did go in or go anywhere and you saw any Aboriginal people, you weren't allowed to speak to them. So you had to live that isolated life. We never, ever got our wages or anything like that. It was banked for us. And when we were 21 we were supposed to get this money, you see. We never got any of that money ever. And that's what I wonder: where could that money have went? Or why didn't we get it? (HRC 1977: Submission 11)[3]

While some interviewees acknowledged the education received in certain missions and homes, the Report mainly reveals gross mistreatment and degradation of children in numerous institutions and foster homes. The statistics on crime and substance abuse are much higher for people who were taken away from their parents than for Indigenous people who were not. The statistics on physical and sexual abuse in allocated institutions show that almost one in ten boys and over one in ten girls experienced sexual abuse in a children's institution. Recent court decisions over victims of this system have found that the state failed to ensure that children were safe from ill-treatment.

The Report also foregrounds the issue of identity. Clearly, being caught between two worlds was experienced more as a violent and traumatic reality than as an existential problem: 'I was taken there because I was a half-caste.... We were treated differently to white and black people. We weren't allowed to go down to see our Aboriginal people, or go into houses where white people were. We just had to live around the outside of the house' (HRC 1997: Submission 821). Similarly, the loss of culture and language is detailed by the compilers of the Report, and often raised by the interviewees: 'We lost much of our culture, our language and traditional knowledge, our kinship and our land' (HRC 1997: Submission 821).

The Report is not only about children; there is a lot about mothers. One woman named 'Evie', whose fair-skinned children were taken from her by her sister-in-law while she was ill, talks about her life:

I couldn't get my kids back when I came out of hospital. And I fought the welfare system for ten years and still couldn't get 'em. I gave up after ten years.... And with my daughter, well she came back in '88 but tings aren't working out there. She blames me for everything that went wrong.... The two boys know who I am but turned around and said to us, 'You're not our mother – we know who our real mother is.' So every day of your bloody life you just get hurt all the time. (quoted in Bird 1998: 41)

Over and over again, the Report chronicles the breaking of the link between mother and child:

It was wrong the way my natural mother was treated.... My mother was not crazy she was only nineteen. She was the right one and shouldn't have killed herself but she knew no better as there was no one to help her keep her children. I can remember the day she died -that has haunted me for the rest of my life. I remember the police coming to Mrs Sullivan's place where we were and told her that mum Faith died I'm sure I heard that. I turned and said to Mrs Sullivan 'Mummy Faith can't take us away anymore.' The day she died we died. (HRC 1997: Submission 818).

The Report not only uses life stories to establish its evidence, but quotes directly from the victims of the 'Stolen Generation', taking its evidence from 535 people interviewed in all the states and territories of Australia. Here is a government document using testimonials as evidence, recording voices that not only establish historical fact, but whose tone betrays the pain that those events caused. There has been some question over the use of these accounts – which are occasionally unverifiable, owing to culled archives – but it was decided to let the evidence speak for itself. The voices in *Bringing Them Home* speak louder than statistics. In the context of a National Enquiry it is, of course, the truth-value of these stories that holds sway over style or self-reference.

The Report does not reveal the names of most of the interviewees, labelling their narratives 'Confidential Submissions', and it occasionally uses fictional names. The events described by one interviewee, 'Millicent', are a disturbing example:

> My name is Millicent D. I was born at Wonthella, WA, in 1945. My parents were CD and MP, both half-caste Aborigines.... Because my parents were fair in complexion, the authorities decided us kids could pass as whitefellas.... Colin and I were taken to the Sister Kate's Home.... They told me that my family didn't care or want me and I had to forget them. They said it was very degrading to belong to an Aboriginal family and I should be ashamed of myself, I was inferior to whitefellas. (in Bird 1998: 28)

Later, when Millicent was in her first year of high school, she was sent to work on a farm. Here she was raped by the man of the house. When she told the matron at her return, her mouth was 'washed out with soap'. After running away, she was sent back to the farm to work:

> This time I was raped, bashed and slashed with a razorblade on both of my arms and legs because I would not stop struggling and screaming. I wanted to die, I wanted my mother to take me home where I would be safe and wanted. Because I was bruised and in a state of shock I didn't have to work but wasn't allowed to leave the property. (Bird 1998: 30)

As a result, she gave birth to a baby girl:

> I was so happy, I had a beautiful baby girl of my own who I could love and cherish and have with me always. But my dreams were soon crushed: the bastards took her from me.... My baby was taken away from me just as I was from my mother. (Bird 1998: 31)

Millicent's story is about the repeated suffering inflicted upon her in the interests of so-called 'Protection', and the way in which many generations of a family were affected by removal. However, her story is also about speaking out.

Bringing Them Home was listed as the most important book of 1997, and had an immediate impact on national politics, as well as on Australia's understanding of its history. At roughly the same moment, Random House published some of this confidential evidence as *The Stolen Children: Their Stories* (Bird 1998). The timing of these two publications marks an important shift in genre from *report* to *story*. As editor Carmel Bird sees it in her introduction, 'witness' becomes 'storyteller'.

How should we approach these stories no longer presented as evidence? These accounts are reminiscent of first-person narratives from Latin America that have been labelled testimonials. While we should be careful of transposing the genre from one context to another, it may be useful to look at some of the theoretical points they hold in common. Critic Doris Sommer has grappled with the Latin American *testimónio* genre, and has suggested two defining characteristics. The first, she argues in the case of some Latin American autobiographies, is that the 'I' of traditional autobiography becomes a 'we' in these narratives: an implied 'plural subject', either spoken for or spoken to in an act of public 'witnessing' (in Brodzki and Schenck 1988: 108). According to Sommer, this metonymical relationship of one-standing-up-among-others, rather than one-standing-in-representatively-for-others, is typical of testimonials. Her second point is that autobiographies must be defined also by their claim to referentiality (that is, history).

These stories, taken together, have a community-building value, even though each is an individual story of both tragedy and heroism. The president of the Human Rights Commission, Ronald Wilson, has stated: 'Notwithstanding their general similarity, every one was special because it recorded the experience of a particular unique individual' (HRC 1997: 14). Nevertheless, these accounts have been used to corroborate evidence of still other accounts, so that the act of witnessing is used in both a legal and a cultural sense. The compiling of these accounts into an archive tells the story of a people, and the many similarities and repetitions among them contribute to the plural subjectivity of the whole.

The other generic question is that of truth. I hold that these stories, even in their context as autobiography, illustrate Sommer's second point about the testimonial genre. These stories, even beyond the Report, retain their *referential force*, and remain testimonies in the legal sense. The personal accounts, narrated orally to the psychologists working for the National Enquiry, have been made public as story, and have thus become of national concern. We witness the pain, but also the incredible courage, shown by people like Millicent who are finally able to speak after a systematic silencing that would have relegated her to the shadows of Australian history. Here, we are no longer in the problematic realm of the fictional 'I' of autobiography, in the splitting of the autobiographical subject that has become a major question since Philippe Lejeune's work (Lejeune 1975). It is critical when reading these stories to identify the textual 'I' with the referential Millicent. This is not to argue that in this genre there is never any 'self-dramatization', or 'retrospective narrativizing', a necessary aspect of autobiography theorized by Lejeune.

As Mary Graham states, with regard to these stories, 'some are told better than others' – but this is not what astounds us. We are forced to focus on the question of the referent: in Millicent's story as presented in the Bird collection, it is the 'this happened', 'this is how I felt' aspects of the telling that are immediately powerful for the concerned reader.

This crossing over between evidence and autobiography raises many questions about the reception of such texts. While Black activist Roberta Sykes encourages Aboriginal women to write their autobiographies for their advancement, the publicizing of stories of separation is seen by many as an opportunity to face up to past wrongs and enter into true Reconciliation. Indeed, recommendation 4 from one Aboriginal group to the Human Rights Commission asks that the history of forced family separations be made more widely known through avenues such as 'publication of the history of separations and individual stories' (HRC 1997: Recommendations). Reading or hearing about the 'Stolen Generation' is clearly seen as having the potential to advance Australian society as a whole. Ronald Wilson and others have spoken of a 'healing process' facilitated by the telling of these stories (Wilson in HRC 1997: vi).

Graham puts it another way. She reversed my question to her about literature and Aboriginal development, and spoke of developing the wider Australian community: 'These stories help Australia to embark on the long road to understanding itself because at the moment there is no collective self-knowledge of their white Australian society and its relationship with the land in the emotional, spiritual or psychological sense.' It is as if the non-Indigenous Australians are in dire need of help through understanding. While some cannot face their history, others 'are attempting to come to terms with the implications of what the stories are saying about Australian society'. Indeed, the Report's inclusion of such testimonials has had *national* consequences.

Immediately after its release in May 1997, the Report was brought before the Australian Parliament, where the opposition leader, Kim Beazley, called for 'an outpouring of emotion in this parliament' (*Hansard* 1997). Indeed, he wanted to read out some of the examples from the Report, illustrating how the intimate suddenly occupies the central floor of public debate. The release of the Report placed pressure on Australia's Prime Minister to present an apology on behalf of the nation to the victims of separation. Mr Howard, however, declined to offer an official national apology, offering only his 'personal deep sorrow' (Howard in Steketee 1997: n.p.).

The Federal government has recently made a promise of some 50 million Australian dollars to be spent over four years on the health and welfare of Indigenous people, with emphasis on reuniting families. However, no official apology from the Federal government has been forthcoming, and the money is being proffered slowly. The apology, as well as payment of reparations to the victims of the 'Stolen Generation', is part of the larger issue of 'Reconciliation' in Australia. It coincides with the Land Rights issue, in the name of which Indigenous groups have made various claims following the Native Title Act of 1993.[4] However, the limitations set on Native Title by the present government are being examined by the Human Rights Commission of the United Nations. The question of Indigenous rights has finally taken centre stage in Australia at the beginning of the new century, attracting international attention and concern.

A year after the publication of *Bringing Them Home*, a committee rallied huge popular support for a national 'Sorry Day' on 26 May, a commemorative annual event that would highlight awareness of this chapter of Australia's history. This commemoration – also one of the Report's recommendations – was piloted by Link Up, the national Commonwealth-funded association that helps people find family members lost through removal. Both the popular and institutional support for this event shows that many Australians are moved and mobilized by what they have heard and read, and are disappointed by the 'non-apology' of their country's leader. As former Chairperson of ATSIC, Lois O'Odonoghue, has said: 'There is no longer any excuse for people to say that they do not know our story – now they can know our story and can share in our past' (in MacDonald 1995: viii).

In Australia today, the telling of life stories is rocking the political and moral fabric of the entire country. The stories of the 'Stolen Generation' illustrate the use of so-called 'qualitative evidence' in developing social policy. Is this an example of autobiography's revenge? As it was state policy that determined the difficult lives of these citizens, have their life stories come back to haunt the state? Here the dialogue between the personal and the public, between the categories of literature and history – indeed, the blurring of those boundaries – must be understood in the Australian context as expressing the complex relationship between the Aboriginal community and the nation. The voices of members of the 'Stolen Generation' are testimonies; that is, proof that a significant number of lives in Australia did not fall apart as a result of some inevitable process, but were forced apart by state policies of continuing internal colonization and assimilation.

Other texts by Indigenous authors cross over into the testimonial genre. Sally Morgan's best-selling autobiography *My Place*, published in 1987, is an important example. *My Place* recounts a series of secrets and lies that surround Sally's family past, including her own mother's and grandmother's conspiracy to tell her that she was 'Indian'. As she uncovers her matrilineal Aboriginal background, Sally's search becomes a kind of detective story, in which she is called upon to solve the double mystery of the suppressed identities of her grandfather and her grandmother's father.

The story of family secrets, of repression, exploitation and incest in *My Place* has been read in Australia not only as a terrible and well-told individual tale but also as representative of a number of similar cases. The wider social and historical context of Morgan's story is evoked by the text itself: Sally is interested in what she calls 'history', and indeed indicts the white amnesiac historiography of Australia (Morgan 1987: 161). The tale of Sally Morgan and her relatives touched a tender nerve in Australia, exposing not only acts committed against Aboriginal women in particular, but above all the public silence surrounding this past. The grandmother's story is, of course, also that of Australia's 'national history': a narrative of how the pastoral exploitation of the outback of Australia was achieved at the expense of the livelihood and culture of its Indigenous inhabitants. The use of more or less indentured Aboriginal labour hinted at in *My Place* is also linked to the main issue of sexual violence. The rape of women was indeed the enactment of and metaphor for the colonization of Australia. As historian Henry Reynolds puts it:

> The raping and abduction of women and the stealing of children have always been a part of the story of conquest – acts that brutally illustrate new, imposed relationships of dominance, submission and humiliation. (Reynolds in Bird 1998: 183)

As Sally Morgan, in fact, hands over the narration to her uncle, mother and grandmother, *My Place* could be termed a collective testimonial in the spirit of Sommer's generic formulation. Morgan herself stated in an interview: 'The story of my family is not unique. It is echoed thousands of times over the length and breadth of Australia' (Morgan in *The Age*, 10 October 1999). Her text moves self-consciously between story and history, between the personal and the national. Morgan's is a text that effaces the line between testimonial and autobiography.

Some critics have pointed out that the editing of Morgan's autobiography geared the text towards inclusion in the genre of Australian national literature by appealing to generic autobiographical elements:

the pioneering myth, the war hero, and so on. As in the case of other Aboriginal authors, Morgan finds herself having to respond to the national, to the hegemony of non-Indigenous accounts of Australian history. The success of her book nonetheless established a place from which women of mixed descent could speak. Almost in answer to postcolonial critic Gayatri Spivak's challenge – 'There is no place from where the sexed, subaltern subject may speak' (Spivak 1988: 120) – Morgan's title states bravely: 'There is *My Place*'.[5]

Naturally, not all literature written by Indigenous Australians is concerned with historical or personal fact. Indigenous writers do not feel that they should be confined to the 'real'. Traditional Aboriginal literature, of course, has its own history and theory as well as social role, spanning thousands of years of civilization in Australia. Traditional stories continue to be passed down orally in Aboriginal families and communities, and have been published in Australia in various forms (some more authentically presented than others) since the beginning of the twentieth century. Interestingly, these stories from the Dreamtime are often cited in cases for Native Title to show continued attachment to the land by the claimant group.

Several anthologies of Black Australian writing (Davis 1990) illustrate its enormous range and diversity: from autobiography to traditional stories; from 'Bush yarns' (Herb Wharton) to science fiction (Archie Weller); from short stories to poetry (Jack Davis, Lionel Fogarty, among others); song, theatre, as well as experimental genres (Mudrooroo Narogin). Women writers have produced an equally generically diverse body of work. The eminent poet Oodgeroo Noonuccal, formerly known as Kath Walker, whose poetry raised awareness of discrimination in the 1960s and 1970s, has been followed by a new generation of authors. The novels *Steam Pigs* and *Hard Yards* by young writer Melissa Lucaschenko explore the complexities of modern Aboriginal identity politics with insight and biting wit. Alexis Wright's 1997 novel *Plains of Promise*, listed for the Commonwealth Writers' Prize, explores an interaction between the realism of Mission life in Western Australia and the secret magic of traditional Aboriginal spirituality.

The role of such literature in national development is well documented by historian Benedict Anderson (Anderson 1988), as well as by literary critic Homi Bhabha (Bhabha 1990). A literary consciousness can only further the cause of Aboriginal nationalism (Reynolds 1996), and this through what Graham designates as 'the aspirations of Indigenous people to gain some measure of equity'. At the same time, it also plays a role in the consciousness of the wider community – that of testimonial, as I have indicated above. The dissemination of these texts across the nation has been in part a result of changes in publishing practices and priorities – the University of Queensland Press's Black Australian Authors Series, the David Unaipon Indigenous Authors' Prize, Indigenous-run Magabala Books, Allen & Unwin, and Fremantle Arts Press. A similar shift in priorities may be seen within Australian academia as well, especially in the development of Aboriginal Studies departments in universities across Australia over the last twenty years. There has always been an active Aboriginal intellectual literary tradition in Australia, but its growing institutional base and its increasing impact on government policy are crucial evidence of Aboriginal self-determination and, indeed, development practices.

Notes

1. I conducted an interview with Mary Graham in Brisbane, Australia, on 26 October 1999. All citations from Graham in my text are from this electronic interview. Mary Graham's book on Indigenous literature, to be published by University of Queensland Press, is forthcoming in 2001. She currently works for the Aboriginal association *Faira*.

2. Subsequently referred to in my text as HRC 1997.

3. In this submission, a New South Wales woman describes removal to Cootamundra at the age of 2 or 3 in the 1940s, and life from 13 to 16 in the Parramatta Girls' Home.

4. This law followed the ruling of the High Court of Australia in 1992 in the case of Mabo v. Queensland Government, whereby Eddie Mabo was granted rights over his land; the court recognized his claim to traditional rights that preceded British colonization. Before this time, the notion of *terra nullius* was invoked in law to stop Aboriginal land claims. Native Title means that Aboriginal people can make land claims where they have traditionally and continuously inhabited.

5. Other women's autobiographies have had a wide readership and an important political impact, especially Ruby Langford's *Don't Take Your Love to Town* (1988) and Glenyse Ward's *Wandering Girl* (1987). The first volume of Roberta Sykes's autobiography *Snake Cradle*, while it caused some controversy, was nominated Book of the Year by the newspaper *The Age* in 1997.

References

Anderson, B. (1988) *Imagined Communities: Reflections on the Origin and Spread of Nationalism*, London: Verso.

Bhabha, H., ed. (1990) *Nation and Narration*, London: Routledge.

Bird, C., ed. (1998) *The Stolen Children: Their Stories*, Sydney: Random House.

Bringing Them Home, National Enquiry into the Separation of Aboriginal and Torres Strait Islanders from their Families (1997) Human Rights Commission, Commonwealth of Australia.

Brodzki, B. and C. Schenck, eds (1988) *Life/Lines: Theorizing Women's Autobiography*, Ithaca, NY: Cornell University Press.

Cooper, A. (1995) 'Talking about *My Place*/My Place: Feminism, Criticism and the Other's Autobiography', *Southern Review*, July.

Davis, J., M. Narogin, S. Meucke and A. Shoemaker, eds (1990) *Paperbark: A Collection of Black Australian Writing*, St Lucia, Australia: University of Queensland Press.

Graham, M. (1999) Interview with Deirdre Gilfedder, 26 October.

Langford, R. (1988) *Don't Take Your Love to Town*, Victoria: Penguin.

Lejeune, P. (1975) *Je est un autre*, Paris: Éditions du Seuil.

Lucaschenko, M. (1997) *Steam Pigs*, St Lucia, Australia: University of Queensland Press.

Lucashenko, M. (1999) *Hard Yards*, St Lucia, Australia: University of Queensland Press.

MacDonald, R. (1995) *Between Two Worlds*, Australian Archives, Commonwealth of Australia.

Morgan, S. (1987) *My Place*, Western Australia: Fremantle Arts Press.

Morgan, S. (1999) 'White Lies', *The Age*, 10 October 1999.

Pilkington, D. and G. Nugi (1999) *Follow the Rabbit-Proof Fence*, St Lucia, Australia: University of Queensland Press.

Reynolds, H. (1996) *Aboriginal Sovereignty: Reflections on Race, State and Nation*, St Leonard's: Allen & Unwin.

Scott, K. (1999) *Benang*, Freemantle, Australia: Fremantle Arts Press.

Spivak, G. (1988) 'Can the Subaltern Speak?' in C. Nelson and L. Grossberg, eds, *Marxism and the Interpretation of Culture*, London: Macmillan.

Stanner, W.E.H. (1968) *Boyd Lectures*, Sydney: ABC Radio publications.

Steketee, M. (1997) 'Aboriginal Reconciliation: Sorry Seems to Be the Hardest Word to Say', *The Australian Online*, 24 May 1997.

Sykes, R. (1997) *Snake Cradle*, St Leonard's, Australia: Allen & Unwin.

Ward, G. (1987) *Wandering Girl*, Magabala Books.

Weare, R. (1999) *Malanbarra*, St Lucia, Australia: University of Queensland Press.

Wright, A. (1987) *Plains of Promise*, St Lucia, Australia: University of Queensland Press.

'She Breastfed Reluctance into Me': Hunger Artists in the Global Economy

Françoise Lionnet

It is not sufficient to know the personal but to know – to speak it in a different way. Knowing the personal might mean naming spaces of ignorance, gaps in knowledge, ones that render us unable to link the personal with the political.

bell hooks, *Talking Back* (1989: 107)

Different narrative strategies may be authorized at specific moments in history by complex negotiations of community, identity, and accountability. Fiction, as we know, is political.

Kamala Visweswaran, *Fictions of Feminist Ethnography* (1994: 15)

Quietly, unobtrusively and extremely fitfully, something in my mind began to assert itself, to question things and refuse to be brainwashed, bringing me to this time when I can set down this story ... the story I have told here is my own story, the story of four women whom I loved, and our men, this story is how it all began.

Tsitsi Dangarembga, *Nervous Conditions* (1988: 204)

Walk into any supermarket in Mauritius, one of the Indian Ocean Rim countries known among economists as an 'African tiger cub', and you get a picture of abundance: neat rows of packaged foods, aisles crowded with customers, entire families comparison shopping for bargains (*The Economist* 1988: 51). Enter the large parking lot on the first couple of days of the month, and parking is a major problem: those patrons who can shop only once a month (because of transport problems) are busy spending (or overspending) that portion of their monthly budget that they use for food or non-perishable items. The lines at the cash registers are long, even at the French-owned mega-stores Continent and Prisunic, which charge inflated prices, or at the South African-owned Winners and Spar, which import merchandise from not quite as far away as Europe. In a country where the average annual income per capita is approximately $3,700, the disposable income of the middle and working classes is limited, and people will spend their pay cheques in the first few days of the month on the basic necessities of life (*Jeune Afrique* 1998: 55). But what counts as 'basic necessities of life' in the midst of this consumer revolution? How has the concept of individual need been inflected by the availability of imported merchandise, the lure of easy credit, and the promise of a more satisfying lifestyle? How have these issues affected women's lives? And what do we know about the impact of these economic changes on the quotidian practices of a new generation of Mauritian women today? This essay will attempt to answer some of these questions by analysing a fictional text by Lindsay Collen, *There is a Tide* (Collen 1990), and situating it within the context of those changing socioeconomic conditions.

The transformation of the world's markets, and the resulting changes in patterns of consumption, have affected the daily habits of the population and the balance of payments of remote developing nations such as Mauritius. Once adequately fed by multiple small-scale local resources – fish and vegetables – and imported staples such as rice and lentils, the population is now invited by advertising and the proliferation of malls and supermarkets to value imports and fast food: the best of the food grown locally or fished from the sea is reserved for the luxury hotels and their hard-currency-paying guests. At the supermarkets, you can stare at pre-packaged imported apples and oranges (and at fellow shoppers) while dealing with well-groomed, uniformed and politely distant cashiers. The depersonalization of shopping and the promotion of items which have questionable use-value in the general context of the culture and the nation reached exceptional levels in the 1990s. By contrast, the open-air market or Creole bazaar continue to be the preferred choice for cheaper local produce and other staples. Market day in the towns of Mauritius is the shopper's opportunity to discuss freshness and prices with jocular growers who will boast 'pas fin met di sel dans sa legim la' (organically grown vegetables). These open-air markets also serve as outlets for garment-industry 'seconds' and defective items which are sold at cut-rate prices. The unlabelled designer clothes that you find there run the gamut from Ralph Lauren Polo shirts to Gap sweatshirts or jeans and Pierre Cardin ties and sweaters – all made in Mauritius in the Export Processing Zone factories by a largely female workforce. In other words, shopping in Mauritius is now basically the same kind of experience as shopping in any number of American towns where farmers' markets and outlet malls coexist in various neighbourhoods. The difference is in the rapidity with which changes have occurred since the early 1980s, and the radically different relationship which the local consumer has to the modes of production of the items on sale, to the surplus that they represent, and to the workforce that produced it.

Two of the most basic necessities, food and clothing, form part of the range of material practices central to the identity of a people. It is a truism that what we eat and how we eat tends to define us as social beings (Weismantle 1989), and that there is a dynamic relationship between the body, clothing, and the changing self-representations of citizens (Hendrickson 1996). The worldwide expansion of capitalism, and the phenomenon vaguely known as 'globalization', bring about new forms of social interaction which are superimposed on more traditional ones, resulting in stresses on gender roles and familial arrangements, and in conflicted responses to new job opportunities. People's bodies exhibit the mark of their changing relationship to the symbolic realm of culture. Thus, in Mauritius, the new consumerism spells a less complex diet, even causing nutritional disorders of all kinds, like those prevalent in the West: obesity, anaemia, anorexia or bulimia. Women who are employed in the service sector are given tailored uniforms which do minimize their clothing expenses but also affect their self-image and their demeanour. Add to this the omnipresent billboards promoting the products of the offshore garment industry and the tourist sector's objectification of the exotic Mauritian feminine body in its advertising of this 'island paradise', and you have the ingredients for making women appearance-conscious in a more Western way, suspended between their roles as producers and consumers on the one hand, and as lures for both tourists and foreign capital investments on the other.

Women's relationship to food and shopping, work, language and sexuality is shifting rapidly, and creating new pathologies of identification. The social and economic forces which normalize slenderness and gender identity (Bordo 1993) and conflate the exotic Creole or Asian body with stereotypical forms of 'mysterious' femininity become reinforced by public health warnings against the dangers of malnutrition and obesity. Faced with these modern stereotypes, which the well-intentioned government campaigns serve to reinforce, but having to cope with aspects of the traditional culture, which puts a definite premium on 'plumpness', Mauritian women have to sort out conflicting signals about body shape, health and food. From breast milk and baby formula to the preparation of quotidian family meals, everyday choices now carry a heavy symbolic load, and generate stressful reactions. More women than ever are developing symptomatic reactions of alienation and disembodiment, which continue a pattern of psycho-somatic ailments dating from slavery and indentured labour, and amount to internalized forms of social and gender oppression.

In the industrial sector – especially the garment factories – stress-related fainting spells, screaming fits, seizures and spirit possession are not rare. They create disturbances and cause production shutdowns, and can thus be interpreted as tactics of resistance, non-verbal ruses against authority or surreptitious forms of protest (Certeau 1984). They are also physical reactions to and ways of dealing with the traumas of colonial and neocolonial exploitation (Ong 1986). This behaviour is increasingly recognized and disciplined by the medico-cultural discourses which regulate health and normalcy on an international scale. Mental illness has become a big business. It is treated by growing numbers of health professionals who practise at the old Brown Sequard Hospital, aptly named after the nineteenth-century Franco-Mauritian neurologist who became famous in Paris for his research on glandular secretions and hormonal therapy for mental disorders, including hysteria and anorexia (Brumberg 1988: 206–8). Today, among the affluent classes, even Prozac has become a drug of choice for depression. But since psychosomatic reactions are still largely read as narcissistic or hysterical, women have been the primary targets for experimental treatments, drugs and psychotherapy which aim at 'normalizing' their behaviour.

Eating disorders are commonly associated with a warped self-image, and a distorted sense of one's body shape and appearance. Feminist research has shown, however, that these disorders are closely related to larger social issues, including work and wage-labour, rather than being the result of a narcissistic or neurotic focus on personal appearance. Women's self-image cannot be divorced or decontextualized from the use- or exchange-value of the body within the political economy of a given culture. Cultural critics increasingly view the fixation on personal appearance as a result of the relationship we are obliged to have to our productive capabilities, and to the concurrent need to discipline our labouring body. Anorexia and bulimia can thus be seen as the conse-quences of a social need generated not just by unrealistic standards of beauty but also by the conditions governing rules in the workplace, and by the history of the culture and the nation. Mauritius is now a postcolonial and developing nation with a history of trauma related to its past and the demands which were put on its workforce (from slavery to neocolonial exploitation). Somatic disorders linked to the globalization of the economy are thus a multilayered syndrome, symptomatic of the survival of the past in the present.

Social Reality and Personal Stories

Few cultural historians and anthropologists have done work on Mauritius (Arno & Orian 1986; Eriksen 1988; Nirsimloo-Anenden 1990). Only Nirsimloo-Anenden has asked gender-related questions, but her research is limited to the Telegu ethnic group. No one else has used gender as a systematic category of analysis, or conducted extensive interviews with women. Information about popular culture is found mostly in the work of folklorists such as Lee Haring, who bemoans the fact that oral tales are not taken seriously by the educated elites who have internalized Western values and standards of literacy and rationality (Haring 1992). Sociologists, on the other hand, have recently begun to document some of the changes in labour reorganization, while economists have always shown a great deal of interest in the resilience of the local markets and the productive capacity of women workers.

In the 1980s, Free-Trade Zones and Export Processing Zones were set up in Mauritius, as in a number of developing countries, as an instrument of economic stabilization and structural adjustment. Export Processing Zones (or EPZs) have been devised by the international banking community to help indebted governments to redress their balance-of-payments deficits by producing goods for the international market. As Cynthia Enloe describes it: 'Governments lure overseas companies to move their plants to these EPZs by offering them sewers, electricity, ports, runways, tax holidays and police protection. Most attractive of all is the governments' offer of cheap labour. Women's labour has been the easiest to cheapen, so it shouldn't be surprising that in most Export Processing Zones at least 70 per cent of the workers are women' (Enloe 1989: 159). In Mauritius, women's share of manufacturing employment was 6.6 per cent in 1962, climbed to 57.4 per cent in 1982 (Pearson in Nababsing abd Kothari 1996: 25), and hovers at around 66 per cent today. These new forms of industrialization have helped to create a precariously affluent middle class. If the new shopping malls exemplify this affluence in the urban areas, the garment factories which have sprouted in the middle of sugar-cane fields have transformed the rural areas, providing employment where the poorest people live. Sociologists Vidula Nababsing and Uma Kothari, who have studied these patterns in

Mauritius, Bangladesh and Sri Lanka, note that the socioeconomic
benefits to women have been considerable, even where employment
conditions, wages, labour laws, and low unionization levels have created
less than optimal working environments. Their findings indicate that in
Mauritius, 'new employment opportunities were taken up either by
those who would otherwise have gone into an already declining agricultural sector or domestic service' (Nababsing and Kothari 1996: 134),
or would not have been job-seekers in the first place.

For the sociologists, the single criterion of 'new employment opportunities' is a value, since it is helping women to acquire a measure of
independence which can allow them to escape some of the more rigid
religious and patriarchal traditions, to support themselves and their
families in ways that improve upon the arduous labour in the sugar-
cane fields. The benefits of modernization should not be discounted,
their argument goes, even when the mobility of international capital
renders industrialization ephemeral: consciousness-raising has been an
important impact of industrialization. 'In fact, the empowerment of
women in terms of their increased participation in social, economic
and political arenas [became] a primary objective for many development
agencies and projects' (Nababsing and Kothari 1996: 152), as women
pushed for reforms in the areas of social and welfare services. The
'moral panic' (Nababsing and Kothari 1996: 148) expressed by some
religious leaders at the prospects of liberalization, and their fear that it
would impact negatively on 'family values', have been largely unfounded
as women have organized to support one another and strengthen community bonds.

The psychosocial aspects of this industrialization process, however,
have been largely neglected by development 'experts'. The intimate
feelings of the women and their working conditions have recently been
articulated in fictional texts. These feelings must give us pause as we
listen to the worker's own voice against the sociologists' account of
empowerment and participatory democracy. As Lindsay Collen's autobiographical character Shynee reports in *There is a Tide*:

> I'll be twenty-three soon and I've got already ten years' experience behind
> me. Ten years making woollen threads out of bundles of wool or sewing
> collars, collars and more collars. Don't know who I'm making it all for, not
> even what'll become of it. I feel old and tired. Don't we all. Some of us
> climbing up and down. It is like an animal, that I feel? Like an ox, to be
> more precise, working bowed and cowed. Over a sitting machine. Others
> like me in my first job, watch the thread on the machine, and when it
> breaks, which it does every few minutes, they climb up on the stool and tie

it up again fast, and do this day in and day out, on an eight hour shift, ever-rotating. Seven to three, three to eleven, eleven to seven. And then again.

And I've never moaned. Please don't misunderstand me. Even now I am not moaning. In any case I prefer working on the twister running backwards and forwards after the 'mule' like my mates have to. Other workers work harder than I do. Especially now that I am a machinist, bottom to my chair, back aching, sewing away at collars…. Sometimes I feel all angry inside about it. I don't know what it is. I am humiliated by my turning this eight hours into my bread.

I had to eat a lot. We all do in the factory. I was quite proud that I got a bit round…. And being a machinist, I jumped about less. Much less than on the twister…. So a general plumpness rounded me off. (Collen 1990: 44–5)

The manipulation of the body of the worker, and her feelings of anger and humiliation, convey the concrete consequences of exploitation. Food becomes a substitute for free expression and freedom of movement. It compensates for the physical discomforts of wage-labour: food is what one works for, but also that which can soothe the humiliation of 'turning this eight hours into bread'. It is the sign of one's alienation. As women are made more conscious of the 'shape' they are in, yet use food to take comfort in the soothing quality of its sensual aspects, their individual anguish is made visible and shared in these non-verbal ways of coping.

Women writers who bear witness to their efforts document their vulnerabilities and strengths as the new exploited class of global capital. Struggling to become the subjects of their own stories, the narrators of their own history, women workers engage with the public scripts that attempt to define them. There is a Tide fictionalizes the material and symbolic changes of the 1980s by reinterpreting current somatic symptoms in terms of a history of social and political events. As the 'labour politics of postmodernity' (Ong 1986) infiltrates communities which had remained largely rural and self-sufficient, ethnicity, gender and class are redefined and intertwined with shifting economic relations of domination and insubordination. Fictional and personal narratives become the sites where contradictions are worked out and solutions begin to be imagined.

A polyvocal text which looks back on twenty-five years of post-independence Mauritius, There is a Tide is a testimonial narrative which stages and authorizes different perspectives on this contested reality. There are three parallel testimonies: 22-year-old Shynee Pillay, an anorexic Hindu worker in a shirt factory in the free-trade zone, writes an 'auto-analysis' (Collen 1990: 7) for her psychotherapist at the Brown Sequard Hospital; Fatma, a midwife, recounts the life of Shynee's grandmother and father, and the latter's public role as union and strike organizer during the revolutionary struggles for independence; finally, the unnamed psychotherapist's stream-of-consciousness diary reveals a disconnected and disaffected postmodern subjectivity. These three voices are themselves embedded within a futuristic frame which projects the reader into the twenty-first century and a utopian post-globalization world. The narratives provide a multifaceted critique of social victimization and agency during what the framing story calls the pre-revolutionary 'dark ages'. Two autobiographical modes are constrasted with a historical and biographical one, and their relative status as sources of information is foregrounded by the utopian quest for useful and enabling knowledge. Each narrator's act of witnessing articulates for the reader the interconnectedness of the local and the global, of gender, ethnic and class subject positions. Taken together, the stories add up to counterhistory and visionary feminine ethnography. They perform identity and citizenship on three levels across time and space, rewriting the history of independence movements, exposing the complacent attitudes of local elites, denouncing the politics of female labour in the Export Processing Zones, and questioning neocolonial consumerism as well as religious fundamentalism.

In her study of the testimonial genre, Doris Sommer has shown how Latin American *testimónios* are related 'to a general text of struggle ... written from interpersonal class and ethnic positions' (Sommer 1988: 129) which engage the reader in a relationship of 'respectful distance' where difference is acknowledged, and the goal is 'to raise the reader's consciousness by linking her to the writer's testimony' (Sommer 1988: 130). In *There is a Tide*, the plurality of subject positions which cannot be collapsed into one another challenges the reader to consider more inclusive definitions of citizenship and to question the clichés of democracy. Each story foregrounds coping mechanisms and ways of witnessing directly linked to the social practices that are implicitly being critiqued. Sommer makes the point that 'one of the most fascinating features of [*testimónios*] is their unpredictable pattern, the sense that the discourse of analysis and struggle is being created in an open-ended and syncretic process of trial, error, and surprise' (Sommer 1988: 120). The three alternating narratives of *There is a Tide* provide this sense of 'surprise' as they function as interpretative frameworks for one another. Fatma tells of the father's experiences of political solidarity: the historic dockers' strike of 1971 and the general strike of 1979, which culminated in a hunger strike by the jailed activists. Listening to her, Shynee is able to recast her own choices and motivations – to 'name the spaces of ignorance', as bell hooks puts it – and to appropriate the realm of the political. History's hidden scripts gradually emerge, along with an alternative reading of her anorexia not just as individualized protest against social constraints, but also as an echo of the heroism of a previous generation of political agents. The public theatre of nationalist politics and the private realm of women's lives are brought together by the same spectacular gestures of refusal and rejection, and by analogous ways of dealing with inequities and refusing consumption. The narrative thus mediates the performance of self-starvation and its gendered contexts by weaving together the symptons and the cure, the seeming solitariness of anorexia and the public statement of hunger-strikers.

The different styles of each section of the novel force a constant readjustment on the part of the reader, enacting a deconstruction of the seamless narratives of neocolonialism and exposing the postmodern fragmentation of the new nation. Fatma's and Shynee's voices interrupt the ironic and self-deprecating flow of the medical expert. The psychiatrist's breathless style of enunciation, intensified by the lack of punctuation, mirrors the penetrating flow of capital as it infiltrates every aspect of the local economy. While the cumulative effect of his words on the page aestheticizes and 'privatizes' his experiences, his soliloquy is a form of excess that interrupts the narrative or testimonial economy of the women's dialogues, and his tone reveals the disciplining power of money and privilege. The testimonies of the women, on the other hand, their stories of embodied struggle within the regulative discourses of culture, labour and capital, assert the dissolution of the very concept of 'privacy', making visible the concrete material conditions of their existence and the 'collective assemblage' of their enunciation (Deleuze and Guattari 1986). Their conversation thus puts the reader (rather than the psychiatrist) in the position of witness to the cultural and historical trauma of the nation and its working class.

When small oppositional practices of everyday life (Certeau 1984) proliferate outside hegemonic relations, in the interstices of systems of domination hidden from public scrutiny, testimonial narratives help to articulate personal experiences as forms of collective struggle, as 'structures of feeling' (Williams 1977: 128) and emergent sensibilities. The public scenarios of globalization, their norms and disciplining power, are sundered by the multiplication of unscripted behaviours revealed by the dissenting voices of the women. The storytelling in which they engage shifts the focus from 'expert' and professional testimony (medicine, anthropology, sociology, economy) on to their own concrete experiences. The act of telling and remembering is thus part of a process of symbolization, a sharing of values, the logic of which produces more self-aware and politicized subjectivities. As a literary text, *There is a Tide* draws attention to the casualties of the new labour markets while remaining an open-ended and utopian engagement with the desire for long-term political change. As literature, then, it is the space where issues that are not immediately resolvable politically can be articulated and symbolized, leading its readers towards both a personal and a national confrontation with the issues and traumas that have occluded discussions about the past, the histories of colonialism and independence struggles, their gendered subtexts, and the way these issues continue to have an effect in the present.

Blood, Milk and Money

At the hospital where she begins her narrative, Shynee is required to decline her identity using a questionnaire meant to establish the 'facts' of her life: name, age, occupation, education, and so on. When she gets to the last line, 'food preferences', she writes: 'I refuse to answer this. This question is, in my case, not in the realm of fact, at all' (Collen 1990: 20). She adds: 'What I am about to write is the reason why I *do not eat*' (Collen 1990: 27). Her first explanation is the obvious one: wanting to conform to new models of beauty, to be 'thin. Slim. Lithe. Svelte. Light as a feather' (Collen 1990: 43), she thinks of it as a necessary 'diet' after becoming a bit too 'plump' on the factory job. Dieting now becomes an issue of self-control, and the focus broadens from body size to contours and appearance in general. Factory workers who have fits are tagged 'wild women'. Shynee's head of 'unruly hair' becomes a symbol of unbridled sexuality which connotes a femininity out of control. It needs to be tied 'up into a neat plait' (Collen 1990: 43), just as her clothing needs to conform to certain rules. Hair and skin imperfections become signs of the 'madness escaped from inside of me' (Collen 1990: 163), as she puts it. The fear of revealing her inner reality translates into a need to restrain and stabilize the inner self within impermeable borders: 'I had two linked worries. Not wanting to take anything in. And not wanting to let anything break out' (Collen 1990: 47). Susie Orbach has shown how anorexia is precipitated by the tensions and paradoxes women experience about their place in the world: 'Anorexia symbolizes the restraint on women's desire. In the most tortuous denial of need and dependency and the most persistent and insistent expression of independence, women with anorexia live out the contrariness of contemporary cultural dictates.... Anorexia is at

once an embodiment of stereotyped femininity and its very opposite'
(Orbach 1986: 29, 30). As she moves out of the sphere of the home,
where the matriarchs of the village praise a well-rounded body, and
goes to work in the factory, Shynee's values are jolted by advertising
dictates and factory rules which encourage uniformity, but succeed only
in generating schizophrenic reactions.

The power to refuse food becomes performative on other levels as
well. It leads to dissent and defiance with regard to the technologies of
identity used by the hospital. Each line on the questionnaire now raises
more questions than it enables Shynee to answer: 'Name. I have already
given my name. It is a fact. A known fact. But facts are difficult. The
fact of *Shynee Pillay* is fraught with problems' (Collen 1990: 17). As
Kamala Visweswaran has pointed out in *Fictions of Feminist Ethnography*, 'facts'
have a way of being misperceived, of contructing the subject 'as' something other than she wants to be seen (Visweswaran 1994: 61). Referring to a woman who 'refused … to be [her] subject', and whom she
calls simply 'M' in her research, Visweswaran asks: 'What if I were to
call this resisting subject Françoise or Ghislaine? Surely my audience,
anticipating the story of an Indian woman, would object knowing that
the anthropological pseudonym connotes place-name if not ethnic
identity.' Shynee's 'paper name' connotes a specific caste and ethnic
identity – and refusing to use it is a proclamation of distrust for printed
information, for government or religious 'archives' (Collen 1990: 19)
that immediately demarcate her as representative of a distinct political
class, with a civil status that she has not chosen. Her musings echo
those of her father, who had pondered the wisdom of 'changing' names
handed down in slave cultures: 'To change it seems to be to sell out.
To abandon the last memory … To somehow bury something that should
not be buried. To forget what should be remembered. And yet, to leave
it the same seems to mean you accept the slave-owners' definition of
you' (Collen 1990: 75). Names are linked to 'blood-lines', but as Fatma's
commentary stresses, the seemingly ambivalent identity (both Indian
and African Creole) of Shynee's father, his double name – Lallmohar/
Larmwar and Laval – was a force in the struggles for independence, a
symbol against the 'race war' (Collen 1990: 29), and a means of avoiding
essentialist notions of self and other: 'Nothing is in your blood, girl.
It's all out there, around you, moulding you, making you. That is the
only moral my story will have' (Collen 1990: 75). The physical and the
social body are conflated in this reminder that religious beliefs encourage arbitrary notions of racialized and gendered purity and posit
definitions of selfhood that can lead to ethnic cleansing. When workers

at the factory break up into race and religious groups to eat their meals, Shynee reacts with 'morbid horror' (Collen 1990: 148–9), realizing that efforts to unionize them are bound to be difficult if even the sharing of food becomes an index of the fragmentations and divisions that the bosses can now easily exploit. Her refusal to be named and circumscribed by the rules of patriarchal logic extends to food choices, and cultural notions of purity and transgression.

In her study of pollution and taboo, *Purity and Danger*, Mary Douglas stresses that 'food is not likely to be polluting at all unless external boundaries of the social system are under pressure' (Douglas 1966: 127). The fear of social destabilization is brought about by the proliferation of new social practices – from pre-packaged and pre-cooked foodstuffs and objects whose use-value is at issue, to new work opportunities. This fear serves to reinforce archaic models of purity at all levels of society. As Douglas puts it: 'If we treat ritual protection of bodily orifices as a symbol of social preoccupations about exits and entrances, the purity of cooked food becomes important' (Douglas 1966: 126). Quoting from commentators who have studied Indian pollution symbolism, Douglas explains that 'cooking may be taken to imply a complete appropriation of the food by the household. It is almost as if, before being "internally absorbed" by the individual, food was, by cooking, collectively predigested. One cannot share the food prepared by people without sharing in their nature' (Douglas 1966: 126). Thus the preparation and consumption of food are symbolically marked, and changes in eating habits can lead to symptomatic disorders at the individual and collective level. Refusing to consume what is external to the household, the culture, the nation, the anorexic appears to be making visible the paradoxical yet logical parallel between self-starvation and the utopian need to feel autonomous in the face of global capitalism.

When Shynee states, 'milk was my first food, and I don't want to drink milk' (Collen 1990: 27), she emphasizes its ambiguous meaning. The most basic food of life, it carries a set of unsettling connotations. 'Milk', Roland Barthes has said, 'is cosmetic, it joins, covers, restores … its purity, associated with the innocence of the child, is a token of strength, of a strength which is not revulsive, not congestive, but calm, white, lucid, the equal of reality' (Barthes 1972: 60). But the production and circulation of milk in rural Mauritius are fraught with taboos which are anything but 'calm' and comforting. The milk-producing cows are cared for by women who collect and sell the fresh milk to a middleman. Shynee's stepfather is such a milkman who circulates in the countryside, puts diluted milk in an 'aluminium tank soldered to his bicycle' (Collen 1990: 164), and resells the watered-down product to other families for a fat profit.

Although milk is generally linked to the notion of purity and mother-hood, in this context it becomes, like bloodlines, the sign of an oppressive system of exchange, and of an imposed identity. It marks the numerous ways in which women lack control over their own labour and bodies, which can be exploited by those who are freer to circulate at will in society. The nature and use-value of milk thus foregrounds the links between production and reproduction, especially unwanted pregnancies: 'My mother did not want me. I was foist upon her.... Nor did she want my father. He was also foist upon her' (Collen 1990: 29). Shynee exposes the notion of 'family' as artificial, and the traditional role of mothers as bearers of culture as damaging to their relationship to the child. 'She breastfed reluctance into me', says Shynee, denounc-ing the corporeal struggle involved in reluctant motherhood, the hard-ships that biology visits upon the women who do not have the luxury of sentimentalizing the maternal instinct.

Resentment against sexuality and reproduction, as well as other 'natural' functions of the body such as digestion, evacuation and menstruation, becomes confused within a symbolic economy that at-tempts to conflate nature and culture. Shynee's refusal to conform becomes a leitmotiv against the perversion of natural needs. When her mother dies – 'in a pool of blood on her bed' (Collen 1990: 59) – from a botched illegal abortion, Shynee is confirmed in her 'reluctant' sub-jectivity, that of a woman who refuses to be defined by the feminine realm of the 'fluid' (Irigaray 1985), by the products of her body: blood and milk. The oppressive structures of religious taboos, in Hinduism as in other religions, associate traditional views of femininity with un-cleanliness and filth. The significations attached to blood and milk, and the role women play in reproducing gender differences, are central to Shynee's developing feelings of repulsion. As Carolyn Bynum has shown in her study of medieval women's fasts, fasting is impelled by the pious need to feel 'clean', 'pure' and 'holy'. The anorexic's wish for disem-bodied spirituality, for a state of being that will be divorced from the pollution associated with the flesh, stems from the religious conflation of the impure with the feminine (Bynum 1987). 'I have stopped eating, doctor, in order to be cleaner. The more I stop, the cleaner. The cleaner, the holier. I want to be holy ... I would prefer never to get my periods, if it's unclean. If I don't eat, maybe I won't', confesses Shynee (Collen 1990: 59). Since menstruation is what banishes women to the realm of immanence, that of the unchaste and the desecrated, it is not surprising that Shynee, 'not wanting to let anything break out' of her, should also resist 'tak[ing] anything in' (Collen 1990: 47). Caught in a double bind, she would 'rather not risk living', since life might mean passing on to a daughter the mark of gender and its weight of shame, guilt, self-hatred and despair. Refusal becomes empowering, since it is what allows her to go against the grain of femininity and motherhood, to step out of the shackles of patriarchal culture.

Self-awareness and negativity finally culminate in Shynee's realization that her behaviour is not simply culturally driven (dieting, fasting), but economically and politically motivated as well:

> I have no objection to eating, to using food. I just happen to refuse to consume food. I am a producer. I work ... I don't always know what I produce. Nor do I know who I produce it for. But I know for sure I am a producer. I make shirts.... I am not a consumer of things.... This refusing to consume is what turns out to be my not eating. (Collen 1990: 104–5)

The distinction between 'using' and 'consuming', between need and want, the necessary and the superfluous, is hard to establish, however, since money corrupts the use-value of things. When even milk becomes a commodity like any other, it can be exchanged for money. Its exchangeability corrupts its inaugural meaning, and perverts its original usage.

For Marx, only 'superfluous products become exchangeable products', only those 'whose use-value falls outside the sphere of mere necessaries' (Marx 1904: 168). Milk, like bread and money, becomes what one works for rather than the source of life. The milkman who collects it from the rural women and sells it for a profit to his high-caste clients is in a position to legislate the standards of 'purity' which must accompany the handling of milk by the womenfolk whose impure nature (according to Hindu beliefs) can cause the milk to curdle when they are menstruating. But Shynee suggests that the man's ability to turn this 'product' into a consumer good, to water it down in order to make more money, contaminates its meaning with regard to the 'basic necessities of life'. Milk thus loses its purity, its 'innocence' (Barthes 1972). It becomes the 'abject' (Kristeva 1986) – something that is both self and other, but feared as foreign; something against which the self must be guarded. The throat contracts against the invasion by this substance, thus rejecting what does not enter into 'the satisfaction of immediate need' (Marx 1904: 208), what is already defiled by its association with the notions of superfluity and excess. No longer the natural means of satisfying a natural need, milk becomes a medium of exchange which further oppresses those who are subjected to its symbolic economy. It becomes that which can be dispensed with, expelled, evacuated – in other words, it becomes, in Freudian terms, linked to faeces and excrements within the archaic economy of the social subject (Goux 1990: 29–31).

Milk becomes a metaphor for what Shynee's body refuses to ingest, and for what the nation's Export Processing Zones symbolize in this new world economy. The EPZs are sites which are both within the country, and yet external to it, regulated by laws which transcend those that govern the lives of the ordinary citizens who labour in those zones, but reap few of their benefits. They are useful to the developing country, but for Shynee they are the means by which her exploitation reaches a point of paroxysm. When the concept of need is perverted, the refusal of food corresponds to a very different logic of starvation from the one prevalent in either Western interpretations of narcissistic 'dieting' or religious notions of purification and 'fasting'. It now corresponds to a paradoxical logic of survival, expressed in the contradiction at the heart of the statement made by Shynee just before her return to a more 'earthy' acceptance of embodiment: 'It is as though I want to say: I don't need to eat to stay alive' (Collen 1990: 168).

With this declaration, Shynee comes full circle and experiences a form of epiphany that grounds her in unmediated nature. In a crucial scene, she is suddenly attracted by a smell: 'I felt my nostrils flare open. I put my head back and sniffed. Loudly. Like a wild deer … I snorted. I panted with excitement…. It was a rotting *tang*' (Collen 1990: 174). The *tang* is a rodent which burrows and scavenges for food, 'the lowliest of creatures' (Collen 1990: 173). This dead animal, the symbol of what is abject in nature, becomes the catalyst that sets Shynee on the road to recovery. In a horrific attempt at ingesting that symbol of impurity, she becomes like a scavenging animal herself, merging with all that is abject, and recovering in this process an identity that she had been taught to deny. She becomes a 'huntress' (Collen 1990: 175), and her appetite returns. She embraces nature and its life-affirming 'filth' and transforms her relationship to culture. She asserts her independence from culturally defined functions of the body, but this is not an illusion of transcendence. Rather, it is her acknowledgement of the *utopian possibility* of being in harmony with unmediated nature, of surviving at the level of raw need, of feeding on wild creatures and uncooked substances. The fact that she then starts to eat normally (that is, processed foods) is an indication of the transformative power of this realization. In other words, she is tempted by, but recognizes the futility of, an escape from the encroachment of global society, from the uneven exchanges metaphorized by the whole process of feeding. She learns from the *tang* that to scavenge and to survive is a perfectly acceptable form of resistance, whereas anorexia and isolationism lead to self-destructiveness. Her discovery about food can be extended to the economic realm as well. If the products of the EPZs are meant for foreign markets, and if the local economy has to make do with 'seconds' or 'rejects', then the local producer/consumer becomes a form of scavenger who undoes the distinction between the local and the global, the pure and the impure, the raw and the cooked. She can decide to survive on the crumbs or leftovers of that global economy, rather than letting it destroy her. She can learn to manipulate the system, and benefit from its contradictions.[1]

Hunger Artists and Hunger-Strikers

In this story, 'normal' or patriarchal narrative logic would have required closure either in the form of death (anorexics often starve to death, as do political prisoners whose sole means of protest is fasting) or in complete separation from the realm of the social. But the initial rejection of food is only a means to a creative end. It permits the narrator's voice to come into its own, voraciously to enumerate possible explanations of her reluctance to be a 'model consumer'. Deleuze and Guattari explain that 'there is a certain disjunction between eating and speaking, and even more, despite all appearances, between eating and writing … writing transform[s] words into things capable of competing with food.… To speak, and above all to write, is to fast' (Deleuze and Guattari 1986: 19–20). In writing her 'auto-analysis', Shynee progresses through different stages of negativity which offer a systematic critique of social 'norms'. She reaches a point of political and critical awareness that allows her to embrace life and affirm her local cultural values. Her fast is a form of consciousness-raising. It clears the path towards higher self-knowledge, even if this knowledge is embedded within multiple contradictions.

Like other 'hunger artists' before her, Shynee *performs* linguistically, and thus renders visible the gap between cultural survival and mere physical subsistence.[2] By contrasting what Maud Ellman has termed the 'wordless testimony of the famished flesh' (Ellman 1993: 17) with the abundance of descriptive language in the local vernacular, Shynee is able to distinguish her anorexia from other forms of self-denial. By articulating her refusal as a form of hunger strike, and then attributing a series of meanings to her refusal, she is able to make her 'self-starvation

readable as protest' (Ellman 1993; emphasis added). The artistry and elo-
quence of the testimony serve to 'master [the] destructive logic' (Ellman
1993: 21) of the act of starving. Rather than denying and disavowing
her eating disorder, as women patients are generally supposed to do,
Shynee's narrative allows her to claim agency and responsibility for the
act of negation; rather than being a denial, her act is one of conscious
refusal. By withholding the basic and 'natural' needs of the body, she
is simultaneously conferring upon it the status of a cipher, a slate upon
which the notion of negation is inscribed – just as her father's body
and those of manual labourers had their work 'engraved' into it (Collen
1990: 34), marked and broken by the weight of the burdens they carried
and the repeated gestures they performed as dockers who loaded sugar
on to the cargo ships. The mechanization of sugar-loading has rendered
the docker's job obsolete, but it is now the female workers of the EPZs
who are put in the same situation of repetitive physical labour. Their
physical trauma mirrors those of the past, and begs the question about
modes of psychological healing that can take this long history into
consideration instead of excising the gendered subject from its representations.

In the chronicle of revolutionary events narrated by Fatma, the heroic
strike of the dockers serves as counterpoint, and introduces another
notion of purposiveness. Fourteen of them starve together, publicly, in
the main park of the capital city (Collen 1990: 212). The collective
aspect of this protest contrasts starkly with the woman's isolating refusal
of food. Since eating and conviviality are very much a part of the
activity of building social bonds, to refuse food would be to become
hopelessly isolated. But if the gift and the sharing of food constitute
the basis for building cohesion, while the nature of the food to be
shared clearly undermines the constitution of the group or the nation,
then it becomes logical to propose that it is in the collective refusal of
the *inappropriate* meal that a proper community can begin to be imagined.
If an earlier generation of workers embarked together on a hunger
strike to solidify the communal means by which they might succeed in
resisting oppression, then Shynee's accomplishment is of a different
nature. By ceasing to refuse food undiscriminatingly, she learns the
difference between the blanket denial of need and the discriminating
approach of an enlightened subject who does not exist and survive
only 'by the gaze of others' (Ellman 1993: 17). She no longer needs to
exhibit her physical body as an instrument of protest, to mortify it. She
can make choices that will not be damaging to her being, just as – it
is implied – the community, too, can resist rampant consumerism,

benefit from the consolidation of its most vital and local needs, and survive by using the resources of its newly prosperous economy.

The narrative attempts to resolve these contradictions by slipping into the realm of utopia. The tone changes to one of prelapsarian reliance on the goodness of nature's bounty, on the quasi-mythic time of Shynee's childhood, when cultural and economic self-sufficiency seemed the norm. The flora and fauna are lovingly described in a style which combines English and Creole with meticulous precision:

> bred murum from trees, bred sonz in the marshes, and bred gandol, and bred batat, and bred martin, and these were our vegetables, they grew by themselves, and were free for the taking.... We would ... cook the karang fish, or the kapitenn, or the madam tonbe, of the vyel, or the kordonye.... Or we'd go down to Belil River and catch and eat the tilapya and carp fried crisp. (Collen 1990: 105)

In those days, the small general store of the village was a site of festive diversity which allowed one to cross cultural borders simply by choosing different kinds of 'French' (franse), 'Indian' (indyen) or Chinese (lasir) sweets according to one's desires, or the holiday being celebrated:

> oven baked cakes called gato franse and sweets called gato indyen. During the cane cutting season, there was gato lakerls.... At Chinese New Year, there was gato lasir, called 'wax cake' because it looks just like wax, somehow made from rice. There was gato papay, which was not made from pawpaw, but from Chinese pumpkin. (Collen 1990: 108)

The linguistic density and the poetry of these lists convey a playful use of language, a freedom from external constraints that seems possible only because the materiality of food is transformed into the materiality and magic of language. The lists go on to include objects of all sorts that used to coexist in the neighbourhood shop tended by Lung Yu. But there, these objects' use-value was indisputable, as though the Creole terms that describe them (paydefer, karay, koton perle, patang, rwa dezer, katora, kalchul, lakord filin, medsinn pis, all in Collen 1990: 110–14) could allow for their integration within a non-alienating symbolic economy. Says Shynee: 'I have nothing against paying for things ... So long as I use them. So long as they are part of our lives' (Collen 1990: 116). As Shynee articulates her understanding of her own resistance to consumption, the logic of the narrative suggests that it is the process of writing and communicating in the local language which produces the possibility of considering choices that might still be within reach of informed, enlightened citizens.

Like Lung Yu's store, an anarchic space of diversity, language becomes a space of creative folly, unlike the well-ordered and uniformed existence

of the pragmatic consumer or practical user of words in the standard
European language. The excess (represented by the numerous recipes,
the descriptions of Creole foods, and the 'private' realm of female
solidarity) becomes a metonymy for the excessive or supplementary
nature of the Creole language – a language that is nevertheless vital for
the continuity and survival of the community. The narrative excess
emblematized by those lists thematizes the theoretical debates over the
status and usefulness of Creole among the local elites. It is often dismissed as mere dialect, superfluous, 'vulgar and disgusting and abusive'
(Collen 1990: 81) – in other words, 'impure' or 'abject'. Yet this is the
language that allows Shynee to name those things that are 'part of [her]
life'. It is the foundation of both her subjective and her social existence, and it allows her to name those basic necessities that reinforce
her sense of identity and community. These passages become meaningful and useful in a way that contrasts sharply with the professional ex-
cesses of the psychiatrist's or 'expert's' voice, and permits the author to
integrate the local culture within the Standard English text.

Collen's fictional text, the women's voices it brings to the public sphere
of English-language literature, and the Creole culture to which it bears
witness are a rich contribution to international discourses on development. It is a provocative look at the complex practices that are transforming everyday life on a global scale, and a call to respect diversity
in all its forms, especially linguistic ones. *There is a Tide* represents the
diversity of contemporary Mauritius, and manages to raise serious
questions about history, gender and society that social scientists and
economists would do well to ponder.

Notes

1. I thank Kathleen McHugh and Tiffany Ana Lopez for pointing this out.
2. See Ellman for a thorough study of the spectacular aspects of starvation:
'Self-starvation is above all a performance ... it is staged to trick the conscience
of its viewers, forcing them to recognize that they are implicated in the spectacle
that they behold' (1993: 17).

References

Arno, T. and C. Orian (1986) *Ile Maurice: Une société multiraciale*, Paris: L'Harmattan.
Barthes, R. (1972) *Mythologies*, New York: Noonday Press.
Bordo, S. (1993) *Unbearable Weight: Feminism, Western Culture, and the Body* Berkeley:
    University of California Press.

Brumberg, J. Jacobs (1988) *Fasting Girls: The Emergence of Anorexia Nervosa as a Modern Disease*, Cambridge, MA: Harvard University Press.

Bynum, C. (1987) *Holy Fast and Holy Feast: The Religious Significance of Food to Medieval Women*, Berkeley: University of California Press.

Certeau, M. de (1984) *The Practice of Everyday Life*, Berkeley: University of California Press.

Collen, L. (1990) *There is a Tide*, Port Louis: Ledikasyon pu Travayer.

Dangarembga, T. (1988) *Nervous Conditions*, Seattle, WA: The Seal Press.

Deleuze, G. and F. Guattari (1986) *Kafka: Toward a Minor Literature*, Minneapolis: University of Minnesota Press.

Douglas, M. (1966) *Purity and Danger: An Analysis of the Concepts of Pollution and Taboo*, London: Routledge & Kegan Paul.

The Economist (1988) 'Mauritius: Miracle in Trouble', 28 February.

Ellman, M. (1993) *The Hunger Artists: Starving, Writing, and Imprisonment*, Cambridge, MA: Harvard University Press.

Enloe, C. (1989) *Bananas, Beaches, and Bases*, Berkeley: University of California Press.

Eriksen, T. (1988) *Communicating Cultural Differences and Identity: Ethnicity and Nationalism in Mauritius*, Oslo: Oslo Occasional Papers in Social Anthropology.

Goux, J.-J. (1990) *Symbolic Economies: After Marx and Freud*, Ithaca, NY: Cornell University Press.

Haring, L. (1992) 'Buried Treasure', *Journal of Mauritian Studies*, vol. IV, no. 1.

Hendrickson, H., ed. (1996) *Clothing and Difference: Embodied Identities in Colonial and Post-Colonial Africa*, Durham, NC: Duke University Press.

hooks, b. (1989) *Talking Back: Thinking Feminist, Thinking Black*, Boston: South End Press.

Irigaray, L. (1985) *This Sex Which Is Not One*, Ithaca, NY: Cornell University Press.

Jeune Afrique (1998) 'Examples à suivre', 31 March.

Kristeva, J. (1982) *Powers of Horror: An Essay on Abjection*, New York: Columbia University Press.

Kristeva, J. (1986) 'Psychoanalysis and the Polis', in T. Moi, ed., *The Kristeva Reader*, New York: Columbia University Press.

Lowe, L. and D. Lloyd, eds (1997) *The Politics of Culture in the Shadow of Capital*, Durham, NC: Duke University Press.

Marx, K. (1904) *A Contribution to the Critique of Political Economy*, New York: International Library.

Nababsing, V. and U. Kothari, eds (1996) *Gender and Industrialization: Mauritius, Bangladesh, Sri Lanka*, Rose Hill: Éditions de l'Océan Indien.

Nirsimloo-Anenden, A.D. (1990) *The Primordial Link: Telegu Ethnic Identity in Mauritius*, Moka: Mahatma Gandhi Institute Press.

Ong, A. (1987) 'The Gender and Labor Politics of Postmodernity', in L. Lowe and D. Lloyd, eds, *The Politics of Culture in the Shadow of Capital*, Durham, NC: Duke University Press.

Orbach, S. (1986) *Hunger Strike: The Anorexic's Struggle as a Metaphor for Our Age*, London: Faber & Faber.

Sommer, D. (1988) '"Not Just A Personal Story": Women's Testimonios and the Plural Self', in B. Brodzki and C. Schenck, eds, *Life/Lines: Theorizing Women's Autobiography*, Ithaca, NY: Cornell University Press.

Visweswaran, K. (1994) *Fictions of Feminist Ethnography*, Minneapolis: University of Minnesota Press.

Weismantle, M. (1989) *Food, Gender, and Poverty in the Ecuadorian Andes*, Philadelphia: University of Pennsylvania Press.

Williams, R. (1977) *Marxism and Literature*, Oxford: Oxford University Press.

Developing Subjects

Celeste Schenck

If I am a poet who is charged with speaking the truth (and I believe the word poet is synonymous with truth-teller), what do I have to say about all of this?

Joy Harjo, 'A Postcolonial Tale' (1996: 19)

And poets get directlier at the soul,
Than any of your oeconomists: – for which,
You must not overlook the poet's work
When scheming for the world's necessities.

Elizabeth Barrett Browning, *Aurora Leigh* (1979: 298)

The point was this: I was going to be developed in the way that Babamukuru saw fit, which in the language I understood at the time meant well. Having developed well I did not foresee that there would be reason to regress on the occasions that I returned to the homestead.

Tsitsi Dangarembga, *Nervous Conditions* (1988: 59)

As the narrator of Tsitsi Dangarembga's novel, Sisi Tambu, knows all too well, she has been 'developed' in the passive, targeted for progress by a missionary development ethos in colonial Rhodesia that will brook no regression. At other moments, she also recognizes her 'emancipation' as a 'process' in which she can negotiate her own educative, economic – even psychological – development (recognizing that this always involves compromise with the powers that be), and have an impact on that of the other gradually politicized subjectivities around her. The five very different women struggling to empower themselves in this collective narrative – Sisi, her mother, Lucia, Maiguru, and her daughter

Nyasha – are developing subjects indeed. The strategies they invent – among them, making the most of all development opportunities, investing in a kin network of women, negotiating skilfully in some cases between the responsibilities of the village and the ambivalent appeal of a missionary education, and, finally, maintaining lucid consciousness of the complexity of their own situation – make of these fictional characters development practitioners, using their own lives as a site from which to bear witness and to advocate change.

The subjects of the fictions I examine in the pages that follow are both being developed by processes they cannot control – according to narratives written for them by colonizing economies, internal structures of hierarchy and discrimination, as well as global flows of capital and goods – and, at the same time, subtly undermining those processes by developing themselves in complex, adaptive, sometimes rebellious, often strategic ways. The title of my essay, relying on the ambiguous participle 'developing', tries to convey some of that in-betweenness, the indeterminacy that literature captures so aptly. Within an international, interdisciplinary dialogue about the practice of development across cultures, I wish to argue here, novels, poetry and autobiographies become compelling archives of the ambivalences of participants in those processes, and they may also proffer a salutary vision of the wider imaginative communities development practices aim at establishing. Literature has always had a dialectical relationship to culture, simultaneously reflecting the economic and cultural ground from which literary productions emerge, and also transforming cultural processes by imagining alternatives to them.[1] Thus I argue – reading all too briefly here two recent novels written in very different registers: Arundhati Roy's *The God of Small Things* and Ruth Ozeki's *My Year of Meat* – that literature must be read not only as an important contribution to interdisciplinary development studies but also as a kind of development practice itself: a site at which local and global issues are disturbingly but profitably blurred, at which individual subjects risk their narratives of poverty, discrimination, violence and revolt in order to testify before a wider community.

Writing as International Development Practice

In recent years, one of the most interesting developments on the global front has been the greatest expansion yet of the reading public for serious books in English. For better or for worse, English has become what Latin once was: a world literature, the language the world speaks.[2]

But there is a world of difference between what comparative literature specialists once called 'English Literature' (the literature of Britain and that taught in its colonies) and 'literature in [e]nglish' (increasingly a world Anglophone literature, often with roots in the national literatures of emergent or settler countries, such as Nigeria, Canada, Australia, and some of the island nations of the West Indies). A number of forces have contributed to this flow of English-language books across the globe: the increased transnationalism of literary publishing and translation,[3] indeed a globalization of publication and distribution processes; the rise of the postcolonial within First World academia as a central critical category (a currently fashionable, highly politicized, even talismanic preoccupation) and the resulting revival of interest in the literature emerging from those so-called emergent economies; the gradual materialization of an international English-reading public for books chronicling the effects of geopolitical change on developing individuals and families; recognition of such fictions by all the major literary prizes; and, finally, the appearance on the literary scene of a generation of young writers with two big things on their minds – the recounting of the complexity of local practices and the building of broader, some times virtual communities on the world map. Such a project involves both a certain ambivalence – even irony – about the achievements of traditional development and a determination to write resistant narratives of developing subjects alongside the record of international agencies, world banks, and world capital. As Native American poet Joy Harjo and British feminist Elizabeth Barrett Browning capture this notion in their poems quoted in epigraph above, fictions may come closest to the complex truth of development. The contemporary writer, bearing witness, has a critical activist role to play.[4]

A case in point is the spectacular publication history of Arundhati Roy's first novel, The God of Small Things, the story of the complex forces shaping the entwined lives of an Untouchable carpenter and a divorced, Syrian-Christian daughter of the fading bourgeoisie. Roy's novel fell into the hands of an editor with HarperCollins in India in the spring of 1996. Within three days, the major British publishing houses were bidding for the rights; before she could make her decision, agent David Godwin flew to Delhi to sign her up. The book was launched in Delhi in April 1997, and received the Booker Prize in London in October of that same year. In the intervening months Roy had received £500,000 in advances, and the rights to the book had been sold in twenty-one countries. By the end of October 1997, just a few months after its publication, some 400,000 copies had been sold all over the world.

Although some may argue that literature is merely taking its place in global flows of goods and capital – a recent IKEA catalogue featured *The God of Small Things* atop a slick Swedish coffee table made for the international market, not-so-subtly aligning its own politics with that of the book – this is, nonetheless, the global publishing network within which we currently read and write. As Beth Tierney-Tello argues in a discussion of the relationship between literature and political action, the fact that literature participates in the kind of commodification it simultaneously protests does not always undermine that protest; it may also 'transform such commodification into contestatory practice': 'It is rather an honest trafficking in what cultural practices have to offer: the possibility of reimagining our world, a step without which any sort of change is virtually impossible' (Tierney-Tello 1999: 93). I hope to place Roy's novel in a group of similar such fictions, constituting, within the framing elements I have sketched above, a new genre in women's fiction.

Clearly, Roy views her work as contributing to an international dialogue about the future of development. Her first undertaking since this novel was a personal essay on the Sardar Sarovar Dam project called 'The Greater Common Good', an exposure of the 'invariably dubious politics of International Aid' (Roy 1999: n.p.). 'Who are the gods that govern us? Is there no limit to their powers?', she asks, briefly setting aside fiction for drainage reports and documentaries, irrigation surveys and journal articles. This question gains in resonance when the echo with her previous title – *The God of Small Things* – sounds. Valley inhabitants' most potent weapon, according to Roy – '*specific* facts about *specific* issues in this *specific* valley' – has been blunted by what she calls the 'Big Issue, the State/International Aid effort of Building Big Dams for a Nation's Development'. For Arundhati Roy, the twenty-first century must usher in a different approach to development. Perhaps, she writes, we will witness the 'dismantling of the Big. Perhaps it will be the Century of Small Things' (Roy 1999). The novels I discuss below aim at deconstructing the totalizing master narratives, those universal and androcentric stories of human redemption and progress rooted in the Enlightenment that have been the staple of both the disciplinary organization of national literatures and development theory. Each exposes the complex, multiple influences on human subjectivity, and each offers a transformative vision of human agency – often in the form of a transgressive interracial or homosexual couple – that gestures towards new social arrangements, the future egalitarian ground towards which all development is aimed. As novels, all these texts focus on the individual subject as the smallest potential unit of change, creating a textual space in which our anchoring definitions of sexuality and race may be overturned. Just as Danga-rembga's women characters multiply official Rhodesian colonial history into a polyphony of subjective accounts, so Roy invites the god of small things into a house where 'personal despair' seemed impotently small in such a 'vast, violent, circling, driving, ridiculous, insane, unfeasible, public turmoil of a nation' (Roy 1997: 19). That 'Big God', howling like a hot wind, had heretofore made the articulation of small, 'contained, private and limited' experience virtually impossible.

The God of Small Things

'Some days he walked along the banks of the river that smelled of shit, and pesticides bought with World Bank loans', writes Arundhati Roy of Estha, one of her twin protagonists (Roy 1997: 13). The river in question is a fluid, blurry boundary – swelling in the monsoon season, draining to a trickle at other times – between the declining family property and the History House where the Untouchable Velutha has made his home. Roy's ironic mention of World Bank loans evokes development pro-grammes as peripheral to the play of forces acting upon and shaping the lives of her characters, those children who occupy 'very little space in the world' (Roy 1997: 11); in fact, the polluted river, in which fish with boils and fin-rot float belly-up, poisoned by pesticides, is only one of the meanings of this complex, ambivalent symbol. This river will come to symbolize all the border crossings and deaths (among which the fact of botched development will figure only as a leitmotiv) that the family will know as it is drawn to the river and the consequences of crossing it.

One of the main issues at hand in this novel is the policing of borders, such as the one the river draws between the divorced, virtually statusless daughter of the declining family in question and the young Untouchable carpenter who offers friendship and nurturance to her children – in fact, Ammu's doubly displaced femininity, in an irony emphasized in the novel, will make her Velutha's near-equal in un-touchability. Her twins, Rahel and Estha, and their portentously figured separation, stand for a sort of originary unity which has fragmented in the South Kerala village they inhabit into a hierarchy of forces as assiduously ordered as the Hindu caste system that governs all social relations, including relations between women and men. 'Edges, Borders, Boundaries, Brinks and Limits have appeared like a team of trolls on their separate horizons. Short creatures with long shadows, patrolling the Blurry End' (Roy 1997: 3).

In a remarkable scene at the book's centre – one that captures some of the complexity of subjectivity, subject formation and identity in post-independence India – the family's imported blue American Plymouth is piled high with family members *en route* to see *The Sound of Music* at a nearby cinema, when its progress is brought to a halt by a Communist march. One of the marchers is Velutha, and his presence there is evidence of the promises made to Dalits by the powerful Communist Party presence in the South Kerala of the 1960s. In the car driven by Oxford-educated, Anglophile Chacko, the family of Syrian Christians waits for the danger to pass. During the long wait for the demonstrators to be subdued by the police, the narrator speculates about the uneasy coexistence of Marxists, Syrian Christians, and Hindus in the most literate province in India, tracing the history of rising Naxalite violence through its uneasy seduction of Untouchable loyalties. The visceral panic of the Syrian-Christian pickle-making landlords in the face of such alliances is personified in this scene by Baby Kochamma, nursing her own fears of dispossession from privilege from the safe vantage point of the closed car. Ammu, Chacko's sister, watches the proceedings laconically, occasionally commenting drily on Chacko's self-seeking Marxism or her son's potential male chauvinism, and overreacting violently to her daughter's call to the loved and recognized Velutha in the crowd. Like 'a rogue piece in a puzzle', her protectiveness of him will become clear to the reader only in subsequent chapters (Roy 1997: 72). Later, while watching the blockbuster American film, that 'World Hit', working its way, via distribution mechanisms, across the globe in the mid-1960s, Estha – the boy twin who sports an Elvis pompadour and pointy shoes – is molested in the theatre lobby by a candy-seller who is all too aware of the economic status of Estha's factory-owning family. No scene better captures the interplay of forces that act on the lives of this family: it is difficult to speak of 'a culture' in this mix of indigenous and inherited political and religious traditions, the complex development of South Kerala,[5] all firmly grounded in the Hindu sanction of caste distinctions.

It is also impossible to imagine that economic forces are the only ones shaping the lives of the subjects Roy breathes to life. For beneath the spread of American capital and goods, the dominance of the Communist Party, the precolonial tradition of gender oppression, the postcolonial – indeed, neocolonial – survival of elaborate social and economic hierarchies, is the caste apartheid that governs human relations everywhere, including Ayemenem House. As if local identities were not complex enough, and precisely because subject formation needs to be understood as having a global frame, Rahel, the female twin, later marries an American, moves to the USA, and experiences banal but analogous racial and gender discrimination while labouring menially in a highway tollbooth. The wider frame provided by the plot element of Rahel's marriage makes the local speak for the global, sets up and addresses a world audience, and permits the novel to participate in the cultural project we call – in this book – development practice.

In the terms established by the novel, these interlocking systems of oppression go back to two things: the gender imbalances that appear ubiquitous here, and the caste system as an emblem for all human hierarchies.

> [I]t could be argued that it actually began thousands of years ago. Long before the Marxists came. Before the British took Malabar, before the Dutch Ascendency, before Vasco da Gama arrived, before the Zamorin's conquest of Calicut. Before three purple-robed Syrian Bishops murdered by the Portuguese were found floating in the sea, with coiled sea serpents riding on their chests and oysters knotted in their tangled beards. It could be argued that it began long before Christianity arrived in a boat and seeped into Kerala like tea from a teabag. That it really began in the days when the Love Laws were made. The laws that lay down who should be loved, and how. (Roy 1997: 33)

The Love Laws, through which the hierarchy of domination and exclusion is articulated, have remained intact across the multiple cultures and experiences of colonization in India. These laws have also been internalized by the Kochamma family, who, in their double role as both masters and slaves within a rigorously policed system of value, simultaneously enforce and break them. 'Chacko told the twins that though he hated to admit it, ... they were a family of Anglophiles. Pointed in the wrong direction, trapped outside their own history, and unable to retrace their steps because their footprints had been swept away' (Roy 1997: 52).

The twins, Rahel and Estha, come to know such discrimination viscerally within the very confines of their house when their uncle's half-English daughter and his estranged wife come to spend Christmas. Among the children's memories of 'small things' (Roy 1999: 3) are their own lived experiences of linguistic, religious, racial and caste exclusion. Sophie Moll's arrival sets into motion a plot worthy of Greek tragedy, and when she drowns in the river that is meant to enforce boundaries, the twins are subjected to a playing out of the Love Laws within the family nexus. In Roy's novel, all power relations reproduce the master/slave dynamic, especially within the family crucible. Thus

Mammachi, shrewd manager of the family business and once-great violinist in her own right, subject to violent beatings in her marriage, takes on the role of victimizer in her relationship to her own powerless – because divorced – daughter. Similarly, Baby Kochamma, denied access to the man she loved by those same Love Laws, sadistically victimizes the twins, and their beleaguered mother. The irony is that Baby Kochamma and Ammu share the same fate as unmarried daughters.

> In the way that the unfortunate sometimes dislike the co-unfortunate, Baby Kochamma dislikes the twins, for she considered them … Half-Hindu Hybrids whom no self-respecting Syrian Christian would ever marry. She was keen for them to realize that they (like herself) lived in sufferance in the Ayemenem House, their maternal grandmother's house, where they really had no right to be. She subscribed wholeheartedly to the commonly held view that a married daughter had no position in her parents' home…. As for a *divorced* daughter from an *intercommunity love* marriage – Baby Kochamma chose to remain quiveringly silent on the subject. (Roy 1997: 45–6)

The same compulsion that leads the family to enforce hierarchy, however, also drives it to test boundaries. Border crossings obsess this particular family, amounting almost to a curse on the house. Baby Kochamma had been in love with an Irish priest, Father Mulligan, in her youth. Chacko goes off to Oxford, where he takes a pale English bride and produces the child, Sophie Moll, whose life and death will be an ever-present reminder to the twins of the inexorability of racial distinctions. These same twins, Estha and Rahel, in a paroxysm of grief after the death of their mother, end up in an incestuous sexual embrace. During the years of their separation, Rahel suffers feelings of dislocation and oppression in America. In the History House across the river, now occupied by Velutha, a British colonist gone native killed himself for the love of an Indian boy. Ammu, the twins' mother, first marries a Bengali Hindu, and then is fatefully drawn to Velutha, for the only joy the book proffers, at a cost that subsumes all the lives that touch theirs. The metaphor for all these transgressive relationships is the Banana Jam that the family factory, Paradise Pickles and Preserves, makes illegally, even after the Food Products Organization 'banned it because according to their specifications it was neither jam nor jelly. Too thin for jelly and too thick for jam. An ambiguous, unclassifiable consistency, they said' (Roy 1997: 30). Looking back from the vantage point of adulthood, thinks Rahel, 'it seemed as though the difficulty their family had with classification ran much deeper than the jam–jelly question' (Roy 1997: 30–31).

Perhaps, Ammu, Estha and she were the worst transgressors. But it wasn't just them. It was the others too. They all broke the rules. They all crossed into forbidden territory. They all tampered with the laws that lay down who should be loved and how. And how much. The laws that make grandmothers grandmothers, uncles uncles, mothers mothers, cousins cousins, jam jam and jelly jelly. (Roy 1997: 31)

But resilience and resistance, Roy seems to be saying, are to be found in the stubborn continued production of contraband banana jam. Although the final chapters of the book count out a toll of unparalleled cruelty and destruction in the triple betrayal, torture and sacrificial killing of Velutha, and although they chronicle the ironic survival of the most villainous family member, Baby Kochamma, at the expense of Ammu and her blighted twins, still the final out-of-order chapter, in which the famished Ammu meets her beloved Untouchable Velutha in a timeless embrace, is a curative gesture in favour of border crossings, an eloquent plea against racism and discrimination in all its forms. Although Roy's project is to expose a caste hierarchy that has outlived its banning by law and the rise to prominence of large numbers of Untouchables within the Indian political system, nonetheless she reserves her most lyrical and compelling gesture for this last chapter. Velutha, ultimately, is the god of small things on whose side Roy comes down, fathering Ammu's abandoned twins with all the tenderness the ambivalent Chacko cannot provide (seeing them, despite himself, as millstones), repairing the boat with which they have come to him in the colonial bungalow, revising by means of the personal that History which has divided them. The children '[make] the back verandah of the History House their home away from home, furnished with a grass mat and most of their toys', companionably watching Velutha carve little windmills and boxes for them, even painting his fingernails red, a detail that will have poignant resonance at the end of the novel as he lies dying on the police station floor (Roy 1997: 264).

When Velutha and Ammu, in the closing pages of the novel, ultimately consummate their relationship, 'they [make] the unthinkable thinkable and the impossible really happen' (Roy 1997: 256). Although Ammu has dreamed this encounter before it happens, and although the novel has already spelled out its inevitable consequences, the embattled, isolated, persecuted daughter of this family 'suddenly rose from her chair and walked out of her world like a witch. To a better, happier place' (Roy 1997: 332). All the accumulated rage of her own impotence, combined with her hunger to take her own life into her hands, drives her to 'love by night the man her children loved by day', and wilfully to inhabit this liminal space, this place of freedom 'in the penumbral shadows between two worlds' (Roy 1997: 44). On the thirteen nights that followed the first one, 'they stuck to the Small Things', the infinitely small human happinesses that transform our experience of the everyday. In an earlier chapter, Estha, his young life already broken, had asked his mother, 'If you are happy in a dream, does that count?' (Roy 1997: 218); when his beloved hound lay dying on his cushion, that same Estha had already learned to prize even a glimpse of joy – the vision of a bird taking flight reflected in the 'smooth, purple balls' of his dog. 'The fact that something so fragile, so unbearably tender had survived, had been allowed to exist, was a miracle' (Roy 1997: 12). Similarly, Ammu and Velutha 'put their faith in fragility', 'stick[ing] to Smallness' (Roy 1997: 339). The astonishing beauty of the novel's last gesture, as Ammu turns to bid her lover goodbye both in Malayalam – 'Naaley' – and in English – 'Tomorrow' – is what stays with the reader, an emblem of renewed relations at every level of their culture.

While the healing union achieved by Ammu and Velutha – 'her brownness against his blackness' (Roy 1997: 335) – is ultimately sexual, it is no coincidence that the chapter is called 'The Cost of Living', and that Roy notes, in passing, that it had grown unaffordably high. In fact, Velutha's sacrificial death is only ostensibly a punishment for crossing caste lines. A whole set of equivalences in the plot show how enmeshed politics and economics remain within the Love Laws, how the erotic is one among many measures of the lived experience of people's lives. Velutha is betrayed first by his own father, whose obsequious worship of the family that exploits him underscores his economic dependence on them. He is betrayed a second time by the embittered women of this family, whose own experiences of gender violence and economic powerlessness (although Mammachi was a better manager than Chacko of the family factory, she could make no legal claim to it) lead them to see the 'enormous potential' in the situation, and to cry rape, transforming the mutuality of the scene described above into a grim parody of A Passage to India (Roy 1997: 257). He is betrayed a third time by his employer, Chacko, a Marxist who simultaneously organizes his workers into a union and sexually harasses economically dependent female employees – an irony that is not lost on his sister Ammu. For all his Marxist leanings, upon his return from Oxford Chacko promptly seizes the factory from his competent mother, jacks up the business thanks to extravagant development loans, and sets his sights on capitalist expansion. Comrade Pillai, the local Marxist leader who runs a printing business on the side, designed the labels for the maladroitly named Paradise Pickles and Preserves, adding of his own accord the picture of a Kathakali dancer, and the even more unfortunate logo: *Emperors of the Realm of Taste*. Defending their marketing strategy to Ammu, Chacko praises the labels for the 'Regional Flavour' they give to the product, something that would 'stand them in good stead when they entered the Overseas Market' (Roy 1997: 47). The uneasy alliances among the gender politics, the Marxist politics, and the imperial economic dreams of this Factory Owner come out all too poignantly in the fate of his bungled business. Finally, Velutha is betrayed a fourth time by the aforementioned Comrade Pillai, who had signed him into the Communist Party by making 'fervent, high-pitched speeches about Rights of Untouchables ('Caste is Class, Comrades')' (Roy 1997: 288). Pillai essentially sacrifices Velutha to his long-term Marxist siege on Paradise Pickles, the same Paradise Pickles which is simultaneously a source of his livelihood, by encouraging Chacko to fire him so that he – 'an excellent carpenter with an engineer's mind' (Roy 1997: 277) – does not incite the envy of other, Touchable workers. He also refuses Velutha asylum when the affair is discovered, quoting pieties about the Party staying out of workers' lives, largely because Velutha is worth more to him dead. Later Pillai would use the firing against Chacko in order to bring the business to its knees, neither his Party affiliation to Velutha nor his shared Marxist sympathies with Chacko fuelling any kind of loyalty to either of them. He would also strike a tacit deal with the Police Inspector on the case – a deal that would deliver Velutha over to the Inspector's Touchable rage. Only in a novel could the interconnectedness of all these forces be so powerfully foregrounded, could the struggle of subjects against such subjection be so eloquently waged – against which the peripheral presence of bank loans, factory waste running in rivers, and failed businesses appears curiously flat.

The strategic *métissage* that characterizes Ammu's and Velutha's relationship, and the alternative family it provides for her children – that is, the politics of racial mixing that drives the novel – similarly characterizes the book's formal construction, its play with varying cultural and generic materials and languages.[6] Modelled as much upon Joyce's wordplay and Faulkner's splayed plots as upon the cyclic patterns of Indian epic, Roy's novel yokes disparate elements into a fragmented but productive whole in her effort as much to capture the complex conditions under which her subjects develop as to reach an Anglophone world audience. The novel's contrapuntal play with English and interleaved Malayalam is part of this process, a simultaneous reminder of cultural boundaries and the possibility of their crossing, the text's bilingualism at once barring and inviting entrance to all potential readers of the novel.

My Year of Meat

Many of the same elements drive another recent novel written by a young Japanese-American, first-time novelist: foremost, the desire to bear witness to the ravages of colonialism, capitalism and – as it happens – their connecting link, cowboys, those perennial producers of meat, by constructing a shared, transforming vision of human subjectivity at century's end. My Year of Meat is as funny as The God of Small Things is tragic – a mongrel compendium, or novel-as-anatomy, replete with faxes, office memos, recipes, treatments, scripts, newspaper articles, journal entries, charts, clippings, documentary interludes, snippets of contemporary poetry and interleaved citations from The Pillow Book by a tenth-century Japanese classical poet, Sei Shōnagon, the protagonist's literary forerunner and favourite author.[7] For all the feisty humour of this brave novel, however, its mission is a serious one. Its protagonist, like the documentarian-turned-author who created her, 'had spent so many years, in both Japan and America, floundering in a miasma of misinformation about culture and race' that each had, in her different medium, 'determined to use this window into mainstream network television to educate' (Ozeki 1999: 35).

The book's politics of métissage, evident on every page, also begins with the main character, Jane Tagaki-Little, born in Quam, Minnesota, daughter of an American botanist and a Japanese immigrant. She is an entirely new subject in fiction: nearly six feet tall, and therefore viewed as a freak in Japan, where she worked as a translator. She 'simply gave up trying to fit in. I cut my hair short, dyed chunks of it green, and spoke in men's Japanese. It suited me. Polysexual, polyracial, perverse ... racially 'half' – neither here nor there – I was uniquely suited to the niche I was to occupy in the television industry' (Ozeki 1999: 13). Recognizing that 'ingenious hybrids and strange global grafts are the local businessperson's only chance of survival in economies of scale' (Ozeki 1999: 72), the starving Jane, forced to take any work she can, occasionally sees herself as a 'hybrid or a mutant', perfectly positioned to serve as a 'cultural pimp' for the American Beef Export Lobby, BEEF-EX, 'selling off the vast illusion of America to a cramped population on that small string of Pacific islands' (Ozeki 1999: 14). Increasingly, however, she views her hybridity as a strength, having learned that we didn't even have cows in this country until the Spanish introduced them along with cowboys. Even tumbleweed, another symbol of the American West, is actually an exotic plant called Russian thistle, that's native not to America but to the wide-open steppes of Central Europe. All over the world, native species are migrating, if not disappearing, and in the next millennium the idea of an indigenous person or plant or culture will seem quaint. (Ozeki 1999: 20)

'Being half', she continues,

I am evidence that race, too, will become relic. Eventually we're all going to be brown, sort of. Some days, when I'm feeling grand, I feel brand-new – like a prototype. Back in the olden days, my dad's ancestors got stuck behind the Alps and my mom's on the east side of the Urals. Now, oddly, I straddle this blessed, ever-shrinking world. (Ozeki 1999: 20)

The 'ever-shrinking world' in which Jane manoeuvres as a subject – that 'network society' that has subsumed national borders, reshaped the material basis of society, and unleashed new flows of capital on a constantly evolving geopolitical map – along with the concomitant resurgence of human searches for community and identity it seems to require – has been exhaustively described by sociologist Manuel Castells in his three-volume collection *The Information Age: Economy, Society, and Culture* (1996). Volume I of his triptych characterizes the network society as an interconnected world of creolizing relations, a world in which the borders of the nation-state have been blurred by the media, the autonomy of electronic communication, transnational business, the decline of the Soviet bloc and the diversification of what used to be called the Third World, new currencies and the alliances that make them necessary, evolving and revised ideas of citizenship, including the rise of migrant lifestyles of all sorts, and, of course, the unprecedented and unchartable flows of global capital. As he concedes, media has become the space of politics in the information age, invading, like capital, the most intimate, and heretofore unreachable, spaces of human experience. His second volume explores the seemingly universal need – given the wealth and breadth of his far-flung examples – to define and redefine human identity which such accelerated change has spurred. 'In a world of global flows of wealth, power, and images, the search for identity, collective or individual, ascribed or constructed, becomes the fundamental source of social meaning' (Castells 1996: vol. I, p. 3).

My Year of Meat fictionalizes simultaneously both sides of Castells's complex dialectic. On the one hand, it makes the link between globalization and its discontents – imaged in the novel by the 'Walmartification of America' – and the entwining of capital, colonialism and cattle-pushing (meat-raising, meat-eating, and meat-distributing, especially to foreign markets). In epigraph and endnotes, Ozeki associates Aryan imperial conquests with the search for land on which to raise cattle, colonialism, and even neocolonial capitalism with the polysemous word 'stock'. In one of the novel's ironies, the Japanese advertising executive who hires Jane to produce 'My American Wife!', a man named Joichi Ueno, rechristens himself John Wayno after a visit to the shoot in Texas. The frontier he seeks to conquer, American-style, is a culture that has never been meat-eating. In fact, the job Jane initially accepts is to market American beef – which has been banished from the European markets for its use of antibiotics and growth hormones – to Japanese house-wives by featuring 'wholesome' American families, replete with well-behaved children and helpful husbands. The unitary, normative construct of American identity Ueno seeks to market in Japan, however, as Jane realizes all too quickly, is far from native. Not only is American culture an amalgam of imported cultural elements, its most interesting and flourishing families have nothing in common with the profile outlined in the BEEF-EX faxes.

On the other hand, Jane is compelled to produce meaningful images of American identities. Her difficulties as a documentarian begin as she discovers how hard it has become to define – and thereby to market – Americanness. Stumbling off the plane during Gulf War Fever, she is accosted in a restaurant by a World War II veteran, who rephrases his brutal question three times: 'Where are you from, anyway?', 'No, I mean where were you *born*?', '*What* are you?' She finally retorts, enraged: 'I ... am ... a ... *fucking* ... AMERICAN!' The shows become increasingly difficult to shoot as her desire to film American culture in all its multidimensionality supersedes her sense of responsibility to her job. First, she smuggles meats other than beef on to the programme, pre-pared in less than American ways – burritos, pork chitterlings, lamb; then she begins filming couples of mixed descent, families of colour, families that have been troubled by financial problems or disabilities, reconstituted or invented families, such as the Beaudroux of Louisiana who have adopted ten children of Asian descent. In the show that tips the balance, and virtually loses her her job, she films an interracial lesbian couple with their two little girls. In addition, this couple cooks pasta primavera, as they are militant vegetarians. Angry as the producers get after each subversion of their economic project, the viewers re-spond ever more enthusiastically to the authentic struggles of the American families she films.

Jane is increasingly driven by a mission, the articulation of a shared world culture that is increasingly *métissée*. The pages of Ozeki's novel are filled with examples of circulating cultural artefacts and vigorously hybrid personalities. Jane's musician lover is recognizable to her crew as the sax-playing actor in the Suntory Dry Beer commercial. Her film company includes her own Japanese-American self, her office producer – 'one of the new breed of *issei*, first-generation Japanese immigrants, who wore his British accent like his Armani suit, casually draped, with a sense of perfect global entitlement' (Ozeki 1999: 34), and the sexist crew, with their own cooler in the van 'filled with mineral water from France'. One of the crew members recognizes the Japanese weed kudzu growing all over the Beaudroux family farm, and introduces the father, Vern, to its various uses: as a starch in batter, a tuber sliced into a salad, and a hangover medicine. The kudzu that had signified mainly metaphorically 'the inroads of Japanese industry into the nonunionized South' comes to thicken the batter for Vern's prizewinning fried chicken, and ultimately to serve as a cash crop on his farm. And these same crew members serve as role models to this family's full spectrum of Korean children. The Beaudroux family also live on a former plantation, on which the renovated slave cabins will house their biological daughter Alison, a soon-to-be single mother.[8] This is only one of the communities described in the book; to them must be added the Dawes family's church congregation and the community named Hope that has mobilized around the Bukowsky family and their injured daughter Christina. As the proliferation of recirculated cultural items expands, all the characters working on the documentary series are altered by its altered mission. The sexist cameramen are changed by a day's filming of this paraplegic girl who had been crushed in a truck accident. The pin-ups from *Hustler* disappear from the van overnight.

The odd but convincing world community forged by Jane's subversive activity also extends to her audience of Japanese housewives across the world. Unbeknown to Jane, Akiko – the abused, apparently sterile, bulimic wife of producer Ueno – watches the weekly programmes and rates them for her husband. Although she gives the early programmes a very low authenticity rating, Akiko's interest – and her consciousness – rises with each programme. The Beaudroux family's brood of biological and adopted children receive a 9 on her scale of 1 to 10, but Lara and Dyann, the lesbian, biracial couple, change her life. Seeing her own closeted desire for other women and for a baby imaged in the loving family on the screen, her husband's violence to her mounting with each subsequent subversive episode of the programme, Akiko walks

determinedly out of her own life, having become triumphantly pregnant during an act of marital rape. In fact, the novel's *development feminism*
emerges most compellingly in the textual pairing of Jane and Akiko,
employee and wife of the book's villain, but textual counterparts in
countless other important ways. The twinning of their stories – each
seeks to get pregnant, although only one will carry her baby to term
– cross-culturally, via the media, will be the occasion for reciprocal
transformation.

The first tie that binds them is their apparently matched set of roles
as documentarian and audience. Until Akiko sends Jane a fax requesting
information about the effects of hormones on male fertility, and the
way to find the Northampton that provides cultural shelter to the lesbian
couple of the series, Jane has had no concrete idea of her real audience
across the globe. Mobilized in a way that she comes to see as 'arrogant
and chauvinistic' by the 'well-being of the American women I filmed
as subjects', thinking of the Japanese woman who might watch her
show as at best an 'abstract concept: at most, a stereotypical housewife,
limited in experience but eager to learn, to be inspired by my programmes and my American wives', Jane has thought of her audience as a
'demographic statistic, a percentage point' to 'rub in a pesky executive's
face'. Suddenly, reading Akiko's writing, Jane is confronted by 'the
audience': 'embodied in Akiko, with a name and a vulnerable identity'.
In the wake of her recognition of other subjectivities, in her abandonment of the construction 'self and other', 'nothing is the same' (Ozeki
1999: 273).

What follows in the novel is a series of reflections on Jane's own
responsibilities as a development practitioner, a documentarian in the
terms of the text. To add to the complexity of these meta-reflections,
boxed inside one another like Russian dolls, is the fact that while Jane
makes television shows in a visual medium, her author, formerly a
television documentarian, attempts a similar project in the medium of
fiction. The difference between the two media – the visual one featured
in the book and the verbal one manifested by the book – is also ex-
plored. Ozeki herself turned from documentary film-making to novel-
writing because, she has said in an interview, she was tired of the
'radical editing and simplification of complex truths' required to produce
films (Ozeki in Swindell 1998). Although Jane herself initially undermines
'My American Wife!' to 'further international understanding', and to
replace misinformation with a 'single, empirical, absolute truth', as she
gains experience as a filmmaker, she comes to see that 'truth was like
race and could be measured only in ever-diminishing approximations'

(Ozeki 1999: 210). What the written medium provides for Ozeki is precisely the capacity to render the broad spectrum of lived human experience in all its detail, its contradictoriness, and its complexity. For all the differences between this novel and *The God of Small Things*, the words Ozeki puts into Jane's mouth at the end of the book echo the metaphors generated by Roy's own novel. Having started her year as a documentarian wanting 'to tell the truth, to effect change, to make a difference', she ends up 'haunted by all the things – big things and little things, Spendid Things and Squalid Things – that threaten to slip through the cracks, untold, out of history' (Ozeki 1999: 424). When a wife on one of the early shows, of whose life she had made a fiction, writes to say that the sordid facts of her life have ultimately aligned themselves with Jane's narrative, the borders between fact and fiction, documentary and life, development practitioner and developing subject become productively blurred.

A second, more important tie is forged between the two female protagonists of the book when Akiko, having left her husband, appears on Jane's doorstep, and the two women meet in the flesh. Although they share the same language, communication is halting at first. Akiko uses polite Japanese, and then tries English. Walking the island of Manhattan from Battery Park to Harlem, the two women talk endlessly. The developer/developed opposition dissolves as each woman recounts her experience of pregnancy, and the two come to realize how the corporate production and global marketing of beef can have an impact on 'something as intensely private as the descent of the egg through the fallopian tubes', as Ozeki herself describes it (Ozeki in Swindell 1998). Jane's research into the meat industry, and her desire to tell the truth about it publicly, takes on new contours as she discovers that she is herself a DES baby, and faces the fact of her own spontaneous abortion. Akiko, conversely, has practically engineered her own pregnancy in the aftermath of her rape, picturing the egg descend into its uterine home as she lies in her hospital bed recovering. When she meets Jane, she finds her 'surprisingly tall', but more life-sized than she had imagined. Expecting her to be 'a woman who is carrying the straight razor' – an image from a country song that accompanied one of the programmes – Akiko finds Jane less tough, less resolute, than the Amazon she pictured (Ozeki 1999: 390). In short, meeting in person allots each woman her appropriate scale, and renders each of them human. Their meeting manifests for the reader an Akiko who has taken her life into her own hands, setting out first for Louisiana and then up to Northampton – and perhaps back to Japan, where she might found an alternative family with Tomoko, the woman who nurses her through her battering by Ueno. Their meeting also enables Jane to pick up the pieces of her own life, face the grief of losing her baby, and begin the process of editing the films saved by her crew in their final shoot in the slaughterhouse. Her first documentary having had its modest impact on the communities she sought to reach, Jane begins compiling note-books, papers, stories, for her next project, seemingly a novel. 'I live at the cusp of the new millennium', she says at the end. 'Whatever people may think of my book, I will make it public, bring it to light unflinchingly' (Ozeki 1999: 426).

Conclusions: Towards Mestiza Consciousness, or, Beyond Development

To tell the full story of this emergent genre in women's fiction, and the new development practices it features, Roy's and Ozeki's fictions must be joined by – to take just two examples – Michelle Cliff's *Abeng* (1995), a novel that features a mixed-race Jamaican daughter who passes for white; and Ann-Marie MacDonald's *Fall on Your Knees* (1996), a saga that traces three generations of family history issuing from a mixed marriage on Canada's Cape Breton Island. Cliff's novel tells the story of Clare Savage, suspended between her white, patriarchal, colonial father and her black Jamaican mother, and speaking the language of each. Moving between the patois of her childhood and Standard English, between the brush and the family house in Kingston, between official history and family histories, she crosses sexual boundaries too, feeling something of her need for her mother in the powerful lesbian desire she feels for her childhood friend Zoe. In one of the central scenes of the book, an inadvertent hog-killing brings to the fore all the difficulties inherent in crossing boundaries, even as it presents them as vitally, self-savingly attractive. MacDonald's book features the dysfunctional marriage be-tween a young Scottish-Irish immigrant and his dark Lebanese bride as an allegory for colonialism. The entwining of racism and incest at the heart of the story is worked out subsequently by the daughters of the family in surprising ways: *métissage* – relationships with men *and* women of colour for the variously coloured daughters of the book – becomes a viable way of recovering the abused, racially othered mother, and of remembering the lost mother country. Just as Cliff's novel includes entire pages in patois, so MacDonald's renders passages in Arabic, the children's maternal language. Just as Jane can accomplish her cross-cultural documentary mission only by speaking a provocative form of her mother's native Japanese, so Roy's, Cliff's and MacDonald's novels depend upon the interweaving of the mother tongue and the text's otherwise-dominant English. This gesture is simultaneously one of inclusion and exclusion, a reminder of the specificity of local experiences and the need for a more global hearing. This family of texts, taken together, shares a body of practices that nudge us to a position beyond that envisioned by traditional development theory.[9]

In a haunting, lyrical, bilingual text that positions itself somewhere between philosophical treatise, political manifesto and autobiography, the poet Gloria Anzaldúa describes an emerging 'mestiza consciousness, *una consciencia de mujer* ... a new consciousness of the Borderlands' (Anzaldúa in Warhol and Herndl 1997: 765). In fact, her prose poem/ article envisions the subject position from which speak many of the authors I write about in this essay. Echoing the Mexican philosopher José Vasconcelos, whose theory of a 'fifth race embracing the four major races of the world' she describes, Anzaldúa envisions the fruit of such cross-pollenization: 'At the confluence of two or more genetic streams, with chromosomes constantly 'crossing over', this mixture of races, rather than resulting in an inferior being, provides hybrid progeny, a mutable, more malleable species with a rich gene pool' (Anzaldúa in Warhol and Herndl 1997: 765). Such subjects-in-the-making, she argues, 'straddling two or more cultures', are 'officiating priestesses at the crossroads' (1997: 767). Tolerant of ambiguity and contradiction, willing to question the subject–object duality, and ready to put history through a sieve, their 'role is to link people with each other' (1997: 770).

Near the end of a book on development practices, a collection that questions the traditional unilateral flow from development programme to developed subject, Anzaldúa's vision strikes me as a salutary one. It binds the novels I have written on in these pages to other such novels written by women of the same generation; it posits a virtual community in which practitioner and theorist, grassroots organizer and female villager, developing subjects all, engage eye to eye. It envisions a world in which everyone is borderline, or crosses borderlines, and in which borders themselves are in constant movement. It lays the ground for a future in which terms such as North and South, First and Third World, will have only anecdotal or historical relevance to our lives. It imagines a world community in which development begins at the level of small things, most importantly the struggling human subject. Finally, it images for us a future in which literature – anticipating, as it always has, the place where we are going next – offers us, in the words of Joy Harjo, 'a map to the next world' (Harjo 2000).

Notes

1. The design of this book – concluding with literary meditations on development processes and practices – emerges from our conviction that the arts, culture – even the humanities – offer, at the current moment, a healthy tonic to the long domination of development studies by political and economic policy-making. A number of authors in this volume make this claim, including Melching, Nnaemeka, Weil-Curiel, Farhat-Naser and Svirsky, Okafor, and all the authors of this chapter [Editors].

2. St. Martin's Press has recently issued both a book and a CD-Rom version of what it calls the *Encarta World English Dictionary*, reflecting the 'new world status of English', particularly that of the composite language that dominates 80 per cent of information stored on the Internet. A mix of US English, British, Canadian and Indian English, as well as dozens of other varieties of [e]nglish proliferating across the globe, the dictionary includes coinages, slang and transnational terminology, as well as common words (Minzesheimer 1999: 1D).

3. These changes correspond to a similar reorganization of world capital; currently, books from the 'Third World' are auctioned in many languages simultaneously, often in advance of publication; books in English from former colonies take their places in series created for them within both university presses and trade houses. While some critics abhor the neocolonial importation of raw literary materials from the colonies into First World academic factories for processing, the truth is that writers and readers of such fictions live in a different world from the one that could formerly be divided into North and South. These writers move, migrate, and move again in a world of transnational publishing and – more important – reading. A good example of such readerly migrations would be the trajectory of Ozeki's book through my own hands. Bought in New Zealand for an American colleague of mine living in Paris, it was brought to my attention, then ordered from Britain for the international students I teach in Paris, and reordered in New York from the American publisher for the students I taught at Barnard College in New York. My own well-thumbed copy has travelled from New Zealand to Paris to the States and back, all the while illustrating both literally and figuratively the global flow of reading, teaching and writing that now affects international publishing.

4. All the contributors to this chapter invoke the genre of the testimonial for its attention to collective plights, plural subjectivities, redemptive or restitutive projects; for a theorization of this genre, see Sommer in Brodzki and Schenck 1988; Tierney-Tello 1999.

5. South Kerala claims a literacy rate of between 90 and 100 per cent, possibly higher than any other state in the world. In 1957, it also became the first state on earth (with the exception of one Italian principality) to form a democratically elected Communist government. It is still under Marxist control. Caste continues to govern social relations in South Kerala, although its importance is greater in the eyes of Syrian Christians than in those of South Kerala's Hindu population.

6. It is beyond the purview of this essay to problematize the notion of *métissage* I invoke strategically here, but that issue is a central concern of my

current work-in-progress. See Note 9 below. The most important feminist post-colonial work on *métissage* has been that of Françoise Lionnet (1995), who brilliantly reworks concepts of creolization articulated by Edouard Glissant and Raphaël Confiant in the context of women writers from Africa, the Caribbean and the Indian Ocean.

7. The only thing that dates this novel, first published in 1998, is the omission of e-mail — its absence suggests the speed with which the network culture Ozeki describes has been transformed by the telecommunications industry in the ensuing period.

8. This transformation of former hierarchy-enforcing housing has its ironic counterpart in Roy's description of the most recent neocolonial renovation of the History House, now a five-star hotel replete with continental menu and truncated Kathakali dances for tourists.

9. My current work-in-progress, *Developing Subjects*, explores this new genre in women's fiction, and theorizes a transnational comparative literature that might be adequate to its analysis.

References

Brodzki, B. and C. Schenck (1988) *Life/Lines: Theorizing Women's Autobiography*, Ithaca, NY: Cornell University Press.

Browning, E. Barrett (first edn 1864; 1979) *Aurora Leigh*, Chicago: Academy Chicago.

Castells, M. (1996) *The Information Age: Economy, Society, and Culture*, 3 vols, Oxford: Blackwell.

Cliff, M. (1995) *Abeng*, New York: Plume Penguin.

Dangarembga, T. (1988) *Nervous Conditions*, Seattle, WA: The Seal Press.

Harjo, J. (1994) *The Woman Who Fell From the Sky*, New York: W.W. Norton.

Harjo, J. (2000) *A Map to the Next World*, New York: W.W. Norton.

Lionett, F. (1995) *Postcolonial Representations: Women, Literature, Identity*, Ithaca, NY: Cornell University Press.

MacDonald, A.-M. (1996) *Fall on Your Knees*, London: Jonathan Cape.

Minzesheimer, B. (1999) 'World of Words Rolled into English', *USA Today*, 5 August.

Ozeki, R. (1999) *My Year of Meat*, London: Macmillan Pan.

Roy, A. (1997) *The God of Small Things*, London: HarperCollins.

Roy, A. (1999) 'The Greater Common Good', in *Frontline*, vol. XVI, no. 11.

Swindell, L. (1998) Review of *My Year of Meat*, Fort Worth Star Telegram, 20 June.

Tierney-Tello, B. (1999) 'Testimony, Ethics, and the Aesthetic in Diamela Eltit', *PMLA*, vol. CXIV, no. 1.

Warhol, R. and D. Herndl (1997) *Feminisms: An Anthology of Literary Theory and Criticism*, London: Macmillan.

EPILOGUE

Resisting Development

It seemed fitting to the aims of this book to close with a creative piece written specifically for this collection. In 'Beyond Child Abuse' Nigerian author Chinyere Grace Okafor has created a short story that recentres development processes within the lived lives and the consciousnesses of those subjected to development at all levels: local, national and international. Her concern is with the impact of so-called modernizing decrees, particularly those which the governments of emergent economies effect in order to secure certain kinds of international aid, aligning, when it is expedient to do so, Western moralizing theories with traditional tribal practices. The story surveys with grim contempt a number of development tactics and theories critiqued within this collection – the imposition of structural adjustment programmes, the targeting of specific scourges (FGM, child abuse) by eradicators from outside the local culture, token appointments – even certain feminist discourses, such as those that exclude men from a community of resisters. It terms 'family abuse' the impact of such development policies on the lived lives of women vendors, in many cases solely responsible – with their children – for the livelihood of the family. Such families are portrayed early in the story as units of strength, economic cooperation and community, held together by mutual purpose, love, verbal banter, and a strong sense of irony about development.

The women whose intertwined stories make up this piece are 'developing subjects' indeed. They have all been subject – in different ways, as the stories from different regions and urban/rural settings attest – to misuse of international development funds; they have been subject to the impact of structural adjustment firings on marital relations; they have experienced the demolition of their homes and the destruction of the fragile balance of coping strategies that formerly made it possible for them to pay school fees for their children. And they actively, efficaciously and indignantly resist such development. But in this story, which imagines solutions that we are only beginning to record across the globe, the women also take development into their own hands. At the intergenerational, intervillage meeting at which grievances are aired, they also take action. Educated daughters-become-journalists in the city support that struggle, and appeal to the international community to support women's local efforts to develop themselves.

Beyond Child Abuse

Chinyere Grace Okafor

Special Announcement

The Federal Military Government of Nigeria has promulgated a new decree. It is decree Number 7, called the 'Child Abuse Decree'. It is part of the government's Structural Adjustment Programme and its main objective is to protect children from abuse. Henceforth, anybody seen employing children in the labour market, or inflicting any kind of abuse on children, will be severely dealt with. A special task force has been set up to enforce the decree. The News Commentary follows immediately after the advertisement. Thank you.

'It is my story, my story!' shouts Christi Anyawu Igwe. Members of the household begin to rush into the living-room to watch the television. The information flies from one sibling to the other, and on to the adjoining houses without television sets in the Aria neighbourhood of Abakpa Housing Estate in Enugu, where Christi is visiting her parents. Relations, friends and neighbours gather in the Igwes' small living room to watch their Christi on television. Mama Christi, as Christi's mother is called, leaves the kitchen, where she is dishing out the dinner, and hastens to the living room. Even the family pet, Sweety, leaves the kitchen, where she is sniffing the food being dished out, to join the gathering.

News Commentary

Dr Mrs Florence Okoko-Aja, the current President of the Association of Environmental Health, has been named Chairman of the task force on the Child Abuse Decree. In a special interview with our reporter, Christi Anyawu Igwe, the doctor reiterated her support of the law. Here is an excerpt from that interview which took place this morning in Dr Okoko-Aja's Floral Garden mansion in the capital city of Abuja.

The camera pans over the extensive landscape of lush trees, trimmed hedges and flowers before it zooms in on the mansion surrounded by that landscape. The living room is as spacious as the Igwes' living room is cramped, and there is another marked difference in the interior decoration. While the Igwes' living room, which is scantily decorated, is filled with people watching the television, the doctor's living room is populated by only herself and the reporter.

'Hei! The house be like heaven', Christi's sister Chinenye declares.
    'Shut up your mouth. Have you ever seen heaven?' her sister Uzo quips.
    'I have prayed about it. It is like that house on TV. Look at…'
    'Shut up.' Their brother cautions her because the camera now focuses on Christi, who is asking a question.

Christi: How do you feel about your appointment?

Okoko-Aja: I am very happy that the government is now doing something constructive about the law against child abuse which has been in place in the country. Following the United Nations' focus on the abuse of children, this country enacted a law against child abuse. The law was hailed by our traditional rulers, who saw it as a promotion of our traditional custom against child abuse. Remember that there are many traditional satiric songs against abuse. In spite of these, people have continued to indulge in all kinds of abuse. Even women who are abused are also guilty of abuse. I am very happy that the military has stepped into the matter.

Christi: Talking about women, do you envisage any problems from market women?

Okoko-Aja: I know that women, particularly the ones who use their children as food-vendors, nannies and domestic workers, will come under the task force's whip. In fact, workers in other occupations such as mechanics, carpenters, building contractors and all who apprentice and use young people should desist from doing so. I seize this opportunity to appeal to everyone who abuses children to desist from this criminal activity. It is a criminal offence which is punishable by law.

The news commentary continues after the excerpt, but the inmates of the Igwes' living room are no longer listening to it, because Christi has been phased out. Their own performance and commentary take over. Papa Christi vocalizes his pride: 'Well done, my daughter. My labourer job and palm-kernel picking for raise school fees for my intelligent daughter don put my name for television today.' Mama Christi hugs her, saying: 'When you arrive today from Abuja, begin sleep for hours, I know say you don do big job wey tire you. And you wake up with your tired body and still teach my other *pickins* their homework. Now, you don put joy for inside our belle. Well done, my daughter.' She goes to bring kolanuts and some dried fish for a customary blessing. The neighbours join in the brief prayer, commend Christi, and help themselves to the fish, which they eat as they leave for their homes. After they have left, Christi's father tells the children to emulate her: 'She don give you good example to follow. No waste my labourer suffer-suffer.'

IK, Christi's younger brother, replies jokingly that he has always taken the first position in his class despite the fact that their father uses him as his bicycle cleaner and their mother makes him wash all the dirty bedsheets and blankets. Papa Christi laughs at the irony of his son, saying that he is being used by those who slave to make him better than themselves. Following IK's example, the sisters begin to voice their own sides of the story.

Chinenye: Too much abuse in this house must stop now or the army boys will strike like thunder. Mama uses me as her kitchen maid. Always, 'Chinenye, wash the plates. Chine, call them to come and take their food. Chine, you did not give your father drinking water. I have told you that once you serve someone food, you must also give the person water to drink in case the food goes the wrong way. Chine…'

Uzo: Wait! You have said enough. What about me? I am the one who sweeps this house every morning. I am the house cleaner. Hei! hei! hei! Wait. I am also the maid of that naughty Sweety who 'peepees' on the kitchen floor when she is angry. Wait…

At the mention of her name, Sweety mews and snuggles up to Christi, who picks her up while making her speech.

Christi: I can't wait no more. I have to join in the family fun which I miss so much whenever I go for outside jobs. Here is my own piece. I am the one who teaches all of you your lessons whenever I am here. Do you know how much I'll be paid if I do it for money? Talk of exploitation in the home! Who pays me for it? Who pays me for buying that old black-and-white television and for putting the family's name on it? When you go to school now, all of you will be bragging about your sister being on the television.

Papa Christi and all of them laugh through the speeches, at the end of which he says: 'I happy too much say all my children sabi lawyer-lawyer for themselves. If I tanda here and listen to ya jokes and no go sharpen hoe and cutlass for tomorrow, wash body and oil muscles, nobody go hire me for laborer work tomorrow morning when I tanda for Holy Ghost corner by Ogbete market.' He leaves while Mama Christi goes to the kitchen with Sweety running after her. From the kitchen she says, 'Chinenye, come take waki to ya papa. No forget to give am water for drink. All of una, come take una waki.' Sweety digs her head into her plate without being told.

Soulful Trip

Mgbeke adjusts her nine-month-old baby on her back, ties her properly, and heads towards the hut where her husband, his brother, and his friend are discussing and laughing about the Child Abuse Decree. She hesitates at the entrance. Their laughter and banter irritate her. She turns round and gazes at the moon, which is almost full. She gazes at it fixedly, as if trying to read it. But she is not really seeing the moon. She is gazing into her soul, and all that has happened in the seventeen years of her life. She folds her arms around the sleeping baby on her back. The baby responds by squeezing her mother and making a happy noise. Mgbeke goes in to meet the men.

'I am ready to go, my husband', she says quietly, her subdued voice masking the turmoil in her soul. The men stop laughing – not because they no longer find the decree funny, but because of the entrance of the woman, who is not smiling. Her entrance is a reminder of her mission. She is one of the women who are going to represent Ndialero village at the women's meeting by the River Niger at its Illah crossing. Anybody brought up in Igboland becomes alert, watchful and antici-patory when women are about to act. This attentiveness has been ex-pressed in a folk song which is a constant reminder of the seriousness of such meetings.

When they whisper across the bitter-leaf hedge,
Look out for danger, my friend, my relation.
When they carry message in song of firewood,
Look out for danger, my friend, my relation.
In the market, their laughter on the outer teeth,
Is a sign of danger, my friend and relation.
In the market, their banter on the upper lip
Is a sign of danger my friend and relation.

When they throng to the meeting place,
Put on the cat's cloak, my friend.
And when they gird wrappers for battle,
Put on the cat's cloak, my friend.
If they yank branches from trees,
Thunder and lightning in hot pursuit.
If they pull fire from the hearth,
Spitting cobra is mother to me.

'I am ready to go, my husband', Mgbeke repeats.

Ogonna, Mgbeke's husband, stretches out his hand and turns off the transistor radio: the only property he has brought home from Asaba, where he lost his job as messenger in the Ministry of Information. He rises from the mat, saying, 'Make we go take Mgbeke to Illah water-side.'

'No, my friend, we want to listen to more news', his friend Nnagbo says. 'They are going to talk about SAP – Structural Adjustment Pro-gramme', he adds.

'No', shouts Nnadi, Ogonna's brother. 'Call it the name you people call it in the city: Suffering Adjusting Poverty. In this village of Ndialero, we call it Suffering Adjusting Poor-People.'

'Yes. All of them na adjustment. Na the same thing di women go dey talk for their meeting this night. So, make we go take my wife to the meeting', insists Ogonna.

Nnagbo has another opinion: 'Let women go and find how they can adjust to the poverty caused by decrees of World Money Bank and Soldier government and Task Force and other big Ogas. Me, I want to listen to them on radio and laugh at them. That is what I want to do now. Na fight I go fight when I get up from this position.' He promptly puts on the radio.

'Stay well', Ogonna says to them, and leaves with his wife.

As soon as they leave, Nnadi expresses his resentment towards his brother's wife, Mgbeke: 'I do not understand why my brother has to take Mgbeke to the meeting. Other women will paddle their boats to the venue, but my brother? He must hang on to his wife's wrapper as if he is a baby.'

'It is not his fault. He has lost his job and is trying to hold and keep what is remaining. Don't you know that once a man has no money, he loses his grip on his woman? But my friend, your brother, is holding on tight.'

'It is not because he lost his job. Many men lost their jobs. Re-trenchment of SAP is the order of the day. Fifty per cent. Almost all the men in this village lost their jobs because of SAP and they have adjusted to poverty and being men in the village. But not my brother. He has lost his job, and his shack in the market has been destroyed. He has also lost his manhood.'

'Do not talk with venom. Your brother is happy with his wife. Mgbeke is a good woman, quiet, gentle and obedient. That is what every man prays for.'

'I am surprised that you say this. You do not tag along your wife. You are every inch a man.'

'Do not talk about what you do not know, my friend. Wait until you get married. As for your brother, he has his reasons for taking her himself in her own boat.'

'It is not her boat. My brother bought it for her. Any money my brother gets, goes into her hand. I no longer get anything from my own brother, who once shared the same breast with me, since he married Mgbeke.'

'And you cannot adjust structurally to the situation?'

Cutlass in Ogonna's hand and baby on Mgbeke's back, the two make their way through the narrow path that leads to the river. Occasionally, the moonlight shines through the foliage and illuminates the path. By the time they get to the river, they can see light on a few boats, so they call out and receive replies from other village women boarding canoes and rafts that will take them to the venue of the meeting. They take off, Ogonna on the paddle while Mgbeke makes a bed for her baby. The water yields gently to the strokes of Ogonna's paddle, and the canoe takes off swiftly towards its destination. As the canoes and rafts of the women invade the water, the frogs let out protesting sounds. Ogonna and his wife do not notice the chorus of frogs, because they are ab-sorbed in their private thoughts. Mgbeke continues to ponder on her life, while her husband curses the government that retrenched him 'for sake of wicked SAP', he sighs bitterly. Somehow the women's meeting gives him a glimmer of hope, though he does not know the exact agenda. Automatically he puts more energy into the task of paddling, so that it takes them less than thirty minutes to get to Iyi Odogwu, the venue for the meeting. A sonorous chorus is reverberating, indicating the exact location of the gathering. The riverside is busy as women fasten their canoes and rafts, and exchange greetings. Ogonna wants to stay with the baby on the boat, but Mgbeke wants to take her.

'She may need to eat from the breast', she pleads, knowing that he knows that the child no longer wakes up at night to eat.

'If you leave her with me, you will be free at the meeting', he replies, knowing that the baby is never a hindrance when she is on Mgbeke's back.

'This place is cold. She will be more comfortable on my back.'

'My body is also warm, and I can carry her in my arms till you return.'

Mgbeke laughs. Ogonna laughs. Both know one another's need for the baby.

'Go in peace, my wife. I shall wait here.'

Ogonna, who relishes every opportunity to be with his daughter since he lost his job, lets his wife have the baby. His daughter is the only thing that makes him feel alive and hopeful since he lost his job. He believes that Chukwu – who created him, and gave him a child just as he was about to lose his job – must open a path for him to take care of her.

The women follow the sound of the chant. They begin to hum the song they all know so well, a song in praise of God.

'Listen, my sisters', Mgbeke commands excitedly, 'the song has new words.'

They keep quiet and listen. The word God, in 'If I narrate what God does for me' in the original, has been replaced by THEY to signify the negative subject of their gathering. The positive attributes and senti-ments have also been changed. The women understand the changes, and begin to sing the modified chorus:

> Day will come, day will die,
> If I narrate what they are doing to me.
> Night shall come, Night shall go,
> If I call the names of their wicked ways.
> Day will pass, night will pass…

The song is melodious and entertaining, but in this particular context the women know that it has assumed a different meaning. It is stirring up all the grievances provoked by the subject that is not named in the song, but whose identity is well known.

Odogwu Creek is one of the tributaries of the River Niger as it flows beside Illah and Asaba on its southward journey through the eastern part of Nigeria to the delta on the Atlantic Ocean. It is remote and normally unnoticed by human beings – except by the occasional hunter in search of game, or the healer collecting herbs. Only animals and birds are the usual inhabitants of the valley. On this night, however, it assumes a new importance as delegates occupy its two sides. It is as if the ordinary inhabitants of the valley understand the importance of the event, and keep their peace. No animals harass the women. Even the birds recede from the place. Only an owl remains adamant and shares the arena with the women, although it hides in the crook of a tree unseen by the assembly. After Mgbeke's team arrives, the singing goes on for quite a while before rising to a crescendo and dying abruptly like a stormy day.

The Meeting

'Umu-nwanyi *kwenu!*' Eze-nwanyi, the women's leader, shouts in a loud voice that echoes from valley to valley.
'*Yaa!*'
'*Kwenu!*'
'*Yaa!*'
'*Kwesienu ike!*'
'*Yaa-a-aa...*'
The women stretch the word as much as they can, its echo reverberating in the environment. The owl buries its head in its shoulders, as if shielding itself from the penetrating sound. Ogonna leaves the canoe and stealthily makes his way towards the meeting place to a vantage point on the branch of a tree.
'Mothers, daughters, my fellow women, I salute you again and again. I welcome you with reverence to this gathering. I thank you for heeding the call for action and for showing that you are always alive. Greeting is for Chukwu and greeting is also for you whom Chukwu created very well. A good greeting is for our big mother, Ochie-Nwanyi, who has left the warmth of the smouldering charcoal of her hut to fight the cold and night in order to be with her daughters and bless our meeting.'
'Umu mu *kwenu!*'greets Ochie-Nwanyi in a voice that belies her septuagenarian age. 'If I die today, I will not turn in my grave. How can

I turn in my grave when I now know that there are women who are walking in the footsteps of women of yesterday? If I die today, I will meet other people who have gone before me and my head will be high because I did not fail them. I have something good to report to them. Thank you my daughters and my sisters.'

Shouts, clapping and cheers greet this heroic speech.

She continues: 'About those who are putting their fingers in our eyes...'

Everybody keeps quiet to hear about the subject of the meeting.

'Since THEY have been passing urine in our shrine and excrement on our yard, we adopted the wisdom of the baboon, which they take as a sign of weakness. Now they are pouring sand into our cooking pot and using the gun to frighten us like children. But we are not children. Are we children?'

'No-o-oo...', the reply echoes and re-echoes.

'I have finished.'

The leader leans on her walking stick, her eyes trained in the direction of the owl hiding in the tree. The owl, finally getting used to the noise, relaxes its shoulders and surveys the assembly. The women look like an army of termites before an operation – numerous, serious, purposeful, destructive. The owl makes out the shadow of the old woman inclining on her stick and rolls its eyes in reaction to the compelling power emanating from her.

The first speaker, Eze-nwanyi, takes over: 'We thank our mother again and again for giving us support and courage. We all know why we are here. We all know that we are angry. Yet we want some people here to tell us their angry stories. After that, we shall take a final decision. Greetings, Mother. Greetings, my fellow women.'

Mgbeke's Story

'My name is Mgbeke, daughter of Onwuemene and Nkemka of Ndieze.'

Representatives from her village clap and cheer Mgbeke. Incidentally, her mother's mother, who is in the assembly, springs up from where she is seated with delegates from her village. 'That is my daughter's child! The snake does not beget something that is short. That is my own blood.'

Mgbeke continues: 'I am the wife of Ogonna of Ndialero village. I am telling my story, which began in Ndieze and continues in Ndialero. I do not know where it will end, because night has descended on my life and I have just given birth to a child.'

Ogonna's sympathy for both his wife and himself is aroused by this opening. He begins to climb down from the branch to get close to his wife.

'Carry on, my fellow woman', says Eze-nwanyi.

'My mother had seven of us before the influenza that took two of us and left five. I was the oldest. My father and mother took us to the farm in Onicha Ugbo, where we lived during the rainy season, cultivating and weeding. I took care of the younger ones while my mother weeded and my father tilled. That was my life until luck walked into our house and Mama James took me as housemaid. My mother said to me: "Mama James is now your mother. You must listen to her." I went to live with my new mother in Onitsha on the other side of the River Niger. That was how I had the luck of going to school, of knowing how to read and write English and of learning how to trade.'

'You are correct, my child', her grandmother chips in.

'Life was not easy, but I got something good. We used to wake up by four o'clock in the morning every day. My duty was to wash the beans, grind them and prepare the ingredients for making bean cakes. As early as six, people come to buy bean cakes. I sell them before I go to school by eight. When I come back, I hawk groundnuts and chin-chin on the streets. When I passed flower, my new mother said to me, "Do not allow any male to see your laps."'

A giggle from a young woman, another giggle, then laughter from several women as each one remembers similar experiences. Ogonna opens his eyes wide trying to make out his wife's figure from the crowd that is faintly visible by the light of the moon. She continues: 'I obeyed my new mother, and no man saw my laps, but Ogonna managed to get me in the family way without seeing my laps.'

Ogonna winces and stops in his tracks. Subdued laughter from a few people. Sympathy from others: 'Poor child.' 'Such is life' 'It's not easy.'

Her grandmother comes to her side to hold her in sympathy: 'It is enough, my child.'

'No, Nne-Nne. My story has just started. Child abuse! Was my pregnancy not child abuse?' asks Mgbeke.

Ogonna's mouth opens in bewilderment. He has never considered his action as child abuse. His wife Mgbeke continues: 'When they did not tell me how not to get pregnant, were they not abusing me? They showed me many things on the map of the world, but they did not show me anti-pregnancy. I knew America. I knew France. I knew China, Russia, Britain, Germany, Japan, and many, many, countries but I did not know how to be a child-mother and child-wife. I was fifteen when Ogonna married me, and I came to live in his village because he had no room in the city.'

Ogonna pleads silently, wanting his side of the story to be heard: 'I be poor messenger wey no fit pay money for room to. I dey share one room with three other men who no allow me bring woman to live with us. I no send her to village for sake of abuse.'

Mgbeke continues with the narration: 'Ogonna is a good man.'

Tears of gratitude begin to form in Ogonna's eyes: 'My wife understand me. She understand me well well.'

The tears drop from his eyes as Mgbeke continues her story: 'Ogonna used to save all his money and walk home to see me every Friday from the city of Asaba, where he worked, instead of paying for bus. We saved all his money for the baby and for me to go back to school. What happened? I had my baby. We thank God for a healthy baby, and for a father who brought money. My mother stayed with me for four weeks, taking care of me and the baby. When she left, they began to talk about child abuse. On the radio, on the lips of men and women, at school, everywhere. Children sing about it. What of me? I do all the work. Nobody helps me.'

Her voice quivers, but she suppresses the tears. 'Nobody helps me because the children sing "child abuse". I put my baby on my back and weed the compound while the children sing "child abuse". I strap my baby on my back and put water pot on my head, while the children sing "child abuse". With baby on my back and basket on my head, I trek to the market, while everybody sings "child abuse". In a tear-filled voice, she shouts: 'My back is so used to this child that I cannot imagine life without a heavy back.'

In his hiding-place, Ogonna flops to the ground, a certain heaviness pinning his heart to the floor. The sleeping head of the baby on Mgbeke's back flops to one side and she grips her mother tightly, still sleeping.

'It is enough, my child', says Mgbeke's grandmother, holding her and the baby.

'Leave her alone', cautions the leader. 'Let her vomit the pain.'

So Mgbeke continues: THEY sacked my husband from his job. He did nothing wrong. THEY commanded them to sack half of the workers, and they did so without caring for their wives and children. Is that not worse than child abuse? Ogonna came home in despair. I said, "Do not worry." I learnt something good from my Onitsha mother, Mama James. I learned how to make bean cakes and fry groundnuts that are good. We used the little money he had to build a shack at the construction site. I made bean cakes and cooked good food. My husband sold them to customers. What happened?'

'It is enough', repeats her grandmother.

'I said, leave her to vomit the whole thing', insists the leader.

And once again Mgbeke continues: 'Child Abuse Task Force destroyed all the shacks, my property, food and all. Now my husband stays at home listening to the radio and laughing the laughter of the hopeless one. I put my baby on my back and keep my fire and bile inside my stomach. Many times I wanted to kill somebody, but I could not kill somebody. It is THEM that I should kill, but I cannot reach them. So maybe I should kill myself!'

She shouts, untying the baby on her back. Ogonna shoots out from his hiding place to restrain her. He grabs her. She laughs: 'No. I shall not kill myself. I shall not kill somebody. If I were a killer, I would have done so when I got pregnant and stopped school. Now, I have a child. How can I kill somebody? I will kill THEM!'

She hastens out of the arena, her husband carrying the child, who starts to wail. Mgbeke's grandmother and a couple of women follow her. Her story has stirred up anger and hopelessness. It is the latter that Eze-nwanyi wants to erase when she salutes the women in a vibrant tone.

'Umu-nwanyi kwenu!'

'Ya!'

'My fellow women, are you people here?'

'We are here.'

'Will it be as we said?'

'It is as we said.'

'Hold your hearts, my sisters. Let us hear another story.'

Aduke's Story

'My name is Aduke. I was born in Ado-Ekiti in the Western state of a Yoruba mother called Modupe and an Igbo father called Echezona of Ama-ndokwa quarters, not far from here.'

People from her village clap and shout greetings.

'I got married to an Igbo man called Mokwenye, from Onicha Ugbo, which is not far from here, but we were living in Patani in the Delta region before he died. The title of my story is "Beyond Child Abuse". My story is about man abuse, women abuse, daughter abuse, son abuse and life abuse. My story is about family abuse. THEY abuse my family from left, from right and from centre, and I cannot take it any more.

My husband died in a boat accident. Without any warning, an oil company ship passed on the sea and sent waves that toppled his fishing canoe. I did not see his body. They did not find his body. Is that not man abuse? I had to leave Patani. I went to Enugu, because they said that there was work in Enugu. Well, that is not the story I want to tell you. I am not a thief. I am not a prostitute. I do not harm anybody. You see these hands?' she asks.

Nobody can see the hands in the night, with only a faint light from the moon, yet a voice answers from the top of a tree. The septuagenarian voice sends a reply to the younger voice: 'You, bird of night, messenger of evil, from the time I entered this place, I knew you were there. Now that you have declared yourself, you must play your part in this matter. Go and tell THEM that you have brought to them the message for which you are known. Go, go. I say, go-o.'

She prolongs the last sound, and the women hear the leaves rustle. 'Yes, go.'

There is silence for a while.

'Continue with your story.'

'I have strength in these arms of mine', says Aduke. 'It is the strength in these arms that I used to do "any work". Every day, I gird my wrappers in war fashion. Yes, why not. Every day is war for me. While I was in Enugu, I used to stand with men at Holy Ghost corner by Ogbete market waiting for whoever would hire me for the day. I did every kind of work that men did. I carried blocks, cut trees, ferried logs across the river, built huts, and still did women's work. Woman abuse. No complaint. I made very little money, although I was able to put food into the mouths of my children. I heard that selling things by the bridge in Asaba was good. I took my children with me, and we made our way to Asaba bridge. I built my own hut beside the bridge, and began to sell every kind of food needed by travellers: fish, bread, maize, plantain and other snacks. My children went back to school. We slept in the hut at night, and used the yard for business during the day. Child abuse? Yes, I am proud to say that I sent my children to school with "child abuse" money, and trained them to be hard-working through "child abuse" work. We do the business together. When it is time for school, they go to school and I continue working. Now! Now!...'

She begins to scream: 'Now, THEY have demolished my hut! Child Abuse Task Force has killed me! My children are out of school because we have no business and no money for school fees.' She breathes in and out as if she has run up a steep hill. Then she continues: 'I have not given up.' She pants. 'Not Aduke, daughter of Modupe and Echezona. Wake up! Wake up!'

Only now do people realize that she has brought her children to the meeting. 'I tell my children that those who are surrounded by enemies do not sleep deeply, for they are always on guard.'

The children, four in number, listen to their mother's instruction and begin a performance. They adopt various kinds of handicap. Mother is blind, one child is lame in one leg while another puts on a raffia wig and acts mad. One leads the way, while the other is the collector of money. They sing a simple song, which they harmonize in many parts that give rise to a pitiful and melodious piece:

Solo: Have pity because of…
Chorus: Mama moo, Mama moo, Mama moo….
Solo: Pity, pity, because of …
Chorus: Mama moo, Mama moo, Mama moo….

They chant it over and over again, moving through the assembly and letting the impact of the performance register on the psyche of the stunned audience.

'This is an abomination.'

'So you understand!' shouts Aduke. 'You now understand when I say that my story is beyond child abuse. I have no hut. I have no property, not even nothing. But I have my children, and we shall not starve. We shall make enough money and I shall build another hut and my children will go back to school. Come, my children. Come and continue with your sleep.'

Mama Christi speaks

'I be Mama Christi. I no belong to no man. Me and Papa Christi don feed many mouths and see many many things for life but this child abuse something don get K-leg for out throat. I know say some people dey really abuse pickins them. Beat pickin for nothing sake when them vex. Some dey do girl pickins them. That na child abuse number one. Me, I go kill any man wey do my girl child! God forbid! So, child abuse dey for ground well well. We no like child abuse. But di abuse wey me and Papa Christi don see plenty pass child abuse. I live for Asaba, di State capital of Delta. Child abuse dey there. Di one wey pass child abuse dey there plenty plenty. Task force destroy huts and shacks as THEM do in other places. So therefore everybody sabi wetin dey happen for di country. My story no soft pass the stories wey you don hear this night from other women mouth. So make me no repeat-repeat story. We don hear enough. If we continue to tell what they do to us...' she intones.

The women complete the chant:

'Night will pass and day will pass. And the story no go finish', Mama Christi emphasizes, and continues with her speech: 'For market, I hear my fellow women say make every woman go back to 'im village for meeting. Me and Papa Christi be Asaba people. I return for Asaba and them say na all villages for this area of the great river go do meeting together for here. Na 'im I come here to warn my fellow women about the new plan wey THEY make for us. Okoko-Aja task force know about this meeting. She go come here by five this morning with police, arrest we. So, I say to myself, "I must come here and say it." Wetin we go do?'

The information that the government's Child Abuse Task Force is going to use brute force to clamp down on them produces consternation among many of the women, and wraps up anger into invisible bullets and bombs in the insides of many others.

'We no go run away!' A male voice shouts.

'Yes! We shall not run away', Mgbeke repeats her husband's assertion.

'Who gave a man the audacity to enter this gathering and open his mouth to talk?'

'Leave him. He is a good man.'

'He is a man. This is women's meeting. Men do not call us to their meeting.'

'It depends...'

'This meeting is a meeting of the oppressed.' This voice is clearly that of Eze-nwanyi, the leader.

'The man also has a lot of bile and fire in his stomach. Let him vomit it, for we shall use all to build our weapons of war.' This is the unmistakable septuagenarian voice.

'They chase me from Asaba. Then they say na message from World Money Bank and Structural Adjustment.'

'SAP.'

'Suffer Africa Plenty.'

'Suffer Add Poverty.'

'My fellow women, let us hear our brother.'

Ogonna continues: 'I never see World Money bank before. I never see di owner of SAP. I never do them any bad thing. Why THEY come chase me from my job in Ministry of Information? I come home to my village and start something with my wife. THEY come chase we from building site. Na Child Abuse Task Force do dat one. They destroy my wife, destroy our business. They want destroy my life, my child. Na THEM! I no go gree!'

'We no-go gree-o!'

The leader, Eze-nwanyi, shouts a well-known war cry. And the response is total as all the women reply and affirm that they shall not agree to abuse, victimization and oppression.

Eze-nwanyi calls for an end to the chant, because of some important information: 'My sisters and my fellow women, we thank all the storytellers, listeners, and all of us sufferers for coming here. We thank our sister from the city who has brought the news of the government's plan to come and shoot us this morning. Some of us already knew about this plan, and have arranged a counter-plan. There is an important part of her story which I want all of you to hear. She told me about the house of the woman whom THEY are using to kill us. The woman's compound is as big as all the land belonging to this big river.'

'Hei!'

'What?'

'God forbid that one human being should live in a land that should be for a village.'

'You have not heard anything, my fellow women', continues Eze-nwanyi. 'Her house is as big as all our houses put together. Yet she does not live with anybody. Do not shout yet, my fellow women. She answers Missis, but no man misses her. She answers Doctor, but does not doctor anybody. There is no sick person in her house. She lives alone.'

There is a murmur as some of the women express concern for the condition of their fellow woman. Some of them marvel at the incongruity of her life.

'Who does she talk with in the big house?'

'How does she sweep the big house?'

'How does she clean the compound that is as big as all the land belonging to this river that extends to the big sea?'

'Machines!' Mama Christi interjects. 'Machines do every job. Machine cut grass. Machine wash clothes. Machine sweep house.'

Eze-nwanyi takes over: 'She can give many of us jobs in her compound and house, but NO! She prefers machines to do our work. Is that not more than abuse?'

'Far above abuse!' shouts Aduke.

'I shall stay here and see that woman with my own eyes. I shall ask her one question before they kill me.' A shrill voice beside Aduke surprises everybody. The women did not know that the children were awake and listening.

'They will not kill anybody. They will kill themselves', the old woman reassures the child.

'Umu-nwanyi *kwenu!*'

'*Ya!*'

'*Kwenu!*'

'*Ya!*'

'*Kwesienu ike!*'

'*Yaa-aa-aa-aaaa…*'

Their voices echo and re-echo from valley to valley.

'This is the time for decision.' Eze-nwanyi begins to take an inventory of suggestions. She finally summarizes the consensus: 'The general feeling is that the person who is flat on the ground does not fear to fall down. We have nothing to lose. Our life is already on the line, so let it stand firm on the line and fight for life. We shall move to the bank of this great River Niger that God gave to all of us. We shall camp between Asaba in Delta State and Onitsha in Anambra State, where they have the long bridge. We shall build our shacks and huts on the banks, not on the road and bridge, so as not to soil their eyes when they pass in their big cars. We shall get water from the river and fish from the river when it is not filled with dirt from their oil companies and their refinery. We shall have farms for the men. But we are market women and this is why we shall not be far from the busy road with big bridge. That is where we shall be selling our goods with our children.'

Special Announcement

The Military Government of Nigeria has reacted sharply against the new village built by market women on the banks of the River Niger. The women have been ordered to go back to their native villages because the new village has been marked for demolition by the Child Abuse Task Force headed by Doctor Mrs Florence Okoko-Aja. The decision is part of the ongoing attempt to enforce the Child Abuse Decree. The government wants to stop people from erecting illegal structures where they conduct roadside trade using children as vendors.

Newsflash

In a surprising twist to the widespread demolition of illegal structures that has been going on all over Nigeria, a group of young lawyers and journalists, led by one Miss Christi Anyawu Igwe, has filed for and got a court injunction restraining the government and the Child Abuse Task Force from demolishing structures. At a special press conference, Miss Igwe said that the government should use the loan from international aid organizations to develop women, their children and families instead of oppressing them. She challenged the Child Abuse Task Force to build houses for women and children instead of demolishing the shelters built by women. She further revealed that the lawyers in her group are working out modalities for taking the case to the International Court if the national courts fail them. We shall keep you informed of further developments. Thank you.

Notes on Contributors

Sophie Bessis, a Franco-Tunisian political economist, is known equally well for her activism, her participation in international debates, her career as a professional journalist, and her graduate teaching at the Sorbonne in Paris. Recipient of the prestigious French diploma in History, the *Agrégation*, she is author of numerous books in the fields of political economy, women and development, and African politics, among them her most recent book, *Women of the Mediterranean* (1995). She has also contributed essays to several anthologies, including *Women of the South: Heads of Household; Poverty;* and *The End of the Third World?*

Vijitha Mahadevan Eyango is chair of UCLA's Institute for the Study of Gender in Africa and a visiting professor at UCLA's Graduate School of Education. She is also principal investigator and director of the Language Materials Project, a US Department of Education-funded research project. Her most recent publications include 'Globalization and International Partnerships in Africa: Defining the "Gender-setters"' (*Development: Journal of the Society for International Development*, vol. 40, no. 4, 1998), and *The Africana Database on CD-ROM, 1981–1992* (National Information Services: Baltimore, MD, 1997).

Deirdre Gilfedder is Lecturer in English and Commonwealth Studies at the University of Paris IX. She has published on history and memory in Australia, in particular on nationalism and memory, but also on Australian writer Sally Morgan, on David Malouf, and extensively on the Human Rights Commission Report on the separation of children from Aboriginal parents.

Sumaya Farhat-Naser is Director of the Jerusalem Centre for Women, the Palestinian branch of the Jerusalem Link. She is one of the founding members of the women's peace movement in Palestine and a founding member of the Women Waging Peace Global Network at the John F. Kennedy School of Government at Harvard University. The German translation of her autobiography, *Thymian und Steine*, was a bestseller. As a professor of botany at the University of Birzeit in Palestine, Dr Farhat-Naser continues to teach and publish as a biologist, particularly in the field of Middle Eastern afforestation. She is also extremely active in a wide variety of development projects in the Palestinian territories. Dr Farhat-Naser has been the recipient of the 1995 Dr Bruno Kreisky Prize for Human Rights (Vienna), the 1997 Mount Zion Award (Jerusalem) and the Ausburg Peace Festival Award (2000).

Françoise Lionnet is Professor and Chair of the Department of French and Francophone Studies, Professor of Comparative Literature, and faculty affiliate in African and African-American studies at the University of California, Los Angeles. She is the author of *Autobiographical Voices: Race, Gender, Self-Portraiture* (Cornell, 1998), and *Postcolonial Representations: Women, Literature, Identity* (Cornell, 1995); co-editor of a special double issue of *Yale French Studies* entitled 'Post/ Colonial Conditions: Exiles, Migrations, Nomadisms', and a special issue of *Signs* on 'Postcolonial, Indigenous, and Emergent Feminisms.' Dr Lionnet directed the 1995 NEH Summer Institute in French Cultural Studies on 'Identities, Communities, and Cultural Practices.' Her research interests and many articles focus on comparative and Francophone literatures, postcolonial studies, autobiography, and race and gender studies.

Activist **Molly Melching** has lived and worked in the West African country of Senegal for more than twenty-six years. She is the Executive Director and founder of the international NGO, TOSTAN, specializing in non-formal education at the grassroots level. Molly Melching has received international recognition for her success in participatory education, social transformation and human rights training. Since 1997, hundreds of villages in Senegal have publicly abandoned the practice of female genital cutting after taking part in the TOSTAN programme.

Obioma Nnaemeka is the Director of Women's Studies at Indiana University, Indianapolis, and the current President of the Association of African Women Scholars. A former Rockefeller Humanist-in-Residence (University of Minnesota, Minneapolis) and Edith Kreeger Wolf Distinguished Visiting Professor (Northwestern University, Evanston), Dr Nnaemeka has numerous publications in women's studies, cultural studies, and African/African American studies, including *The Politics of (M)othering* (Routledge) and *Sisterhood, Feminisms and Power* (Africa World Press).

Chinyere Grace Okafor, academic, writer and artist, teaches in the English Department, University of Swaziland. Recipient of two Rockefeller Humanist-in-Residence Fellowships (at Cornell University and Hunter College), she is a specialist in African festival drama and cultural studies. Her essays have been published in *Okike*, *Literary Review*, *Research in African Literatures*, *World Literature Today*, and *Commonwealth: Essays and Studies*. Okafor was recognized by the Association of Nigerian Authors (ANA) in 1994 for proficiency in the three genres of literature. She received Outstanding Finalist ranking in the Bertram's Literature of Africa Awards in 1996, and a Rockefeller Fellowship for Residency as a Writer in the Bellagio Center (Italy) in 1998. Her creative works include *He Wants to Marry Me Again and Other Stories*, *The Lion and the Iroko* (a play), *From Earth's Bed Chamber* (a collection of poems), *Campus Palavar and Other Plays*, as well as numerous contributions in literary anthologies, journals and magazines.

Susan H. Perry, a political economist and specialist on development, holds degrees from Yale University and the École des Hautes Études en Sciences Sociales (Paris), and currently teaches International Affairs at the American University of Paris. She co-founded and co-organized the international conference on 'Women, Culture and Development Practices' that gave rise to this collection, and is co-editing a special issue of *Signs* on 'Postcolonial, Indigenous, and Emergent Feminisms'. Dr Perry has taught in China as a Yale–China fellow and written numerous articles on Chinese politics, economics and gender. She has most recently been invited to present her research at Indiana University and the JFK School of Government at Harvard University.

Celeste Schenck is Professor of Comparative Literature and Gender Studies at the American University of Paris. She has published widely on women's autobiography, feminist theory, and pedagogical issues, and is a coeditor of *Life/Lines: Theorizing Women's Autobiography* (Cornell, 1988). She was founder and co-editor of two series, the 'Barnard New Women Poets Series', published by Beacon Press, and 'Reading Women Writing', a series in international feminist theory published by Cornell University Press. In recent years, Dr Schenck has become interested in the cultural ground of development, notably the role of literature in recording the experience of participants in the development process. Her current work-in-progress, *Developing Subjects*, explores a new genre in women's fiction, one generated by international feminist interest in development practices.

Elora Shehabuddin is Assistant Professor of Women's Studies and Political Science at the University of California, Irvine. She received a Ph.D. in Politics from Princeton University, with a dissertation entitled 'Encounters with the State: Gender and Islam in Rural Bangladesh'. She is author of *Empowering Rural Women: The Impact of the Grameen Bank in Bangladesh* (Dhaka: Grameen Bank, 1992). Her articles have appeared in *Signs*, *Journal of Women's History*, and *Asian Survey*.

Jael Silliman is Assistant Professor in Women's Studies at the University of Iowa. She has worked on health and reproductive rights, environment, and alternative development issues for the past two decades as an activist, practitioner and founding officer. She is a member of the National Asian Women's Health Organization, the Committee on Women, Population and the Environment, the International Projects Assistant Services and the Reproductive Health Technologies Project.

Gila Svirsky is a veteran peace and human rights activist in Israel. For many years, she was director in Israel of the New Israel Fund, and subsequently director of Bat Shalom – the Israeli side of The Jerusalem Link: A Women's Joint Venture for Peace. She also served as chairperson of B'Tselem – Israel's foremost human rights organization in the occupied territories. She is currently on the board of the Association for Civil Rights in Israel, and continues her thirteenth year standing as a Woman in Black every Friday. Since the 'al-Aqsa Intifada' violence began in September 2000, she co-founded and coordinates the Coalition of Women for a Just Peace, a coalition of nine peace organizations in Israel.

Joanne Sandler is the Chief of Organizational Learning and Resource Development at the United Nations Development Fund for Women (UNIFEM). She has worked as a staff member and consultant to international and women's organizations for the past twenty years, focusing on organizational development and gender justice.

Linda Weil-Curiel, a French lawyer and activist, has been practising law as a member of the Paris Bar Association since 1973. Her practice ranges from the defence of abducted children, particularly those kidnapped by Algerian fathers after their divorce from French wives, to the fight against gender discrimination in the international Olympic Games. Her work has resulted in the signing of a 1988 treaty between France and Algeria protecting the rights of mothers and children, and the establishment of Sydney 2000, an international committee to cut off Olympic funding to those nations that prevent women from taking part in international sporting activities. Her fight against female genital mutilation in France, documented in this volume, has resulted in pathbreaking legislation protecting the rights of young girls living on French soil.

Oidov Enhtuya is a member of the Great People's Hural, Mongolia's legislative body, and a founding member of the Liberal Women's Brain Pool in Ulan Batur (LEOS). She has worked tirelessly to promote the growth of civil society in Mongolia. Her own NGO numbers nearly ten thousand volunteers, a group of enormous political force in this newly emerging economy. She has been both an Asia Foundation Fellow and a Salzburg Fellow, and gave the keynote address at the international conference on 'Women, Culture and Development Practices' in Paris, November 1998.

Aster Zaoudé is the Manager of the Gender Programme in the Bureau for Development Policy at the United Nations Development Programme in New York. An Ethiopian women's rights advocate, Zaoudé holds a law degree from the University of Aix-en-Provence, and a Master's degree from the Sorbonne. She served the Ethiopian government in 1976 as head of the Women's Department before joining the UN Economic Commission for Africa in Ethiopia in 1982. At UNIFEM, where she worked for fifteen years in different capacities, she headed an evaluation unit and served as Regional Programme Director for West, Central and North Africa. She joined the UNDP in 2000.

Index

Aboriginal and Torres Strait Islander
    Commission (ATSIC) (Australia),
    204
Aboriginal Studies, 212
Aboriginal women, autobiographies by,
    200–13
abortion, 95; campaigners against, in
    USA, 177–8
Abu, Katherine, 110
Aburdene, Patricia, 36
Abzug, Bella, 25, 26, 27
adivasi peoples, 72, 76, 79, 80, 81, 85
Africa Special Assistance Programme,
    20
African Charter on Human and People's
    Rights, 33
African National Congress (ANC), 119,
    123
Afrique Debout Unie en Marche, 194
Agarwal, B., 85; A Field of One's Own,
    75–6
Ahmed, Qazi Faruque, 53
AIDS, 158
Akuffo, F.O., 109
Alam, Nurul, 59
alcoholism, 81
Alison, a teacher, 127
All-China Women's Federation, 91, 92,
    93–5, 98; relationship with Chinese
    Communist Party, 95
Allen & Unwin, 212

alliances, building of, 34–8
Alma from Sylhet, 63
American identity, construction of,
    248
Amini, Maulana Fazlul Huq, 50, 58
Ampofol, Gifty, 112
Anam, Mahfuz, 57
Anderson, Benedict, 211
Annan, Kofi, 31, 33
anorexia, 217, 220, 222, 229; as form
    of hunger strike, 229; causes of,
    223–4
Anti-Price Rise Movement
    (Maharashtra, India), 82
apartheid, 179, 191; challenges to, 121,
    122; collapse of, 123; in education,
    120–21
Appadurai, Arjun, 6–7
Asia Foundation, China Programme,
    97
assimilation, of Aboriginal peoples in
    Australia, 203, 209; failure of, 204
Attah, Mrs, 114
Australia, 5; 'amnesiac historiography'
    of, 210; 'Stolen Generation' in, 199,
    200–213
Australian Human Rights Commission,
    5
autobiography, 199, 218–23, 236;
    theorization of, 207
Azizan from Sylhet, 63

Baaliga Declaration, 168
Baartman, Sara, 178–9
Bagadadji Declaration, 169
Balde, Lala, 164
Balde, Oumar, 167–8
Baliga Declaration, 165
Bangladesh, 3, 96, 219; gender politics
    in, 50–70; paper for Copenhagen
    Women's Summit, 54; report to
    Beijing Women's Conference, 51–2;
    secularism in, 55; women's NGOs
    in, 48
Bangladesh Rural Advancement
    Committee (BRAC), 53
banking system, Islamic, 60
Barthes, Roland, 225
basic necessities, 215, 216
Basu, A., 74
Bat Shalom, 4, 133, 135, 136, 138, 139,
    140, 141, 145, 150, 151; Gila Svirsky
    resigns, 146, 148, 149, 153
Baviskar, A., 81
beauty, models of, 223 see also body
    shape of women
de Beauvoir, Simone, 192
Beazley, Kim, 208
Begum, Sultana, 65
Bessis, Sophie, 3, 9, 41–4
Bhabha, Homi, 211
Bhatia, A., 74
Bhatt, Ela, 25, 26, 27
Bilaela, 175–6
biodiversity, 85; loss of, 71
Bird, Carmel, 206
blood, meanings of, 223–9
body shape of women, plumpness,
    216–17, 223, 224
borders, policing of, 239
Bringing Them Home report, 203–6, 209
Brown Sequard Hospital (Mauritius),
    217, 220
Browning, Elizabeth Barrett, 237; Aurora
    Leigh, 235
bulimia, 217
Bundestag (Germany) vote on
    circumcision, 178
Burkina Faso, 195
burqa: buying of, 66; wearing of, 64,
    65
Bynum, Carolyn, 226

Caritas organization, 53

Castells, Manuel, The Information Age...,
    247
CEDPA, 166, 167, 169
Chen Mingxia, 98
child abuse, 257, 259–76 passim
child labour, 185
childcare, 18, 61, 113
children, custody of, 81
children's rights, 192
China, 3, 4; Law on the Protection of
    the Rights and Interests of Women
    (1992), 98; One-Child Campaign,
    93, 95; Programme for the
    Development of Chinese Women,
    93; religious organizations in, 96–7;
    White Paper on Chinese Women's
    Status, 97; women's NGOs in, 48;
    women's organizations in, 89–103
    (proscribed, 90)
China-AIDS Network, 94
China Family Planning Association, 94
Chinese Catholic Church, 96
Christianity, 63, 137; conversion of
    Muslims to, 58; in China, 96–7
circumcisers, 174, 175; punishment of,
    190
circumcision: female, 171–89 (use of
    term, 5, 195, 196); infection after,
    158; reasons for, 182
circumcision hut, 180
civil disobedience, 141–2
Clark, Gracia, 113
Cliff, Michelle, Abeng, 252–3
Clinton, Hillary, visit to Bangladesh,
    50, 52, 57, 58, 59
Coetzee, J.M.: Disgrace, 130; Waiting for the
    Barbarians, 122
Collen, Lindsay, 199, 232; There is a Tide,
    215–32
Commission for the Abolition of
    Female Genital Mutilation (CAMS)
    (Senegal), 192
Communist Party of China, 91, 92, 93,
    94, 95, 98–9, 100
Communist Party of Kerala, 240
complexity, 3, 180, 237; of diet, 216
condolence calls to Palestinian families,
    141
consensus, techniques of, 162
consumption, resistance to, 231
cooking, as appropriation of food, 225
credit: access to, 41; Islamic attitude to,

61; micro-credit, 22, 56, 60, 62, 64
(criticism of, 61)
creolization, 247
critical mass, 34–8
critical thinking, development of, 157
cultural practices, 184–5
cultural relativism, 47
culture, as positive force in
development, 184–8
curriculum: content of, 125; national,
in South Africa, 129; relevance of,
111–13
Curriculum 2005 (South Africa),
124–5, 128

D., Colin, 206
D., Millicent, 206, 208
Dangarembga, Tsitsi, 214, 239; *Nervous
Condition*, 235
David Unaipon Indigenous Authors'
Prize (Australia), 212
Davis, Jack, 211
The Day Kadi Lost Part of Her Life, 174
Deblé, Isabelle, 110
decision-making, 159–66
declarations to end female genital
cutting *see* public declaration
Deleuze, Gilles, 229
Demba Diawara, 164
developing subjects, 235–55
development, 65; as process, 171–2; as
Westernization, 53; attitudes to, 50;
cultural turn, 7; feminist theories
of, 6; genealogy of, 6; language of,
172; literary accounts of, 5;
resistance to, 257–8
development aid, 3
development theory, rethinking of, 1
Diabougou Declaration, 161, 163, 164,
165, 168, 187
dialogue, 141, 157, 161–2, 182; as
means of peace-making, 134–48;
prevention of, 135; training in, 137,
138;
proscription of, 145
diarrhoea, 158
Diawara, Demba, 163
dignity, respect for, 173
displacement of peoples, 73–6; effects
of, 76–7 (on tribal women, 78)
distance, as a political statement, 149
division of labour, gendered, 17, 83

Douglas, Mary, 225
dress of women, 54, 64
La Dûperie, 196–7

East India Company, 58
East Meets West Feminist Translation
Group (China), 98
education: costs of, 110–11;
demographic spread of schools,
107; enrolment rates for girls,
107–11; in Senegal, 162; key role
of, in South Africa, 130; of women,
higher, 105; reform of, in South
Africa, 115–16, 119–32; single-sex,
16 *see also* girls, education of *and*
missionary education
Ellman, Maud, 229–30
empowerment, of women, 1, 4, 25,
27, 28, 29, 31, 60, 62, 75, 165,
187, 219
English: as world literature, 236–7;
constructed as academic subject,
123–4
[e]nglish, literature in, 199, 237
Enhtuya, Oidov, 3
Enloe, Cynthia, 218
environmental impact assessments, 72
environmental issues, and World Bank,
11
environmental movements, 72
environmental problems, of Narmada
dam, 78–9
ethnography, feminine, 221
Eurocentrism, 6, 122, 171
Evie, woman who had her child taken,
205
evil, non-cooperation with, 142
excisers, 174, 175, 190; law in France,
193; reconversion of, 195;
sentencing of, in France, 194
Export Processing Zones (Mauritius),
215, 218, 221, 228, 229
Eyango, Vijitha Mahadevan, 4, 105, 129

Fall, Madame, 179–80
Falungong movement (China), 96
family: reducing size of, 14; urban,
disintegration of, 17
family law, 16
Family Magazine (Zhongguo funu zazhi), 94
family planning, 167
Farhat-Naser, Sumaya, 4, 134–48,

149–54; letter to Gila Svirsky,
152–4
fatwas, politics of, in Bangladesh,
50–70
female genital cutting (FGC), 2;
abandonment of, 156–70; as
prelude to marriage, 192; laws
against, 166; Public Declarations to
end *see* public declarations; use of
term, 195; use of term
'abandonment', 180–81
female genital mutilation (FGM), 2, 3,
5, 28, 257; as crime, 155, 190–97;
opposing views of, 190–91;
(re)contextualization of, 155
female organs, representation of, 159
female-headed households, 74, 75
feminism, 2, 6, 15, 16, 47, 78, 84,
91, 109, 125, 142; and female
circumcision, 171–89;
development-, 2, 7, 250; in India,
73; instrumental, 10–24, 47;
international, 3; of international
institutions, 9
femocrats, 36
fertility, decrease of, 13, 14
Final-Status Negotiations, in Israel/
Palestine, 147, 148, 150
Firoza from Jessore, 63
fluid, feminine realm of, 226
Fogarty, Lionel, 211
food: as substitute for free expression,
220; refusal of, 224, 228, 230, 231;
sharing of, 225; women's
relationship to, 216; women's role
in producing, 41
footbinding reform, in China, 164
Ford Foundation, *Reflections and Resonance*,
97
forests: produce of, 81; tribal people's
dependence on, 79
Forster, E.M., *A Passage to India*, 244
fostering, of Aboriginal people, in
Australia, 200, 203
Foundation for Women's Health,
Research and Development
(FORWARD), 175
France, 190–97; laws on physical
assault, 191; new Penal Code in, 192
Fremantle Arts Press, 212
Frimpong, Mrs, 114
fuel, access to, 79

garment industry in Mauritius,
symptomatic reactions in, 217
gender: and the politics of fatwas,
50–70; as alibi, 21–2; as
depoliticizing term, 47; discovered
by World Bank, 10; mainstreaming
of, 25, 27, 28–9, 30, 42
gender analysis, 28, 29, 42
Gender and Development, 12
gender equality, 9, 22, 25–40
gender inequality: effect of parental
influence, 109–10; explanation of,
109–11; relation to poverty, 20
gender units, dismantling of, 29
germs, transmission of, idea of, 158
Ghana: education in, 4, 129;
educational reform in, 107; higher
education of women in, 105;
survival strategies of women in,
106–18
Gibran, Kahlil, 151
Gilfedder, Deirdre, 5, 199
girls: education of, 4, 16, 17, 18, 19,
106, 107–11 (and falling fertility
rates, 14; and productivity, 15; in
South
Korea, 20; rights of, 161
'Give Peace a Chance' meeting between
Palestinian and Israeli women, 135
global, reading of, 199
Global Knowledge for Development
Partnership, 33
globalization, 216, 247; dangers of,
172; of publishing, 237, 238
Godwin, David, 237
Gordimer, Nadine, *July's People*, 122
Gore, Mrinal, 82
governance, good, 44
government, local, women in, 72
Gréou, Hawa, 193, 194
graduates, job opportunities for, in
Ghana, 112–13
Graham, Mary, 201, 208
Grameen Bank, 52, 53, 57, 61, 62, 64
grassroots organization of women, 48
Green Belt Movement (Kenya), 26
Green Gang (Shanghai, China), 99
Green Revolution, 21, 22
growth, economic, 43
Guattari, Félix, 229
guilt, 138; white, 129, 147, 151
Gwala, Mafika, 122

Harjo, Joy, 237, 254; 'A Postcolonial Tale', 235
HarperCollins, 237
Harriet, a teacher, 127
Hashemi, Syed, 56, 57
health huts, provision of, 169
Hinduism, 80; caste system, 239, 240, 243
Holt, Harold, 204
homosexuality, 238
Hong Kong, 98
hooks, bell, 214
Hoskens, Fran, 183, 184
housework, 77
Howard, Mr, 208
Howell, Jude, 95
Hui minority, China, 96
human rights, 166, 169, 171–89, 191; as mantra, 172; as means of promoting gender equality, 27, 31–4
Human Rights Commission (Australia), 199, 202, 203, 204–5, 207, 208
Human Rights Commission (UN), 209
Human Rights Education, 160–61
hunger artists, 214–32 passim
hunger-strikers, 229–32
hybridity, 246–7
hygiene, 157, 158, 166, 180

Ibrahim prophet, 194
illiteracy, 55; of women, 107 see also literacy
incest, 252
India, 3, 20, 26; women's mobilizations in, 71; women's NGOs in, 48
indigenous peoples: idea of, 247; rights of, 200; stories of, 201
indigenous women, in Australia, 5
industrialization, in Mauritius, 218; psychosocials aspect of, 219
infanticide, female, 95
informal sector, 15, 43, 106, 111, 113; women in, 3, 20, 41, 114
information, rights to, 81–2
initiation rites, 162–3
institutionalization of women's associations, 19
(I)NTACT organization (Germany), 176–7
interest: charging of, 60; Islamic

attitude to, 62
International Conference on Population and Development, 30
International Covenant on Civil and Political Rights, 91
International Criminal Court, 32
International Development Association, 13, 16
International Islamic Relief Organization, 53
International Labour Organization (ILO), 77
International Monetary Fund (IMF), 11, 46, 57, 185
international organizations, and gender equality, 25–40
International Planned Parenthood Federation, 29
Internet, 33, 37
Intifada, 135
Iran, veiling in, 181
Islam, 49, 50, 53, 54, 55, 56, 59, 60, 183, 197; burials exhumed, 58; fundamentalism, 181–2; in China, 96–7; perceived incompatibility with modernity, 50
Islamic Association of China, 96
Islamic law, 59
Islamic state, 55
Israeli government, against dialogue with Palestinians, 134
Israeli–Palestinian relations see Palestinian–Israeli relations
issei Japanese immigrants, 249
Itzin, Catherine, 38
Ivory Coast, 33; female circumcision in, 180

Jahan, Rounaq, 28
Jamaa-i Islami (Bangladesh), 57–8, 59, 65
Jerusalem: as open city, 135; as shared capital, 139; dialogue on, 136–7
Jerusalem Centre for Women (JCW), 133, 135, 136, 139, 140, 142
Jerusalem Link for Women, 4, 133, 139, 145, 148; changes founding principles, 146, 149; declaration of, 150
Jewish Cultural Centre, 134
Jharkhand movement (India), 76
Joanna, a teacher, 129

Kabeer, Naila, 31
Kadi, circumcision of, 174–5
Kapur, 76, 84
Kenya, 26
Ker Simbara, 163, 186
Khan, Maulana Mohiuddin, 59
Khomeini, Ayatollah, 182
Khundker, Nasreen, 57
Koita, Mariatou, 193–4
Kothari, Uma, 218
Kudzu weed, 249

land, women's access to, 41, 65
land rights, 73–6; given to men, 75
language, as space of creative folly, 231–2
leadership skills, 159–66
League for the International Rights of Women, 192
Lejeune, Philippe, 207
Lesbian and Gay Comrades Beeper Hotline (China), 98
Levin, Tobe, 176, 186
liberalism, economic, 11
Lilly-Rose, a teacher, 127, 129
Link Up (Australia), 209
Lionnet, Françoise, 5, 199
literacy, 55, 62, 108, 165, 186, 218; classes, 61; multiliteracies, 125; of women, prevented by husbands, 109; visual, 125
literature: as development practice, 199; relationship to culture, 236
livestock, tended by women, 80–81
local, reading of, 199
local practices, complexity of, 237
Lorde, Audre, 177
Love Laws (India), 241–3
Lucaschenko, Melissa: Hard Yards, 211; Steam Pigs, 211
Lusanda, a lecturer, 126; rejection of, 128–9

MacDonald, Ann-Marie, Fall on Your Knees, 252–3
Mackie, Gerry, 164
madrasa religious schools, 60
Magabala Books, 212
Maheshwar Dam, 85
Malatun from Dinajpur, 63
Mali, 195
Malicounda Bambara village (Senegal),

157, 186, 187; declaration, 161, 163, 164
Malign, a driver, 187
Manresa, Kim, 175
market mammies, 113–14
market traders, women as, 113–14, 260–61
marriage, 114; age of, 110, 111; early, 106, 195
Marx, Karl, 227
Marxism, 240, 244, 245
master narratives, deconstruction of, 238
Mathai, Wangari, 25, 26, 27
Mauritius, 5, 33, 214–32
meat industry, 246–52
Medina Cherif Declaration, 161, 168
Meehan, Donna, 'Joy Ride', 202
Melching, Molly, 2, 5, 155, 186, 195
menstruation, 226–7
mestiza consciousness, 252–4
métissage, 199, 249, 252; valorization of, 5
milk: as metaphor, 228; loss of innocence of, 227; meanings of, 223–9; production and circulation of, 225–6
missionary education, 235, 236
modernity, 65; attitudes to, 50
modernization, 13, 20, 100, 219; in China, 90
money, meanings of, 223–9
monogamy, 183
Morgan, Sally, My Place, 210–11
Mtshali, Oswald, 122
Muslim Aid organization, 53
mutilation, female genital, use of term, 196

Nababsing, Vidula, 218
Naisbitt, John, 36
names, changing of, 224 see also misnaming
Nancy, a teacher, 126, 127
Narmada Bachao Andolan (NBA), 71–88; gender issues within, 83–6; involvement of women, 82
Narmada Dam, 3, 48; environmental problems of, 78–9; opposition to, 71–88
Narmada Shakti Dal, 85

Narmada Valley, gender silences in,
    71–88
Narmada Water Disputes Tribunal, 73–5
Narogin, Mudrooroo, 211
National Commission for Women
    (NCW) (India), 85
national identity, 137
Nationalist Party (South Africa), 121
Native Title Act (1993) (Australia), 209
Naxalites, 240
Ndebele, Njabulo, *Fools*, 120, 121
ndey-dikke (sister, friend), adoption of,
    160
networking, 37, 247; of women, 94, 99
Neville, A.O., 204
Newfield, Denise, 4, 105, 115–16
Nigeria, 259; rights in, 173
Nirsimloo-Anenden, A.D., 218
Nnaemeka, Obioma, 2, 5, 155, 196–7
non-governmental organizations
    (NGOs), 3, 25, 37, 38, 45, 50,
    184; access to UN, 36; in
    Bangladesh, 96 (impact on rural
    women, 56; numbers of, 52;
    perceived as anti-Islamic, 55, 59,
    60; perceived as tool of Western
    imperialism, 56; physical attacks
    on, 59; resistance to, 50, 58–9, 60,
    62, 63); campaigning of, 185; in
    China, 90, 91, 93, 97–9, 100
    (women's organizations, 94); in
    Palestine, 144; in Senegal, 156–70;
    Islamic, 53; lack of financial
    accountability, 56; NGO Affairs
    Bureau (Bangladesh), 53; politics
    of, 48; provision of social services,
    57; use of resources, 57
Noonuccal, Oodgeroo (formerly Kath
    Walker), 211
normalization in Palestinian–Israeli
    relations, 142–3, 144, 145, 149,
    151, 152
North–South relations, 6, 11, 14, 199
novels, 5, 199, 236, 245, 253
Nu Shu sisterhood, 89, 90, 99

O'Donoghue, Lois, 209
OFAD/NAFOORE, 166, 167, 168, 169
Okafor, Chinyere Grace, 3; 'Beyond
    Child Abuse', 257, 259–76
Okri, Ben, 119
Oppong, Christine, 110

Orbach, Susie, 223
Osei, Headmistress, 112
Oslo negotiations, 138, 148
Oxfam International, 29
Ozeki, Ruth: *My Year of Meat*, 236,
    246–52; shift to novel-writing,
    250–51

Pakhi from Dinajpur, 63
Palestine: establishment of state, 139,
    150; GDP in, 141
Palestinian Authority, corruption in,
    144
Palestine Liberation Organization
    (PLO), against dialogue with
    Israelis, 134
Palestinian refugees, 141, 153; right of
    return, 147, 150; rights of, 153
Palestinian Women's Association, 136
Palestinian–Israeli relations, 4, 133,
    134, 136; mutual deterrence, 140
Palestinians, destruction of homes, 142;
    Israeli acquisition of land, 153
Panchayat system, 30
Parma, Pratibha, 175–6, 179–80, 181
participation, 187
participatory form of education, 162
partie civile, role of, 193
Parveen from Sylhet, 64
Patkar, Medha, 73, 84–5
Paton, Alan, *Cry, the Beloved Country*, 122
patriarchy, 115, 144, 182, 183, 219, 229
peace, as concept in Senegal society,
    159
Peace Process between Palestinians and
    Israelis, 136
peace-making, as development practice,
    133; dangers of, 152
Perry, Susan, 4, 48
Peru, 26
Pilkington, Doris, *Follow the Rabbit-Proof
    Fence*, 202
Pillay, Shynee, novel character, 219–22,
    223–32
Pioneers Project (China), 95
Plaatje, Sol, *Mhudi*, 122
poetry, 236
pollution, 225
polygamy, 81
population control policies, 14
postmodernity, politics of, 220
poverty, 20, 76; feminization of, 17;

struggle against, 13, 22, 47, 62; women as agents in fight against, 15

power-sharing between men and women, 110

pregnancy, 106, 109, 110, 111, 115, 250; unwanted, 226

prenatal programmes, in Bangladesh, 60

problem-solving, collective, 157–8

property, women and, 16, 17

Proshika organization, 53

prostitution, 80, 113

Protestant China Fancheng Church, 96

PROWID/USAID, 166

public declarations against female genital cutting, 165, 166, 167, 168–70

purdah, 61, 62, 80; shedding of, 54, 59, 63, 64–5

Queensland, University of, Black Australian Authors Series, 212

racial mixing, politics of, 245

Randall, Bob, 202

rape, 33

Rawlings, J.J., 107

rehabilitation of peoples, 73–6

renaming, as misnaming, 177–81

resettlement of peoples, 72, 73–6

resistance of women, strategies against, 177–81

revenue gap between men and women, 18

Reynolds, Henry, 210

Rhodesia, 235, 239

Rioja, Isabel Ramos, 175

Rizwana, a teacher, 129

Roach, Archie, 202

Robertson, Claire, 111, 112

Rockhill, Kathleen, 109

role-play use of, 159

Roudy, Yvette, 191

Rowlands, Jo, 53

Roy, Arundhati: The God of Small Things, 236, 237–8, 239–46, 251; 'The Greater Common Good', 238

Rural Women Knowing All (Nongjia nu baishi tong) (China), 94

Saadawi, Nawal El, 183; The Hidden Face of Eve, 181–2

Said, Edward, 6

Sakhina from Jessore, 63

Sandler, Joanne, 3, 9, 45–7

Sardar Sarovar Dam, 71, 72–3, 238

scavenging, 228

Schenck, Celeste, 5, 199

Schuler, Sidney, 57

Scott, Kim, Benang, 202

Sei Shônagon, 246

self-assessment in education, 128

self-determination, of Aboriginal peoples, 204

Selina from Rajshani, 65

Senegal, 5, 28, 33, 35, 37; ending of female genital cutting in, 156, 186, 195

Serote, Mangane Wally, 122

sex-selection of children, 95

sexual abuse, in children's institutions, 204

sexual harassment, 33

sexuality, 216; female, 223 (control of, 196); resentment against, 226

Shaanxi Women's Theories, Marriage and Family Research Society (China), 98

Shafi, Allama Mufti Ahmed, 58

shari'a law, 59, 60, 193

Sharif, Ahmed, 56

Shefali from Jessore, 63

Shehabuddin, Elora, 3, 48, 96, 99

Shommilito Shangram Parishad (Bangladesh), 50

Shramik Sti Mukti Sanghatana (SSMS), 81

Siddiqi, Abdur Rahman, 59

Silliman, Jael, 3, 48, 90, 99

sisterhoods in China, 89–103 passim

Social Development Summit (Copenhagen), 45

Sommer, Doris, 207, 221

'Sorry Day' (Australia), 209

South Africa: educational reform in, 115–16; higher education of women in, 105; new constitution of, 124, 129; postgraduate education in, 119–32

Southern African Development Community (SADC), 30; Declaration on Gender and Development, 30

Spivak, Gayatri, 211

Sri Lanka, 219
Stanner, W.E.H., 201
Staudt, Kathleen, 37
sterilization of women, 95
The Stolen Children: Their Stories, 206
stories, oral, among Aboriginals, 211
street-vendors, organizing of, 26
strike of dockers, portrayed, 230
Stromquist, Nelly, 109
structural adjustment programmes, 12,
    17, 19, 21, 263–4, 273; effect on
    family, 258; humanization of, 18
Suppression of Communism Act (South
    Africa), 122
survival strategies of women, 12, 89,
    106; of Ghanaian women, 106–18
sustainable development, 71
Svirsky, Gila, 4, 134–48, 149–54; letter
    to Sumaya Farhat-Naser, 149–51;
    resignation of, 146, 148, 149, 153
sweets, eating of, 231
Sykes, Roberta, 208

taboo, 225, 226
Tansel, Aysit, 110
Tantura, massacre of, 153
target-group strategies, 53
Telugu ethnic group, 218
terrorism, of the state, 140
testimonial genre, 221, 222
theory and practice, 1, 3, 199
Tiananmen protest movement, 91
Tierney-Tello, Beth, 238
Tohura from Dinajpur, 64
tokenism on women's issues, 45
Torres Strait Island people, separation
    from families, 203–4
TOSTAN organization, 156–70, 184,
    195; training by, 162
tradition, 183; as justification for
    female genital cutting, 181
Traore, Bobo, death of, 191–2
tribal lifestyles, changes in, 79–81
tribal peoples, women, 78, 84; needs
    of, 83
Tucker, Vincent, 6, 7, 171
Tunisia, 135

unemployment, of women, 17, 77
United Nations (UN), 16, 26, 29, 32,
    33–4, 47, 65
UN Convention on the Elimination of

All Forms of Discrimination Against
    Women (CEDAW), 32, 33, 55, 173
UN Conference on Women (Beijing,
    1995), 4, 27, 30, 91, 93, 97;
    Platform for Action, 26, 36; review
    of, 38
UN Development Assistance Framework
    (UNDAF), 37
UN Development Fund for Women
    (UNIFEM), 9, 27, 28, 29, 32, 33,
    36, 37, 47; *Battered Dreams*, 31; 'A
    World Free of Violence Against
    Women', 33
UN Development Group (UNDG), 37
UN Development Programme (UNDP),
    14, 27, 37
UNESCO, 186
UNICEF, 14, 164, 167, 168, 169, 186
UN Interagency Committee on Women
    and Gender Equality (IACWGE), 37
UN International Decade for Women,
    11
UN Resolutions on Palestine, 147, 148,
    150–51, 153
UN Special Rapporteur on Violence
    Against Women, 32
UN Women's Conferences, 13, 26;
    Third Conference on Women
    (Nairobi 1985), 28
Universal Declaration of Human Rights,
    32, 46, 173
Untouchables, 239–46
USAID, 169

vaccination programmes, 158, 167; in
    Bangladesh, 60
Vasconcelos, José, 253
veiling, rise in use of, 181–2
Verwoerd, Hendrik, 121
Vienna Conference on Human Rights,
    45
Villanueva, Alicia, 25, 26, 27
violence: against women, 31, 32, 33,
    34, 37, 38, 95, 97, 98, 173–4;
    rejection of, 134, 135, 140
Visweswaran, Kamala, 214, 224
voice, strategies against, 177–81

Walker, Alice, 178; *Possessing the Secret of
    Joy*, 179; with Pratibha Parma, *Warrior
    Marks* 179–80, 183–4, 187–8
Walmartification, 247

Wang Shuzhen, 98
water, access to, 72, 79, 140, 184
Weare, Romayne, *Malanbarra*, 202
Weil-Curiel, Linda, 5, 155
Weller, Archie, 211
Westergaard, Kirsten, 57
Wharton, Herb, 211
widows, treatment of, 73–4, 172
Wilson, Ronald, 207, 208
Witwatersrand, University of, 119–32;
    English Master's degree, 121–4,
    124–5; recruitment of black faculty
    members, 122
women, as agents in fight against
    policy, 15; as graduates, 130; as
    vectors for modernization, 13;
    domestic burden of, 15;
    emancipation of, 17; exhibition of
    body parts of, 173–4, 178–9; in
    parliament, 28, 35; in waged work,
    15; invisible labour of, 18;
    involvement in politics, 82 *see also*
    government, local, women in;
    labour codes regarding, 16;
    marginal representation of, 46;
    survival strategies *see* survival
    strategies; trained in political
    analysis, 137
'Women, Culture and Development
    Practices' conference, 2
Women for Women organization
    (Bangladesh), 59
Women in Black vigil, 143
Women in Development, 12
'Women Making Peace' meeting
    between Palestinian and Israeli
    women, 137
Women Targeting the World Bank
    organization, 22

Women's Conference Copenhagen, 183
Women's Empowerment Program, in
    Africa, 165
Women's Issues Communication and
    Services Agency (WICSA), 184,
    185–6
women's movement, achievements of,
    43
women's rights, 25–40, 71, 100
women's studies, 91
women's work, 62, 78; alleviation of,
    169; attitude of Islam to, 59; lack of
    control of, 226; political (ignored
    by
Israeli media, 143; measured in small
    steps, 144); waged, 20, 77, 218–20
    (as teachers, 114; cheapness of, 218;
    encouraged in China, 93; in
    Bangladesh, 60–61)
WomenWatch organization, 38
World Bank, 9, 33, 41–4, 46, 57, 61,
    65, 72, 76, 239, 263, 273; and
    women's issues, 10–24, 46;
    discovery of gender, 42; *New Plan of
    Action for Women's Health and Nutrition*,
    19; *Reinforcement of Women's Participation
    in Economic Development*, 13
World Trade Organization (WTO), 46
Wright, Alexis, *Plains of Promise*, 202, 211
writing, as international development
    practice, 236–9

Xie Lihua, 94

Yi Nianhua, 89
Yunus, Mohammad, 61

zakat tax, 60
Zaoudé, Aster, 3, 9, 41–4, 45–7